THE NARRATION OF DESIRE

THE NARRATION OF DESIRE
Erotic Transferences and Countertransferences

Harriet Kimble Wrye
Judith K. Welles

THE ANALYTIC PRESS

1994   Hillsdale, NJ   London

Earlier versions of the following chapters are reprinted here, in revised form, by permission of their copyright holders: ch. 3, from H. K. Wrye & J. Welles (1989), The maternal erotic transference. *International Journal of Psycho-Analysis*, 16:673-685; ch. 4, from J. Welles & H. K. Wrye (1991), Maternal erotic countertransference. *International Journal of Psycho-Analysis*, 72:93-106; ch. 7, from H. K. Wrye (1991), Hello the hollow: Deadspace or playspace? *Psychoanalytic Review*, 80:101-122; ch. 8, from H. K. Wrye (1993), Erotic terror: Male patients' horror of the early maternal erotic transference. *Psychoanalytic Inquiry*, 13:240-257.

Excerpts from Dylan Thomas's "Poem on His Birthday" and "Twenty-four Years" are reprinted from Dylan Thomas: *Poems of Dylan Thomas*. Copyright 1939, 1952 by Dylan Thomas. Reprinted in the English language only by permission of New Directions Publishing Corp. (US); the Trustees for the copyright of the late Dylan Thomas; and David Higham Associates, Ltd., 5-8 Lower John Street, London W1R 411A, England, for J. M. Dent, Publishers (UK).

Set in New Caledonia type by Magazine Graphics, Westwood, NJ

Library of Congress Cataloging-in-Publication Data

Wrye, Harriet Kimble
The narration of desire : erotic transferences and countertransferences / Harriet Kimble Wrye, Judith K. Welles.
p. cm.
Includes bibliographical references and index.
ISBN 0-88163-147-7
1. Sex (Psychology). 2. Desire. 3. Love. 4. Transference (Psychology). 5. Countertransference (Psychology). I. Welles, Judith K. II. Title.
BF692.W75 1994
155.3—dc20
93-46946
CIP

Printed in the United States of America
10 9 8 7 6 5 4 3 2 1

To the memories of my mother, Martha Prescott Kimble, who gave me dreams; and my father, James Clinton Kimble, who always said, "Write a book!"
                                                                    –HKW

To my mother, Edith Weiner Kingsburg, who loved me without question; and to the memory of my father, Robert Herbert Kingsburg, who taught me to question everything.
                                                                    –JKW

Acknowledgments

Many people helped us formulate the ideas and stories in this book. First and foremost, we thank our patients for the privilege of knowing them and for their generous willingness to let their stories be told so that we and others could learn. For the sake of confidentiality, we have changed some aspects of identifying data while doing our best to preserve the integrity and spirit of their clinical material.

We are deeply indebted to our teachers, our students, and all our colleagues at the Los Angeles Institute and Society for Psychoanalytic Studies (LAISPS). Among them, Ernest Lawrence, Ph.D. has been our mentor and abiding friend. Hedda Bolgar, Ph.D. and Jean Sanville, Ph.D. together pack as much role modeling as any woman analyst might wish for. Thanks go to our LAISPS study group— quizzically named Adamant—in which gender was the passionate subject for discussion.

Joyce McDougall, D.Ed. has been a champion for the body erotic and an inspiration; James Grotstein, M.D. has lent us his singular voice on primitive phenomena and his generous encouragement. Elaine Caruth, Ph.D. provided a blueprint for scholarship and independent thought. We also appreciate the lively interest and responsiveness of our colleagues in the American Psychological Association, Division III, on Women and Psychoanalysis, who first provided a public forum for our ideas on Maternal Erotic Transference and Countertransference, and then the Carole Dilling Memorial Lecture and the International Psychoanalytical Association, who gave us wider voice.

We owe a debt of gratitude to The Analytic Press and its Editor-in-Chief, Paul Stepansky, Ph.D., whose devotion to clarity and cogency was aimed at keeping us as often as possible out of the primordial mire . . . in short, a sapient editor; and to Eleanor Starke Kobrin, who knows the difference between that and which and has a fine eye for the well-crafted sentence. Here at home, Liz Atlas indefatigably provided spell checks, support, and order out of chaos throughout the many versions of this narrative.

Before we thank our families, we need to contextualize the size of their contribution. When we began this project, we had no idea of the scope of the task of writing a book, nor what it would demand of our daily lives. In the book, we speak about the development of love from primitive impulses to its full flowering and the capacity for mutuality, intimacy, and attunement to the subjectivity of the other. We feel that each of our families has loved us well during this process. We thank them for endless patience, limitless encouragement, and late-night trips to Federal Express.

I (HKW) wish especially to thank James Wheeler for his love, encouragement, delicious interruptions, and humor when I ran out of it myself. Gabriel Wrye, my firstborn, introduced me to the power of these notions in the first place. Ariel Wrye, now a savvy and supportive adult, expanded my experiences with jouissance. She was a child when we started this project and told her friends she thought I was doing "something about the eternal neurotic transference." And Brooke Wheeler, my daughter by choice, has brought a new dimension to mother–daughter bonding.

I (JKW) want to express my deep love and appreciation to Steve Welles for all the many ways he makes what I do possible. Over the course of this writing, he made himself available for discussion, deliberation, and debate, and his keen wit and penetrating questions contributed much to keeping this enterprise honest. To my daughter, Jennifer Robyn Welles, who was happy to provide ample opinions and insight about the ways of young women and whose good opinion matters to me above all things, I offer my abundant and heartfelt appreciation.

And, finally, we must acknowledge each other, without whom, never . . .

Contents

Introduction

Nothing in the entire range of human relations is more richly rewarding and fascinating, and yet makes us more vulnerable, than love and desire. Life's essential and most precious elixir appears in many guises, transforms, and then disappears.

The ability to love develops quite late in the story of the first love affair in any human life, the relationship between baby and mother. Although, from the earliest stirrings of the baby in her womb, mother can feel love and desire, the baby cannot reciprocate until she[1] develops complex capacities far beyond the purely impulsive and reflexive. The baby must recognize her bodily separateness from mother, identify her mother as the satisfier of her needs, and then recognize her desire to be held and cared for by her mother. Before the ability genuinely to love another person is possible, the baby must be able to respond to her own inner world and the world of her mother; to internalize, to symbolize, to understand and express meaningfully; and to participate within an intersubjectivity enlivened by the unconscious of both parties. Only then does love in all its richness become possible.

In this book, we focus on the *origins* of love and desire, starting at the earliest, most primitive end of a developmental spectrum

---

[1] Our use of the feminine pronoun does not indicate that this is a "female" condition. Instead, our narrative purpose is to call attention to the unwitting implications of the generic use of masculine pronouns. If there were an ungendered pronoun that did not deanimate (such as "it" does), we would prefer it. For now, we lean toward the use of "she" because "she" has waited a long time for her turn to be commonly seen as a narrative protagonist. We also hope to call attention to the fact that such small changes in narrative formation can have major therapeutic implications.

that moves toward the capacity for desire and ends with the ability to love. As early as Apuleius' *Metamorphoses*, and down in time through Chaucer's *Roman de la Rose* and Dante's *Divine Comedy*, the rose has symbolized love, encompassing the range of complex feelings that can exist between lovers who appreciate each other both as separate and as subjects.

> As regards the rose, because of its complex symmetry, its softness, the variety of its colors, and the fact that it flowers in spring, it appears in nearly all mystical traditions as a symbol, metaphor, allegory, or simile for freshness, youth, and beauty in general . . . the erotic symbol. (Eco, 1992, p. 57)

Considering the rose as a universal symbol of love, we can also look at what precedes and prepares for the flower—not only the stem and the leaves, but the roots, enmeshed with the soil of mother earth, rich with nutrients, yet crawling with worms and snails and abounding with possibilities. We must look at the whole rosebush. Developing this literary image as a metaphor for the narration of desire, we can trace the unfolding of human desire in the story of each person's capacity to grow from a primal sensory enmeshment into full bloom.

To grow into full bloom means not merely to survive, but to flourish, to be able to enjoy the "rose of love" reciprocally. We must, however, differentiate between the defensive "beautification" exemplified by the picture-perfect rose and dreamed of by many patients as "ideal love," and the rose as an integrated symbol, as a whole plant with its roots in the earth. In our psychoanalytic narrative throughout this book, we portray the development *not* of the idealized and unattainable perfect rose, but metaphorically of a *real* rose, vivified by the realities of life, by the worms, humus, thorns, bugs, and scent of real human sagas of desire. We will be "rooting about" in the mother–baby relational matrix, in the humus where roots and earth, worms and moisture are intermingled.

Of particular interest to us is how the emerging capacity for desire and love is shaped through words and storymaking. We are interested not only in the origins of the sensual feelings and the psychological implications associated with the flower in full bloom, but also in the powerful shaping of those feelings and capacities first in the language of the sensual body and then through the language of the mind—in the words, stories, and songs of desire that give experiences meaning. In this book we explore our interest in and offer narratives about the inchoate origins of adult passionate love.

Our narrative focus moves on from the point where our metaphorical rosebush breaks through the soil (where the newborn separates from the mother's body, represented by the earth). Once in the "fresh air" of more individuated experience, impulses become conscious and unconscious desires—more intertwined, more directed toward loved ones, and finally more integrated as the young child develops the ability for ambivalence and sublimation. Arousing our poetic or artistic sensibilities and our love of beauty, flowers are universal symbols of the pleasurable and painful feelings of love and desire; they evoke the richness of the intersubjective field of love. In this populous realm, we encounter the lovers and the rivals of the oedipal domain, and it is here, in the saga of "Oedipus and the Spruce Goose," that we conclude our narration of desire.

THE NARRATION OF DESIRE IN THE CLINICAL SETTING

Love and desire are replayed in the clinical encounter. With profoundly disturbed patients, the capacity for love often does not appear until near the end of treatment. In psychoanalysis and psychoanalytic psychotherapy, the narration of desire emerges through the vehicle of the transference and countertransference. The early and most primitive part of a patient's narration of desire is preverbal and typically emerges and expresses itself not in words, but through bodily sensations and feelings that an attuned and receptive therapist[2] can pick up. Analysts and patients alike have unconscious fantasies about intrauterine experience before birth, about the fetus enveloped in the body fluids of the mother. Both have pleasurable and painful inchoate memories; we call them "body loveprints." Repressed to a greater or lesser extent, body loveprints are remnants of the earliest bodily contacts, expressed through the vast preoccupation of mother and child with body fluids (urine, milk, feces, mucus, saliva) in the first year or two of the child's life.

---

[2]Throughout the book we refer both to "therapist" and to "analyst." While the latter specifically refers to one who has completed formal psychoanalytic training, it is our conviction that the issues we address in the book are equally relevant to, and appear both in, psychoanalysis and psychoanalytic psychotherapy. They can be worked with in both as long as the therapist works within a carefully bounded therapeutic frame and within the transference.

A mother's acceptance of her own and of her baby's bodily processes and body fluids creates the medium for bonding. Her ministrations to her baby optimally create a slippery, sticky sensual adhesion in which the infant feels itself contained. In the clinical situation, the flow of words and the evocation of feelings between patient and analyst create an associative transference and countertransference link to that early maternal care. The analyst's acceptance of and tolerance for the patient's preoedipal fantasies create the matrix for the patient's consolidation of self and for the advancement toward an oedipal transference. These are the early maternal erotic transferences and countertransferences we discuss in this book.[3]

The classical view of transference is that it is oedipal. When it is erotic (typically from female patients to male analysts) it is viewed as disruptive and requiring "management." In the classical psychoanalytic literature, there has been considerable emphasis on the pitfalls and dangers created by Eros in the treatment. Consequently, many believe that erotic transferences represent a mine field that should be assiduously avoided. Blum (1973) has described the erotized transference that has gone awry: erotic preoccupation with the analyst is used defensively by the patient to avoid the analytic work. Kumin (1985) focuses on the need for analysts to restrain their erotic desire for their patients, a desire that poses a threat to treatment.

Freud (1933) recognized preoedipal erogeneity. Writing of the origins of erotic feeling, he stated that it was "the mother who by her activities over the child's bodily hygiene inevitably stimulated, and perhaps even roused for the first time pleasurable sensations in her genitals" (p. 120). Even here, however, he emphasized his fundamental view of erotism within the Oedipus complex and more narrowly associated with genital sexual drives seeking discharge. His view of female sexuality was that it is stimulated in the female primarily by her longing for the strength, excitement, and power of the phallus to fill the void left by her castration. The most widely known classical view of erotic transference remains rooted in Breuer and

---

[3]In scientific meetings and in previous articles in journals, we have developed our understanding of these transferences and countertransferences; we have also followed their permutations with different types of patients and with the variable of patients' gender. In this book, we endeavored to integrate and weave our ideas, together with new conceptualizations, into an inclusive narrative of desire. Bibliographic references for those of our previously published articles and presentations which are developed in this book are listed in the reference section.

Freud's (1893–1895) paradigmatic and problematic case of Anna O. It was there that Freud first conceptualized transference on the basis of the erotic wishes that disrupted the ability of both Anna O and Breuer to tolerate the treatment. We hope that by dramatically expanding the meaning of erotic transference and by focusing on the preoedipal origins of erotic feeling within an object relations context, we will make it clear that these transferences represent a "gold mine" (Person, 1985) for rich therapeutic transformational work, rather than a mine field to be managed or avoided.

Gold mine though it may be, some patients, particularly males and male and female patients with a psychotic core experience a primal panic—"erotic terror," if you will—in the face of an early erotic transference. They and, unfortunately, sometimes their analysts struggle to avoid erotic terror. When, however, these transferences are recognized, tolerated, understood, properly interpreted, and worked through, they can provide access to the only true intimacy many very seriously disturbed patients have ever experienced.

The sensuous bond between mother and baby and its appearances and permutations in the analytic dyad has piqued the interest of psychoanalysts ranging from classical to object relations theorists, from Kleinians to self psychologists. Questioning basic assumptions from all these different perspectives has opened the doors and windows, so to speak, on the nature of transference in general and erotic transference in particular. Thus the early classical paradigm of erotic transference has had to be radically amended. The burgeoning field of infant research and our newer understandings of preoedipal development have contributed dramatically. Further impetus to questioning it has come from the women's movement and postmodernist thinking.

THE ORIGINS OF OUR NARRATIVE

What do we mean by, and how have we come to write about, the narration of desire? This book has grown out of our ongoing discussions of certain of our clinical experiences. It is both a chronicle of our need to comprehend and give form to disturbing primitive encounters with our patients and, at the same time, a narration of the dialogue from which it emerged. This book is one step in the process of our continuing collaboration.

The stories of the vicissitudes of desire in the analysis, especially as they relate to the transference and countertransference, are the general subject matter of this book. It is also about narratives as they evolve in clinical practice, are embodied in psychoanalytic theory, and establish the working truth of the psychoanalytic situation. We began to appreciate the extent to which erotic desire in its broadest sense is integral to the narrative process during our initial project together, studying early maternal transferences and countertransferences. We have also come to appreciate how erotic desire leads to very interesting complications in analysis.

When we first began collaborating ten years ago, we turned our attention to understanding aspects of the inchoate material that was emerging in some of our clinical work. These inquiries led to our formulating the concepts that we grouped under the rubric of "maternal erotic transferences and countertransferences." A series of journal articles and individual book chapters resulted from those early efforts. As we have lectured, analyzed, and supervised on the basis of these ideas, we have come to realize that it might be useful to convey more of our own process—to retrace the sometimes tangled pathways from the "primordial swamp" of maternal erotics to clinically usable concepts. In a way, this book is an atlas, offering a record of the pathways of desire.

THE STORY OF EROTIC DESIRE

In the "narration of desire," we are particularly interested in its beginnings, in the earliest, most primitively based hungers, impulses, and longings oriented toward the mother's voluptuous and sensually experienced body. These longings, which can be described as the baby's almost spilling into the mother's body, and her reciprocal sensual feeling and pleasure, become, under normal developmental conditions, or through the offices of a good-enough analysis, the basis for mature genital sexual relations. Here we will describe the vicissitudes of early desires which are polymorphous, libidinal-aggressive, and perverse as they are focused and diffused in the mother–infant relationship and are rekindled in analysis. Throughout the book, we use the word "perverse" to describe engagements that are avoidant of mutuality and genuine vitality. Essentially schizoid, perverse enactments represent derailments from a pathway toward generative procreative erotic sexuality marked by love and erotic desire, which we define as follows.

Fully elaborated "erotic desire" is further along the developmental continuum; by mature desire we mean the passionately felt longing for the other and for the other's body. While certainly physical, it is also enriched and deepened by subjectivity and awareness of the uniqueness, separateness, and difference of the other and of the exquisite fragility of attachment.

We are also concerned with tracing the climates in which these desires are eradicated or deadened, blocking the pathway to felicitous adult sexuality. One area we have been exploring has to do with the connection between these primitive bodily desires and patients' wishes for transformation. We see striving for transformation as the basic underlying impetus motivating patients to undergo analysis. We will be speaking more about that at the end of chapter 3.

Desire for transformation is often expressed in wishes for a freer, less problematic love of self, significant others, work, and play. These desires reflect unconscious inclinations and attributes about what creates the conditions for loving and transformation to occur. Unconscious desires about what constitutes the conditions for loving may also, however, be antitransformational and lead to deadlocks and psychic paralysis. This is our subject in chapters 2, 4, 6, and 7.

THE THERAPIST AS NARRATOR

Each of us came independently to the importance of narration in the process of writing cases, and found this a common focus for our mutual storytelling in peer consultation. Initially, I (HKW) had come to think and write about narration by way of my background prior to becoming a psychoanalyst, via a graduate degree in literature. In the process of my subsequent studies as a psychologist, psychoanalytic training and writing up cases, a narrative perspective took shape. While writing a clinical case report on the analysis of a seriously disturbed patient, I began to think more about the therapeutic meanings in storymaking in therapy. My analysand, then an unproductive would-be writer, completed his analysis many years ago and became a successful writer. The construction of his "histories" and stories itself intrigued me. In retrospect, I think I started writing about him because analyzing him was a profoundly disorganizing experience for me because of the extraordinarily primitive level of his material and his own fractured experiences of living. This patient entered my office like a "wild man of Borneo," chaotic, acting out, on drugs, and virtually unable to sustain meaningful contact.

As I launched into writing what became a lengthy case report, I began to sense a parallel process. My patient struggled to communicate to me his chaotic experience and tried slowly and painfully to find some coherence in a very disjointed family and life situation; I took to writing to detoxify the primitive and chaotic countertransference identifications. I became absorbed by the notion of the "story of his stories" and the levels of storymaking involved in conducting any analysis. For the analyst, these levels include thinking, writing, and theorizing about one's work with a particular patient, discussing and formulating meanings with colleagues, and the reverberating effects of these activities on the analytic process.

At the outset, his material was so disjunctive and his referents so concrete and iconographic that I felt disoriented and unable to make any sense of his experience. I felt I was in the presence of what Bion (1957, 1959, 1962) would describe as fractured "beta" elements with no "alpha" elements to provide meaningful links. I believe I needed to write to soothe myself and make sense of his overwhelmingly primitive, often psychotic states. Writing about this case and drawing on my background in literature led to my growing interest in narrativity and its relation to psychoanalysis. Experiencing the onslaught of surreal experience that was my patient's life, I wrote to gain perspective; assuming a narrator's point of view helped me maintain equanimity in the face of chaos. I needed an observer's distance to keep from total "descent into the maelstrom," in the words of Edgar Allan Poe. In this sense, the writing introduced the essential triangularity requisite to creativity that Ogden (1989) speaks of. Through the very process of writing, we are often able to separate ourselves from feeling inundated by the concreteness of our patients' communications, to experience a "room of one's own" as Virginia Woolf called it, a "narrative space" in which to think. This process replicates the coherence making that occurs in supervision, collegial consultation, the "Ah ha!" experiences of scientific presentations or journal articles that can suddenly reveal a new perspective and bring the therapist's "third ear" to life.

I (JKW) came to the concept of narration through a different route, from my interest in philosophy and the philosophy of science, spurred on by basic questions about psychic "reality" and analytic "truth." As a doctoral candidate in psychology, hoping to gain understanding of consciousness, I studied the brain but found consciousness of no interest to the physiologists. My continuing interest in the psyche and philosophical questions regarding the nature of the mind propelled me toward psychoanalysis. My patients' struggles and triumphs in the realm of meaning keep me fascinated. This experience also fueled my orientation within psychoanalysis away from efforts to identify it with the hard sciences and more toward its association with artistic struggle.

While psychoanalysis has always included a narrative or rhetorical focus, this focus has only recently attracted widespread notice in the mainstream. And it is no accident that it is most often associated with the "newer" schools and has an emphasis on countertransference, because it demands a different sort of accountability from the analyst than was true in the more classical models.

I think it is undeniable that in the analytic process we are unable to obtain data that is in any sense free from the constraints of human discourse. Thus it is virtually impossible to separate the data from the observer. The analytic observer (not unlike the patient) is subject to myriad and simultaneous influences that are not susceptible to isolated examination, let alone anything resembling calibration. Another complication is the human propensity to find what is expected and known, rather than to deal with what is inchoate and therefore threatening.

For both of us, the most interesting and important aspects of the analytic process are what the participants are able to understand and teach each other and how their story grows and develops. It is the nature of the psychoanalytic enterprise that this occurs mostly in words. Fundamentally, this book is about our efforts to bring to words those experiences—primitive, body oriented, inchoate— which were not included in our patients' narrative. We are attempting to develop a vocabulary of desire; basic to this is the idea that desire is the symbolization of wishes and needs. Desire is impulse made meaningful and is an intensely human characteristic. Our own collaborative process has provided each of us with the experience of the benign, sapient conarrator, which we both have come to hold as a model for analytic work.

THE VICISSITUDES OF DESIRE

It was tempting in writing a psychoanalytic book, particularly about such primitive transferences and countertransferences, to take a safer "high road" to the theory that evolved. We might have preferred to circumnavigate some of the chaotic disarray we had experienced with patients. As analysts, we ordinarily prefer to avoid revealing much of ourselves, particularly in the midst of confusion. As we are writing about the most intense and intimate of relations between analyst and analysand, however, it seems essential that we try to convey as fully as possible how we felt in that experience and how we came to understand such experiences theoretically through our own collaboration.

Long before we ever considered framing new conceptual formulations a number of years ago, we were impressed by the prevalence of themes of anal intrusion in several clinical cases we happened to be discussing. As we look back, it is obvious that we felt anxiety in dealing with this kind of material; this anxiety led us to select these particular cases to discuss. Initially, we viewed the material as centering on elements of sadomasochism and paranoia, with accompanying obsessional and manic defenses. Over time, we began to recognize a distinctly erotic insinuation in the stories and to describe these transferences as erotic. Eventually we decided we had been struggling to conceptualize clinical findings that we could not fit into prevailing theoretical narratives.

A surprising number of the patients we were discussing had been subjected to enemas in early childhood. Enemas were in part an artifact of the age of these men and women in their 40s to 60s and corresponded to hygienic practices prevalent during their early years. Partly because the enemas had been justified as medically appropriate, many patients told us these stories split off from their feelings. But pathological aspects of intrusive mothering emerged in their reports of anal penetration, rationalized as in the child's best interest. Although neither the patients nor we were initially aware of it, we were dealing in some cases with acts tantamount to anal rape and carrying many of the lifelong consequences of other more overt forms of child abuse. From our current vantage point, a large number of reports of strikingly intrusive and anally directed acts seem to have been necessary to call our attention to the then relatively unexplored area of anal erotism in the transference–countertransference dance.

In retrospect, we believe that the limitation of our perspective was twofold. We had been constrained in our thought by conventional paradigms of oedipal transferences and constricted by our countertransferences to the patients in question. It occurred to us that this double helix was not peculiar to us but might reflect struggles or deadlocks being encountered by others. We looked for material written on pre-oedipal erotic transferences and found it conspicuously absent. Those few writers who noticed this lack often attributed it to issues in the countertransference, which are undoubtedly a consideration. There is, however, another and perhaps a more basic impediment to the conceptualization and report of maternal erotic transference and countertransference. Classical psychoanalysis tells stories from the point of view of the child's desires; mother's subjectivity is not included. Within such a discourse, from which the mother's experience is absent, the mother/analyst has been "without the words to say it"(Cardinal, 1983). Hirsch (1989) has elucidated this narrative limitation within the established discourse of psychoanalysis.

> Freud's narrative, even if we take it on its own terms, contains a pro-
> found paradox, one that he does not and cannot see. On the one
> hand, he insists that female fulfillment lies in the relation between
> mother and child; on the other hand, he posits a necessary and hostile
> rupture of that relation by the child. What he fails to look at, and what
> he cannot look at, is how the mother herself experiences the rupture
> on which he insists. . . . The mother herself is and remains absent
> even to herself. The place she inhabits is vacant. Although she pro-
> duces and upholds the subject, she herself remains the matrix, the
> other, the origin . . . Is it possible to tell the untold tale of maternal
> participation in the psychoanalytic narrative, staying within psychoan-
> alytic terminology? Can we invest with speech the silence that defines
> maternal experience? (pp. 168-169)

As we began to struggle within the constraints of the existing analytic narratives, we ultimately understood that we were going to have to reformulate aspects of clinical theory, in order to do the work as we understood it needed to be done. Of course, in a way, every therapist must do this. Each analysis deserving of the name, and every profound therapeutic experience, produces a theory tailored to the patient, rather than ready made in a book, even an excellent book. And there are excellent books.

PREVIOUS NARRATIVES: SEEKING PATHFINDERS

We read Leonard Shengold's (1967, 1971, 1985, 1988) work on rat people and on anal narcissism. His writings are provocative and illuminating; however, his clinical formulations were derived primarily from his experience as a classical male analyst working with male patients. We were greatly influenced and guided in our inquiries by several female colleagues, among them McDougall (1986a), Chasseguet-Smirgel (1978, 1986), Joseph (1982), and Sanville (1987). At that time, for female analysts working in an object relations perspective, there was almost no published literature on erotic countertransferences. We realized that we were swimming in relatively uncharted waters and wanted to understand why this should be so. Kumin's (1985) work on erotic horror helped to illuminate the reason so little had been written in the area of preoedipal erotic engagement in analysis.

We saw that countertransference was probably the sticking point. One benefit of our ongoing collaboration has been the freedom it provides to explore aspects of our own unsettling countertransferences in the presence of the other. The sustaining influence of each other's mind joined in the struggle to know helped us verbalize what was happening in our respective treatment conundrums. This process brought us understanding that led us to new technical approaches to these impasses.

Perhaps it was our growing appreciation of the *sustaining/containing* aspects of the maternal influence that led us to recognize the power of narratives in the early maternal infant relation. It is the mother who holds, listens, tells, and retells for the young child (here we mean mothering person, as the function can be fulfilled by the father or anyone who speaks and listens with attunement to the child). These early stories are about the inner world and the outer world. Stories of witches, dragons, and monsters, developed into myths and legends, are cultural attempts to give shape and order to overwhelming anxiety and primitive fantasy.

We began to appreciate anew the tremendous transformational power of the mode in analysis, as the analysand and analyst shape, through countless tellings and retellings, the stories of the analysand's life. The making of stories is a major mutative factor in analytic growth and change. Here, we were particularly influenced by the work of Schafer, Spence, Ogden, and Bollas. Any book on the subject of desire and language must acknowledge Lacan's (1977) fecund and controversial contributions.

Finally, to the extent that we ourselves have felt free to weave new theoretical narratives, to set out in a new corner of territory, we have been influenced by the unique training experience we both had at the Los Angeles Institute and Society for Psychoanalytic Studies (LAISPS). Perhaps because it has been in itself a pioneer, the first free-standing interdisciplinary institute to be established west of the Mississippi, LAISPS engendered an openness of thinking, a questioning orientation that we hope marks the tone of our narrative. All these experiences have encouraged us to try to move freely in mental spaces not too closely bounded by established paradigms.

I
Story Making

1

Words and Stories in Narrative Space

Until we can make room for the problem of subjectivity in our theory, we'll never be able to separate the singer from the song.
(Spence, 1992)

As human beings, we are distinguished by the need to make meaningful sense of experience. One way we do so is through language and the creation of stories, that is, through narration. For our purposes in this chapter, we define narration broadly as the developmental capacity for verbally describing internal and interpersonal experience.

Language, acquired in the crucible of our earliest relationships and refined along the continuum of human development, colors and defines our constructions of reality. As unfamiliar sounds, themes, and patterns emerge, new experiences are tested against previously held constructs. Preexisting narratives form verbal and conceptual templates through which data are filtered and shape our perception of experience. This method of data collecting and organizing underscores the relative subjectivity of the narrative process and the plasticity of meaning. Some define the emergence of a sense of self as the individual's gradual accumulation of beliefs and desires containing the word "I." As our beliefs and desires eventually assume a recognizable and cohesive quality, they make a coherent, plausible story. Thus, self emerges by way of narratives.

NARRATIVE SPACE

The universal human quest for meaning is replicated in the analysand's search for and creation of a narrative story in analysis. Patients come into therapy with a life story that may be more or less

1

conscious and may seem to them cohesive and apparently complete. In fact, children at different developmental stages typically construct their stories differently; when the stories are retold in analysis, it becomes the analyst's task to tease out the syntax and cognitive style that characterizes each developmental period so that each story can be located developmentally. Narratives that were constructed during different periods in childhood are evoked in treatment and minutely examined. When retold in the context of the analytic relationship, much of what seemed cohesive and complete proves to be muddled and disjointed because of unconscious distortion and defense. The sudden recognition of discrepancies and disconnection in the stories of one's life is a disconcerting event that creates anxiety and calls for either the creation of new defenses or, with the analyst's help, the emergence of new life stories. Kristeva (1982) calls these "privileged moments," fissures in ordinary symbolization, where new symbols can emerge.

Analysis is, in some ways, the discovery, progressive retelling, and emendation of these stories. More importantly for us, the process of analysis is inseparable from a growing understanding that the making of meaning is the fundamental human enterprise, and there are as many stories as there are tellers, listeners, and occasions. The analysand must feel sufficiently supported in the analysis so that discrepancies can be discovered and the processes of "linking" (Bion, 1959, 1962) and the "making of multiple histories" (Schafer, 1980, 1983) can occur. The construction of a reliable analytic space is a creative, collaborative act; it is neither a given nor something that can be provided entirely by the analyst.

> Analytic space can be thought of as the space between patient and analyst in which analytic experience (including transference illusion) is generated and in which personal meanings can be created and played with. It is a potential space, the existence of which can by no means be taken for granted. (Ogden, 1986, p. 238)

The analysand actively contributes to the construction of the analytic space through collaboration in the working alliance (Greenson, 1967). The analyst's contributions include keeping boundaries, providing important new perspective while refraining from intrusive and premature interpretation, and constantly monitoring countertransference interference. Both therapist and patient collaborate by employing their capacities to reabsorb, defuse, or detoxify certain projections that would threaten to contaminate and destroy the work space. Provision of the needed reliable and clear therapeutic frame fosters the key mutative aspects of treatment. By our recognizing and exploring our own and our patient's anxieties about safety and attendant resisting, the analytic space is slowly created. Within this space and within the transference–countertransference matrix, the participants become able to retell the past instead of reliving it.

Adding to the meaning of the term "analytic space," we have coined the phrase "narrative space" (Wrye, 1991) to describe the process and outcome of the analyst and analysand becoming "coauthors" of a new story. Their quest for meaning occurs in much the same way that parent and child, or lovers, develop a reassuring and familiar personal language and set of shared remembrances. If as children we experienced the soothing, frightening, organizing, and explanatory functions of fairy tales and nursery rhymes, as analysts and analysands we enter eagerly into the storymaking aspect of analysis. A common childhood wish to have the same story told the same way, over and over, owes to the great comfort in the familiar and a fear of the unknown. If the storyteller's lap does not feel safe, the listener may not be persuaded to consider a new story with unfamiliar elements. In that case, only the same old story can be told— no change occurs. With safety, however, the new can become intriguing and expand horizons.

In functional, "good-enough" families, parent and child together develop a reassuring and familiar language and set of shared remembrances. We know that in some families the stories that are told are horror stories—told not to reassure and delight, but to intimidate, coerce, and demean. When children from such families come into treatment, they pose special demands on the therapist. Some particular difficulties in establishing safety with such patients and the consensual frame necessary for creating narrative space for them are taken up in chapters 6 and 7.

For analysands, a critical difference between the analytic encounter and their family of origin is that the analysand is deemed the primary storyteller. Many analyses begin with the expectation that the analyst, like the parent, will be the maker of meaning, the law, and the word. Analysands, however, often look to their analysts to be the primary storytellers. Complicity with this expectation contributes to the infantilization of the patient and the preempting of the patient's primary authorship of his or her narrative. Respect for the patient's integrity is a prime requisite of any analysis; zealous interpreting, like intrusive parenting, can force the analysand into a Procrustean bed, requiring narrow, defensive patterns of response. Inexperienced analysts are very susceptible to being pressured into acting like experts, to earn their keep by making interpretations. Thus, considerable work in the transference and countertransference arenas is required for the deconstruction of infantile wishes for an omnipotent parent that are embodied in the wish for the analyst to be the expert with the last word. The countertransference wish to "make right" and to maintain theoretical correctness is elaborated in chapter 4.

STORIES CHILDREN TELL

What do we mean by narrative? According to linguists, there are at least three kinds of narratives. One is a literary construction that is relatively fixed and smooth running and has a single author. Another simply records a sequence of events, without the whys or wherefores—like a police report. The third is a conversational narrative that reveals the speaker's position and relationship to experiences; this kind of narrative is ephemeral, full of fissures, breakdowns, and repairs. It is not considered to be fixed and stable but can be "reentered" and changed (Wolf, 1992). We are primarily concerned with the last kind, particularly as it makes possible self as the center of narrative gravity.

Narratives are traditionally constructed through language, although there are such nonverbal expressions as art and music. As we grow from wordless infancy to language acquisition, our first words name our most beloved objects and locate them in relation to us. First we learn simple family names, colors, and shapes of everyday life; later we name more complex feelings, foreign objects, and strange shapes to make cognitive maps and derive meaning. Such "word maps" contribute to the establishment of self–other boundaries, a sense of identity, and the maintenance of a cohesive sense of self. Those who lack such a core sense of self exist as if in a black hole of annihilation anxiety (Grotstein, 1990a; Wrye, 1993a) By acquiring emotional or psychological "literacy," we transform the nameless dread of inchoate primal terror into the named, known, and tolerable. Some of our patients come to us with very limited psychological literacy. They have been deprived of the empathic attunement by the primary caregivers that helps children to name their feelings and experiences—they lack "the words to say it" (Cardinal, 1983).

When parents and teachers are able nonjudgmentally to name psychological states that accompany action, they help growing children become emotionally competent and attuned to their own and others' internal feeling states. Many people, however, grew up in some kind of emotional vacuum, where empathic attunement was lacking. Worse, they were made to feel ashamed of their moods and feelings.

In so-called normotic families (Bollas, 1987), feelings are robotically denied and children experience themselves as things among things instead of as persons. When such people enter treatment, the acquisition of even a basic language of psychological states often becomes a primary therapeutic goal. Once acquired, this basic vocabulary can then be expanded to include nuances of meanings. It can be developed to compose more and more complex and descriptive narratives of inner life and experience.

In our view, the achievement of emotional literacy in treatment is accompanied by structural development and psychic growth. Change occurs by working through the conflicts and deficits in the transference and by the provision of transitional opportunities in which the patient takes up again delayed developmental tasks. Of course, the mere development of a simple capacity to name inner states is not a satisfactory therapeutic outcome. Without the structural change that occurs through the analysis of the transference–countertransference matrix, such naming can devolve into empty linguistic exercises .

Developmental linguist Wolf (1992) describes "narrative attunement" as the facility the "good-enough mother" has from the very earliest face-to-face contact with her baby to mirror her infant's facial expression and to give words to it: "So you're sleepy now" or "You look ready to play!" We can posit that the growth of patients who lack competency in describing their internal states was derailed somewhere along the line during the four critical stages and processes Wolf identifies as crucial in the child's development of narrative attunement. These processes appear between caregivers and children at staggered points, and each is at least two sided: a "glorious negotiation" and a bleaker outcome. Awareness of the four stages can illuminate this aspect of our clinical task in helping to foster our patients' capacity for narrativity.

The first stage in the development of narrative attunement

appears when the caregiver, even before the child has language, starts to build "scaffolding" for language as if the child were really already capable. For example, when the nine-month-old wakes up cranky from her nap, her mother, attuned to her distress, may say, "Oh! you want to get out of that crib!" as if the child's capacity for verbalization were already there. There is also the possibility of misreading the cues and of misattuning's leading to a bleak outcome. A truly communal narrative hangs "suspended between caregiver and child" (Wolf, 1992) and allows for a mutual kind of construction. This first stage, characterized only by person and action, is relatively primitive, although the mother does not respond to the primitive aspect but responds as if the infant were more mature and already capable of narrative. This stage culminates in the child's ability simply to verbalize subject and object ("Mommy car?") and to elicit the caregiver's elaboration of the emotional shadings of the moment ("Yes, you're happy to hear Mommy's car drive in! She'll be here in the kitchen any moment").

Next, by the time the child is three years old, comes the use of verb tense and the ability to cocreate more complex narratives. While playing in the mother's presence, the child can describe who, what, where, and when, like a sportscaster, and then shift into questions: Why? Where did it used to be? Thus the child invites the caregiver to participate and elaborate with even more subtle shadings, adding meanings and motivations and historical references. There is an interactive movement, as child and caregiver move back and forth from straight reporting to the building of narratives with meaning. The stage is set for the next phase when there has been adequate mutual following of the child's verbalizations by an empathic caregiver.

The third stage typically occurs when the child is moving out from the sphere of the family into day care or school, usually at three-and-a-half to five years of age. Stories become triangulated; there is an awareness of different points of view and audiences. The child develops the sense not only of her own experience of what happened and what the teacher may report, but of what mother or father wants to hear ("family myths" and cultural and gendered role expectations have already been grasped). Thus, narratives are quickly edited and shaded *in situ*. The precarious aspect here is that, lacking empathic narrative attunement on the part of caregivers, the child may develop a false self to accommodate these demands. By contrast, the empathic caregiver is able to say, "Yes, you're afraid that if you tell me that your brother pushed the boy on the playground, I'll punish him, and you'll feel ashamed. Also, maybe you're worried, because you're his little sister, that he'd get mad at you, too". Finally, in the fourth stage, if such empathic attunement has been available, the child becomes able to narrate complex psychological conflicts while maintaining a sense of self and audience.

Holding these critical stages in mind in clinical encounters with patients who have suffered impediments in the development of narrative attunement and empathy adds a deficit-recovery model to concrete material that we might have been inclined to interpret as aspects of defense.

Stern (1985), whose interest in the influences on and development of narrative memory developed out of infant research, recently embarked on an intriguing study that traces the creation of narrative reports by children as they are being constructed. Attempting to explore children's shaping and construction of stories of experienced events, he developed a design in which he videotaped three-and four-year-olds accompanied by a researcher as they entered into a dramatically scripted "play" about a topic of great concern, separation. As each child comes into the playroom, he or she encounters a clown playing with a big teddy bear, who then invites the child to play. After a time, the play is interrupted by an ominous dark figure, who says she has come to take the bear away to the land of the robots. The clown woefully parts with the bear, offering the child an opportunity to do the same, and the bear is removed. At this point, the clown cries over the loss of her friend, the bear. The child watches, or may share in the grieving, or may choose to comfort the clown. The drama ends, and the child is immediately asked to recount what happened and then to tell his or her mother, who has been waiting in another room, about the experience. A week later the child is again asked to tell the story, and then a year later.

The videotapes of each child's behavior reveal such a differing range of reactions to the separation drama that they offer dramatic evidence of narrative distortion as it is happening. Some children became anxious: one hid under a table; others moved to comfort the bear and the clown about the pain of separation; another little boy dealt with his discomfort with a flurry of motoric activity so distracting that when he told the story immediately afterward there was no mention of the separation at all, only a clown. Once each mother entered as an intervening variable, her own calm, attunement, anxiety, or mechanisms of defense further shaped the child's apparent memory and retelling of the story. Time further molded the telling; some children's versions remained relatively consistent, while others departed considerably. Although these data have not yet been analyzed and Stern (1992) points to the methodological difficulties of a study that can only observe behavior, not subjective internal experience, nonetheless, the study appears to provide observational evidence of the profound impact on memory of personality, defensive style, and the quality of the mother–child relationship. This research study gives credence to the fundamental questioning of Freud's early hypothesis that analysis is a tool to uncover psychic bedrock. If dozens of child–parent pairs conjure at least as many different versions of a scientifically controlled event (and even more versions longitudinally over time), there is no "bedrock" version.

FATHER AND MOTHER AND LANGUAGE

Lacan attributes differing roles during infancy to father and mother as bearers of language (Moss, 1989). The search for meaning carries the search for reunion with both the symbolically soothing mother and the containing father. Father introduces and fosters separation from the physical at-onement with mother (Grotstein, 1978, 1980, 1990a). Mother, bearing the language of everyday experience, of nursery rhymes, songs, and fairy tales, names the monsters and ogres of the night while holding her child safe, thus making the fear of those monsters endurable. Father broadens the path to symbolic thinking, abstraction, and metaphoric language.

    The Lacanian construction is interesting but, in our view, greatly abstracts and to some extent disembodies the complex early interactive maternal/paternal, sensory-bodily matrix in which language develops. Van Buren (1991) takes Lacan to task, reinstating the flesh and blood mother's role in developing symbolic discourse with her baby. Ogden (1985, 1989) sees the entry of father as transforming the rhythm of the dyadic "dialogue of cooing engaged in by mother and infant" (p. 53) into the "triangularity within which space is created. That space between symbol and symbolized, mediated by an interpreting self, is the space in which creativity becomes possible and is the space in which we are alive as human beings" (Ogden, 1985, p. 133). Stern (1985), describing the complex sensory-bodily matrix in which language develops, notes the positive achievement and power that language acquisition represents, as well as the loss of the ineffable, unnamable mystery and magic of the world before words. What happens, he asks, to the *experienced* patch of yellow sunlight dancing in the crib, when it is named?

NARRATIVE THEORY

Without words we have no analysis. Yet words themselves are limiting. Is there any way that a verbal description can really replicate sensory bodily experience? Translating any experience into words limits the infinite shades and nuances of both unconscious fantasy and preverbal and nonverbal sensory experience. When we name the inchoate, we bring it order—temporal, spatial, textural, contextual. This is why naming makes the unknown less threatening for children. Rumpelstiltskin lost his horrible power over the fair young maid once she named his name. Naming has the profound power to shape and alter experience.

Attempting to gain closer access to the unconscious, Freud (1913) developed the idea of free association, urging his patients to say "whatever comes to mind." But, inevitably, selection, focus, and an unavoidable editing process occur in even the most genuine attempts to report free associations faithfully. And for the analyst, a mode of "narrative listening" is inevitable. Ironically, when the patient is most faithfully following Freud's rule of free association and speaking in incomplete sentences, expressing unformed associations and disconnected thoughts, we tend to fill in the syntactic links in our minds. Spence (1982) reminds us that if we could listen with only free-floating attention to a patient who is truly free in his associations, we would hear nothing more than a series of words.

> To register the utterance with some kind of understanding we must supply a wide range of background assumptions and listen in an active, constructive manner, making assumptions about incomplete sentences, filling out ambiguous references, and otherwise supplying what the patient leaves out. (p. 29)

The way we interpolate any meaning into human action is heavily dependent on our conceptual system as observers. There is no bona fide method independently to verify or falsify our interpretations. Thus, Spence argues, we simply have to accept the linguistic and grammatical construction of psychoanalytic narratives as a given. We must acknowledge the "veridical" limitations of psychoanalysis together with the way it implicates subjectivity and creativity.

CLINICAL THEORY AND METATHEORY
IN RELATION TO NARRATION OF DESIRE

We make the assumption that human beings strive toward meaning and the ongoing construction of reality from moment to moment and in their lives as a whole. In both conscious and unconscious experience, the new is continuously evaluated in comparison with the known. Current events are weighed and tested against lifelong assumptions, attitudes, beliefs, and those encapsulated aspects of experiences known as memory, common sense, or reality.[1] The most familiar outcome of this process is a story, or narrative; the cumulative effect is the creation of a system of meaning.

Our further assumption, indeed, the *analytic* assumption, is that critical aspects of the linking process and its results remain unconscious under ordinary conditions. This assumption implies the existence of an inner world, contemporaneous with and unevenly connected to conscious experience and the world of consensual reality. This inner world is the world of primitive wishes and objects, where primary process reigns. With the possible exception of introspection, we have no *direct access* to this inner world; what Spence (1982) would call the "stuff of the mind."

As analysts, we deal primarily with derivatives, those aspects of patients' inner beliefs and processes which can be gleaned from the analytic material as it emerges in the analytic process. The analytic situation is specifically framed to maximize the emergence of these derivatives, leading to the carefully considered set of interpretations that are seen as mutative. The emergence and weaving of these derivatives and the progressive meaning assigned to them also take the shape of a story, told and retold over the course of treatment.

Although there is a fair amount of agreement on the proper framing of an analysis, the rules for interpretation and the content of interpretations considered effective vary drastically according to each analyst's theoretical orientation. The making of meaning in the analytic situation requires the examination of three sets of meaning systems: that of the patient, that of the analyst, and that

---

[1] We mean by this a process similar to Schafer's (1983) "refined common sense . . . which serves as the storehouse of narrative structures and remains the source of intelligibility in human affairs" (p. 214).

which they may teach each other over the course of the analysis. It is this third system of meaning with which we are primarily concerned. Before we examine the specifics of this situation, we want to discuss epistemology, that is, the study of how we know what we know.

A prime requirement for the application of the scientific method is the issue of falsification, that is, the possibility that a hypothesis can be disproved. It is not yet clear to what extent psychoanalytic hypotheses are susceptible to falsification. Clearly we lack the essential methodology for purely scientific explanations, and we must look elsewhere for our paradigms.

In this book we present the position that by leaving aside claims to objective truth and scientific methodology and looking instead at narratives and how they evolve, we may be able to investigate the processes by which analytic pairs achieve the sense that *something is known* and, equally vital, the sense that something has *changed*. As analysts, we strive to listen without prejudice but must necessarily listen within the context of our own system of meaning, including the very real filter of the countertransference. No special claims can be made for the pure reality of the analyst's observations, which Spence (1982) has called the "doctrine of immaculate perception." Yet we cannot simultaneously question every aspect of our belief system without incurring the paralysis of the obsessive-compulsive and essentially ignoring the patient. Having acknowledged the biases of our theories and keeping in mind the fallibility of our ideas and capacity to live up to our own ideals, we still need a working truth to be getting on with.

Freud remained convinced that memories, embedded in the unconscious, could be coaxed or compelled to speak for themselves through the synchronous processes of the patient's free association and the analyst's evenly hovering attention. Contemporary analysts, rejecting the notion of splintered shards of memory lying pristine and undiluted under an obscuring mantle of repression, have questioned Freud's basically archaeological perspective on the nature of memory.

NARRATION AND RECONSTRUCTION

Freud, who compared the analyst to an archaeologist digging to archaeological "bedrock" to reconstruct the truth, nonetheless suggested the notion "most momentous of all . . . though [the event] never had a real existence and is never remembered. It is a construction of analysis"

(Freud, 1919, p. 185). To our way of thinking, this is the crux of the argument about aspects of theory purportedly "derived" from clinical practice. A narrative is a *construction of the analysis*, not the only one possible; but once it is formulated and accepted by both participants, it moves the analysis in certain very definite ways. What does and does not have "a real existence" in the analysis is produced by transference and countertransference, both of which are susceptible to many influences. To the extent that each participant in the analytic dialogue is preoccupied with demonstrating the validity of a theory, each will be less available to the influences of current experience.

As a concept, narrativity resembles, yet must be differentiated from, the psychoanalytic technique of reconstruction. Like reconstruction, its purpose is to enable the analyst to understand and formulate aspects of the patient's infantile life and their contribution to adult dysfunction. Throughout the analytic process, stories or reconstructions are continually reshaped. At different phases of treatment, the patient's life, childhood objects, and experiences look different to the analyst and the analysand. What Harold Blum (1980) says of reconstruction can also be said of narration:

> Because of defensive distortion and areas of ego immaturity, accurate reconstruction is a gradual process involving conjoint efforts and analytic collaboration; usually initiated by the analyst, it is more likely to be valid and effective later in treatment. Reconstruction as a process involves remolding by analyst and analysand with approximations that have ever greater cohesion and explanatory power. (pp. 39-40)

The classical term reconstruction implies the existence of a basic relatively veritable historical truth that can be uncovered, as in an archaeological quest for artifacts. Narration emphasizes the literary or creative element in the pursuit. It is not that the analyst and analysand set out to develop a fictional account; it is that their most arduous and objectively faithful studies of the infantile past through transference enactments and constructions can at best only approximate a "relative truth." Blanks are inevitably filled by creative imagination, warped by the unattainability of the "blank screen," and colored by the intersubjective human/breathing matrix in which they occur. The criteria for preferring one particular construction over others include its plausibility in the context of what is known about human development, anxiety, and defenses in general; its believability in relation to the psychological picture of object relations that has been enlivened in the transference; and its utility in the patient's own terms. Thus, for narrative theory, the emphasis is on construction rather than reconstruction.

Further, all our theoretical paradigms, like lenses, shape and color the construction of our narratives. Analyst/writers, like the proverbial blind men and the elephant, inevitably observe only aspects of the beast. We also subscribe to the notion that case reports, like the analytic narrative, however objectively and faithfully reported, are a kind of fiction. They represent descriptions of selections of the subjective experience of the participant-observer. Similarly, multiple levels of storymaking are at work right here in this book. On one level, each patient constructs his or her own narratives in the analysis; simultaneously each analyst is constructing his or her version of the narrative of the analysis; when we write about that narrative, yet another edited construction emerges. Reading our version, each reader will produce another version. When the therapist discusses with the patient the issue of permission to use clinical material and write about it, what is written will further influence the patient's version of his story. And so on.

SEARCHING FOR A PARADIGM

In recent years, there has been a shift in many scholarly disciplines away from the positivistic, natural-science model. The shift is toward a focus on semiotics, hermeneutics, the study of meaning and interpretation and the concept of narrativity as a kind of paradigm of inquiry (Kuhn, 1962). Although psychoanalysis has always included the narrative or rhetorical focus, this focus has only recently attracted widespread notice in the mainstream.

We take as our model of psychoanalytic inquiry the currently accepted idea that analytic "truth" is relative and subjective. Analysis, a human science, is in some ways closer to art than to physical science. Its "truths" can never be fully tested and absolutely known. Whereas Freud took as his scientific model the energic forces associated with 19th-century mechanical physics, if we were even to stay with that scientific model, our paradigm would have to be in the form of a metaphor based on relativity theory and quantum physics.

This century has seen a revolutionary shift in scientific paradigms. Quantum physics, for instance, shows that rather than discrete particles revolving around a nucleus, all particles in motion have wave properties (*The New Columbia Encyclopedia*, 1975, p. 180.)

Bateson (1972, 1979), in his efforts to understand and elaborate "living systems" theory, challenged the efficacy of the model of Newtonian physics with its linear notions of causality. Referring to Korzybski's maxim "the map is not the territory," he argued that we cannot have an "objective reality." The meaning we ascribe to any event is determined by the assumptions, premises, and presuppositions that constitute our cognitive maps of the world. Bateson compared these "maps" to patterns and maintained that the interpretive reading of any event is determined by how it coincides with previously known patterns of events.

Kumin (1986) relates these shifts in scientific paradigms to psychoanalysis. He conceptualizes object relations

> in their endopsychic as well as their interpersonal vicissitudes, as having the qualities of both "particles" and "waves"; that is, in being both discrete and differentiated psychic images as well as being "smeared out" over a self/object field of complex "shape." Thus, representations of self and object, in addition to being thought of as differentiated entities . . . could also be thought of as complex configurations . . . in dynamic interaction and reversibility with each other throughout life. (p. 660)

We can take a theoretical position based on the metaphor of quantum physics and relativity theory to a parallel notion of the relativity of the intersubjective/intrapsychic field. Speaking within this metaphor, we argue that facts are not simply "out there" to be gathered but, rather, occur as a complex, wavelike interaction of inner and outer realities, the intrapsychic and the interpersonal. Two major shifts in clinical emphasis inevitably ensue. First, analysts must be more aware of contextual considerations; and second, there will be greater emphasis on the countertransference. It is our thesis that the notion of an "analytic or narrative space" expands this metaphor. Narrative space provides the contextual setting in the analytic search for meaning.

Wallerstein (in Spence, 1982), described Spence's work as leading

> to a whole series of transformations of our usual analytic thought conventions: of reconstruction into (new) construction, of acts of discovery into acts of creation, of historical truth into narrative fit, of pattern finding into pattern making, of veridical interpretation into creative interpretation, of all interpretation into a species of

(more or less) inexact interpretation, of analysis essentially as a science of recovery of the past into a science of choice and of creation in the present and future. (p. 13)

Spence points out the vital relationship between what is recalled in the context of the current analytic situation, including the transference and countertransference, and the language that has evolved between the participants.

In Schafer's (1980) conception, psychoanalysis is an interpretive discipline, where a particular and systematic account of human action, the narrative, is developed. He argues that the life story told and apprehended by the analyst changes in an ongoing manner throughout the course of the analysis. This change is partly the result of the analytic question being pursued; eventually, "one might say that in the course of analysis there develops a cluster of more of less coordinated new narrations, each corresponding to periods of intensive analytic work on certain leading questions" (p. 204).

That statement echoes Schafer's conception of multiple histories, the creation of analytic narratives that are progressively refined in the analytic discourse. In a similar vein, Schafer (1976, 1978, 1980) insists that the analysand, like the analyst, must be viewed as a *person;* not as the repository or passive agent of events, or drives, or metapsychological structures and forces, but as one who actively (both mentally and physically) finds and makes the world in which he·acts. In this sense, both analyst and analysand are active agents, authors of the patient's life histories. In the psychoanalytic collaboration, which he calls "the construction of multiple histories," Schafer (1983) emphasizes that there is

no single, all-purpose psychoanalytic life history to be told, for the account of that life keeps changing during the course of analysis. This continuous change occurs . . . because the history gets to be told more insightfully, . . . more completely, more consistently, and with a greater sense of relevance regarding the variables that are crucial in analysis, such as the varieties of sexual, aggressive, and defensive activity during different phases of development. (p. 204)

FROM RECONSTRUCTION TO DECONSTRUCTION

In psychoanalysis, the most important sources of understanding are reverberating rather than predictive. Reverberation is inherent in the ideas of repetition, reconstruction, and transference. What the patient once was, he will be again; what the patient desired, believed, fantasized, and has forgotten will again be visible as derivatives, plucked from dreams, associations, slips, symptoms, and, especially, from the interwoven threads of the transference and countertransference. Over time, these reverberations result in narratives that, in turn, influence and shape the analysis. Narratives may support mutative change, or they may obscure and impede it.

A patient comes in with a story, including ideas about the way life works and the way her own life, in particular, works or fails to work. Individual responsibility for outcomes and the ownership of action are key aspects of these stories, as are cohesiveness and self-consistency. The quality and character of the object relations the patient describes are equally vital. In the analytic process, the patient discovers, selects, and elaborates symbols, objects, and memories. As these are grouped together in a more or less complete narrative account, they may serve as a kind of working truth of the analysis. Such a narrative would contain within it a summary of the state of the self, the state of the object, and the state of the analysis. Thus, narration is inextricably linked to analytic growth.

Narration is a form of internal organizer through which a person attempts to balance and orchestrate narcissistic, aggressive, and sexual intentions. Narration also names and defines important internal objects and potentially reveals a great deal about internal psychic structure. It is no easy matter to "read backwards" from a narrative and find statements about impulses, objects, self-states, and belief systems. First of all, there is the distortion and limitation inherent in translating thoughts into words, especially when the content is images and affects, which may not be available to the patient in anything like a speakable language. Second, once a story is narrated, anxiety and disruption follow the effort to change it. Third, there is the issue of unconscious compliance, the ways in which patients tend, over time, to dream and produce material to confirm the theories of their own analysts. Finally, and specifically on the analyst's side of the couch, there is the double helix of analytic theory and countertransference, which is the frame of comprehension through which constructions are created. All these factors, which we see as endemic aspects of resistance, make it difficult to deconstruct the existing narrative in the service of analytic change. Theory may be similarly resistant to change.

The construction of any psychoanalytic paradigm, such as Freud's elaboration of the Oedipus complex and all the subsequent emendations and applications of it to patients' material, is another, more overarching level of narrative construction. Clinical case reports such as those contained in this book embody the very process of the transformation of inchoate clinical experience into particular, at times arbitrary, narratives. This process includes selective editing, point of view, highlighting themes, and paradigmatic constructions.

A question must be raised as to the ontological status, or truth value, of a series of stories. Is the last story always the best, the most complete, the one in which the earlier stories are subsumed? It is not the story itself that interests us, but rather the process of story-making, the exploration of meaning. If the only requisite for psychoanalytic cure were a better story, it would be easy enough to provide, possibly computer generated. The storytelling itself, the relationship in which the analyst and analysand construct each other in the process of making meaning is, in our view, also critically important.

A similar question is, will a false story cure a patient? A whole popular literature of codependency, for example, has been seized as a "better story." When one examines the popularly proclaimed codependency saga in detail, however, it soon is apparent that it applies generically in often superficial, indiscriminate fashion. It is undeniably of heuristic value and a major stimulus to many who feel they now understand things about themselves. It may also simply reflect the "reparative story hunger" many feel who do not have access to the more refined, individually tailored reparative stories that would emerge from individual therapy.

Our continuing interest is to be mindful of the various psychological and cultural influences that impinge on the making of stories. We try to address bias, the tendency to believe the story one has rather than deal with the anxiety inherent in the deconstruction of that story and the ensuing fragmentation of meaning. Schafer (1992) puts it this way: "Freud's clinical dialogue alters in crucial ways the analysand's consciously narrated presentation of the self and its history among people by destabilizing, deconstructing and defamiliarizing it" (p. 156). These terms, taken from the field of literary criticism, mean the ways in which the analytic process challenges defenses (destabilizes); discovers hidden meanings and hidden inconsistencies (deconstructs); and introduces novel and intersecting storylines (defamiliarizes).

There are, nevertheless, progressive narratives, many of which we recount in this book as case studies, that free the mind from debilitating and warped stories and move toward more playfulness and openness of mind, more creativity, more freedom, greater pleasure in living. Thus, we emphasize that the content of the stories is not nearly so important as the opening of the mind to a multiplicity of perspectives and a freeing and enrichment of desire.

How do the analyst and the patient determine when the story is good enough? Again, Schafer puts it well:

> But here the therapeutic goals of the analytic dyad intervene. Analyst and analysand make a judgment, based on shared health values, that any attempt at further change might create more problems than benefits or might just lack adequate momentum; it may also be judged that the patient is in a more or less adequate position to continue the work of analysis independently, as the need arises and to the extent necessary. At this point, the joint work of deconstruction and new construction comes to an end. (p. 158)

WORKING ASSUMPTIONS

The narrative space, then, is a kind of transitional space in which new narratives can emerge. It is related to the elusive, enigmatic, and paradoxical aspects of the "analytic space . . . where fantasy and reality stand in a dialectical relationship to each other. (Ogden, 1986, pp. 238–239). Winnicott (1967) wrote that a quotation from Tagore, "On the seashore of endless worlds children play," haunted him for years before he used it as the epigraph to his essay "The Location of Cultural Experience." The phrase poetically embodies much of what Winnicott strove to convey about the numinous area of transitional phenomena. To him, the phrase "endless worlds" suggested the opening of creative possibility; "children's play" became the focus of his work; "the seashore" was the perfect metaphor for transitional space, which is metaphorically the meeting of two elements: outer world and inner world, conscious and unconscious"(Winnicott, cited in Siegelman, 1990, pp. 177–178). Parallel to Winnicott's transitional space between mother and baby, therapist and patient share "narrative space" in the search for that which was heretofore unknown, the cocreated narrative.

Although sometimes we say "a narrative," we are really interested in the succession and interplay of multiple narratives in the course of long-term treatment. These original narratives of treatment are elaborated through enactments and mutative interpretations of transferences and countertransferences. Different and recognizable positions, which we describe as deadspace, deadlocks, and primitive eroticism, to name a few, should be understood as narratives and worked with accordingly. When the capacity for storymaking has, for whatever reason, turned in on itself in the form of constricted, deadened fragments, then the way out seems to pass regularly through a certain kind of therapeutic dialogue in which primitive desire can be incorporated. Later in the book we suggest the existence of a kind of "natural progression" from narratives that chronicle deadness, detachment, and omnipotent punishing control over an internal object, to narratives chronicling something more fluid, wet, and erotic, and finally more differentiated "triangulated narratives," which include a third party and which signal articulated oedipal themes.

The area that has captured our interest, the "narration of desire," is the myriad ways in which "love stories" first diffusely emerge on the mother–infant playground (Sanville, 1987, 1991a). These earliest stories evoke the preverbal media of contact, the gaze, smell, taste, touch, holding, feeding, bathing, cooing, recorded in "body loveprints."

In the analytic construction of narratives of desire, new kinds of narratives regularly start with primitive urges involving body parts. This is the first level of preverbal narrative we shall be considering in chapter 2. Some patients use nonverbal expressions of art or music in therapy to communicate their experience. These idioms reflect phenomena along the developmental continuum from the most primitive, concrete forms to refined expressions of sublimated impulses. From this starting point, we turn our attention to the primitive origins of erotic desire that ultimately become elaborated in each analytic dyad's narration of desire.

2

When the Story Doesn't Flow

As clinicians we all experience periods of disruption, stalemate, and clinical dumbness. Experiences of blockage and dislocation are extremely unsettling for analyst and patient alike and can precipitate an abrupt dissolution of the therapeutic alliance. Sometimes, however, the very frustration and anxiety engendered by these therapeutic quandaries stir us to new and more useful formulations. This was the process by which Freud, and later others, transformed the face of psychoanalytic theory from within the consulting room.

In this chapter we describe a few such encounters with our patients and with the patients of therapists we train and supervise. In the course of our doing that work, our thinking about the primitive preverbal erotic transferences and countertransferences has evolved. Through these experiences we have come to elaborate our concepts of maternal erotism. Many of these illustrations are of cases in which the patient provided the opportunity to work with and through the impasse. We will return to these in various chapters throughout the book, to provide an overview of the larger treatment process. However, we are not always so fortunate, and in some cases, impasse resulted in annulment.

SOME PRESENTING FACES OF THE
MATERNAL EROTIC TRANSFERENCE

A female patient brought to her analytic session a rather malodorous package from the fish market and informed her therapist that the package would require refrigeration during the hour. A male patient came to his session with a taped version of his film for the analyst to take home "at leisure" and play on her videotape player. In another instance, a meticulous woman, while ostensibly emptying her purse into the wastebasket, quietly left bits of debris on the couch. In a subsequent session, the same woman brought in a rose for her therapist, who chose to talk about rather than accept the gift. The patient stomped the flower underfoot and walked out.

A male patient came to his analytic session dressed for a costume party. Another patient anxiously requested that her analyst accompany her to a tiny anteroom so that she could reveal a secret. In the fourth year of treatment another male patient suddenly and inexplicably failed to recognize his therapist when she came for him in her waiting room. A loquacious female analysand fell into a week of silence in her sessions, while stroking and rubbing the textured rice paper wall covering beside the couch. At another point, ostensibly because of excruciating back pain, she asked if she could have her session lying on the floor of the office rather than on the couch.

Although obviously many meanings can be read in each of these events, a common denominator is the concrete quality of the transference enactment. Also, we noted over time that these events often occurred at a point when treatment seemed stalemated. Typically the patient was unable to carry on in the analytic mode, was unable to talk about feelings, and felt compelled instead to action. Something primitive, preverbal, and maybe even terrible was going on. As it could not be talked about, or perhaps even named, the patient and the therapist were unable to bring it into the room except by enactment.

Such actions tend to shake our composure and severely strain analytic neutrality. When confronted with these events, we analysts are apt to feel surprised, confused, even flummoxed, and we are likely to behave as defensively as our patients. By reacting rather than reflecting, we implicitly entrench their defenses and strengthen their disavowal of meaning.

The erotic meaning of such enactments is often blocked from elaboration by both the patient and the therapist. There are important defensive reasons for this, which we will deal with more fully in subsequent chapters. Primarily, this kind of erotic enactment is of such a primitive and preverbal nature as not to be readily recognizable as erotic. If it were to become conscious, it would typically result in shame and humiliation on the part of the patient and in anxiety about its management on the part of the therapist. While neither party directly experiences these events as erotic enactments, the analyst can view them through the template of maternal erotic transferences. This view prepares the analyst to deal more effectively with her own defensive responses. In the next section we explain how the concepts of maternal erotic transferences (MET) and maternal erotic countertransferences (MEC) were used to further the treatment.[1]

It should be clear that we are also talking in some cases about patients who, at times, do not fit the traditional psychoanalytic model of verbal symbolic communication and can make meaningful contact only through some form of attack on the traditional frame. Goldberg (1989) refers to the

> patient who cannot fit the verbal-symbolic mode, for whom experience and meaning are registered in some alternative code . . . always acting against the therapeutic framework, so that this framework is in one way or another attacked, rejected, corrupted or foreclosed.. . . Paradoxically, it is precisely here, at the point of attack, that initial meaningful contact may begin between therapist and patient. (p. 449)

The reparative aspect of a patient's wish is often hard to see when the patient insinuates it into the treatment with a concretely disruptive act. The therapist, confronted by a sudden, urgent demand, may be inclined to react defensively. Not all analysts have access to continuous supervision and consultation, as we did, but all therapists can learn to monitor the transference for clues to reparative motivation within apparently disruptive acts, and the countertransference, for important and informative resonances.

In this section we offer examples of clinical crisis to indicate the broad range of phenomena we classify as relating to maternal erotic transference. We are not focusing here on the very important clinical task of enabling the analyst to restore analytic equilibrium; issues of countertransference are more fully developed in chapter five.

---

[1]Throughout this book, for the sake of brevity, the two transference constellations (maternal erotic transferences and countertransferences) are sometimes referred to by the initials MET and MEC. Transference–countertransference is a highly individual matter, typical of each analytic pair at a certain stage in their ongoing relating and, in some key way, not reproducible outside their relationship. We conceive of MET/MEC then, simply as an organizing construct, useful to the extent that it does not preempt or exclude other models or become reified. Wishing to emphasize the complex plurality of the phenomena, we also refer interchangeably to maternal erotic transference(s) and countertransference(s).

WHEN EROTIC TRANSFERENCES
CRY OUT TO BE KNOWN

In the first instance cited in the previous section, the therapist who was confronted by her patient's "smelly package" sought supervision. She had recently moved from one office to another, taking this severely depressed patient, Maureen, with her. Maureen became suicidally depressed following the office move. She could not tolerate the separation anxiety raised by her doctor's moving and actively raged at Dr. A for making her so dependent that she had to follow her from place to place "like a humiliated and demeaned puppy." This phase of treatment lasted for some months, with Dr. A feeling assaulted and at times panicked. Maureen was furious because, as she put it, it "spreads to other parts of my life. . . . I have to develop a very tough shell to keep it all in." Note that the "smelly package" she had brought with her to the session was a loosely wrapped, hard-shelled lobster, which she asked Dr. A to keep in her refrigerator during the session.

In supervision, Dr. A reported her disgust at Maureen's bringing this smelly, clawed creature into her new office and her feeling of being invaded by the lobster to be put into her "icebox." Exploration in supervision made it apparent that Maureen's desperate wish was for safe haven and for access to Dr. A's body, something she had been deprived of with her own psychotic mother, who had repeatedly abandoned her before her early death. Sensing Maureen's craving for bodily connection, but not "knowing" it, Dr. A was pulling away in a kind of panic, presenting her own "hard shell." Dr. A's office move and defensive withdrawal both lent weight to Maureen's fear that she would be "aborted" by Dr. A, as Maureen knew that her own mother had sought to abort her. She seemed to feel that there was no way to gain safety other than to attempt to claw her way into Dr. A's womb, to be a lobster in her icebox. Moreover, neediness and hunger were her constant companions, and she was now so apprehensive that Dr. A would withdraw from feeding her that she had to bring her own food. Further, she wished, and yet feared breaking the treatment frame with the hard-edged object.

Learning of Maureen's early history of maternal abandonment, I (HKW) posited that Maureen's rage about displacement from the familiar office had stirred the symbolic prospect of being separated from her mother/analyst's body. I also offered that a patient's perception of her therapist's anxiety may elicit panicked feelings of loss and bodily disintegration, rekindling her earliest longings for containment in her mother's sensual body.

When Dr. A began to see the transference as a primitive maternal erotic transference enactment, she was able to regain her composure and understanding. Thus able to empathize with Maureen's panic, she emerged from her own largely unconscious horror and fear of being eaten alive by this needy baby or anally penetrated by a smelly fecal baby desperately searching for access to the interior of her mother's body. With interpretation of Maureen's separation anxiety and attendant annihilation anxiety and her longings for containment, the treatment panic subsided. Confirming and elaborating material from Maureen's early history of maternal abandonment emerged in subsequent sessions. With Dr. A's new appreciation of MET/MEC phenomena, the material could be explored without the need for further such enactment.

Although apparently less raw and primitive an act than bringing a malodorous lobster, the patient's enactment of bringing the videotape of his movie to his therapy session was also connected to primitive wishes. This young man, Paul, wanted Dr. B to view the film that he had been laboring on over the previous year, ostensibly to enable her to understand him better. Ordinarily, she would have handled this seemingly ordinary oedipal invitation simply by proposing that they explore together the meaning of his request. She felt in this instance, however, that something more primitive was being communicated, something threatening to her that she could not understand, and sought a supervisor (HKW).

Feeling agitated, and carrying an intense feeling that some illicit proposition was being offered, Dr. B felt embroiled in something she could not make sense of. In contrast, her patient maintained a blasé tone, assuming that his request was reasonable on the face of it and ought to be accepted. He could see no problem in it. Dr. B's sense that she was overreacting was a clue that something primitively powerful was being denied by her patient. At the same time, the treatment had droned down to stale reportage of his work and requests to engage her in "problem solving." Impelled to unconscious enactment, Paul brought in the video when words failed.

Through supervision, Dr. B discovered that behind Paul's more conscious wish for her to understand him and admire his production as a filmmaker was a fantasy that her VCR was in her bedroom. Behind the more obvious and accessible oedipal wish to be sexually intimate with her in her bedroom was a deeply repressed and powerful urge.

Paul had a primitive wish literally to slide his whole body into her body through her vagina, to disappear inside like a baby, and to take up residence within her womb. This fantasy in his unconscious mind would be enacted symbolically through having his film inserted inside her VCR.

In supervision, Dr. B reported that Paul had been rejected at birth by a very depressed and later physically abusive mother who had repeatedly told him that she hadn't wanted him and that he was the cause of her depression. He desperately wished for repair through a magical rebirth from the body of a longed for, warmly sensual mother/therapist. When Dr. B made contact with Paul's wish for rebirth, her own countertransference horror of an erotic invasion subsided. She was able to resonate with his longing, interpret the meaning of his action, and provide the needed containing and transformational function within the analytic frame.

The third patient, Gillian, who brought and then demolished a rose for her analyst (JKW), was a mathematician in her 60s. At the beginning of each session, Gillian would exclaim about the flower arrangements in the office. She was, in fact, something of a naturalist. I was astonished by Gillian's rage when I declined to accept the proffered rose. Gillian had never shown much passion before. As this event occurred early in my analytic career, I was simply and perhaps dutifully following the usual rule of abstinence, to explore the meaning of such an action rather than participate in it. Both the gift offering and the patient's subsequent rage provoked enough worry in me that I began to put together pieces of observations I had made of other bodily centered events in Gillian's analysis and began a more thorough investigation of the transference and countertransference.

At the time in question, Gillian was two years into analytic treatment and had often come into the room with blood-red wet fingernails, which she held suspended above her abdomen and occasionally waved around. This behavior usually stirred my worry about the safety of my very new analytic couch. Although there were many examples of intrusive transference enactment, such as Gillian's using the restroom before and after the sessions and waiting immediately outside the office door instead of in the waiting room, I had not appreciated and linked them to Gillian's history. Gillian had had rectal parasites throughout childhood and had been given enemas. She had grown up in a family who gave themselves daily enemas and talked incessantly about bowel movements. Not grasping their specifically erotic nature, I initially considered Gillian's actions to be indicative of the family's characterological intrusiveness. My conception of "erotic" at that early point in my analytic career was associated with genitality. (A much expanded description of this analysis is provided in chapter 4.)

Besides being confused by my own countertransference, I was also hampered by theoretical paradigm binding. I conceptualized Gillian's material within prevailing classical theory, and it was not easy for me to think about it from a totally different perspective. For this reason, access to a rich and evolving clinical theory is imperative. Otherwise one risks the Procrustean limitation of attempting to fit the body of the patient's experience into the short bed of the known, rather than allowing the anxiety of not knowing to let something entirely new emerge.[2]

Marcus, the patient who came to his analytic session dressed for a costume party, was very concerned that I (JKW) take it "the right way," which meant that I was to laugh rather than scold him. It also meant that we were not to explore the event. It was not until I presented this case at a conference that another therapist suggested that the patient was possibly a cross-dresser. Thus the act in question could be understood as the patient's attempt to wear on his body a wish he could not verbalize, namely, the wish to be transformed into a woman. This patient's erotic transference had appeared in an obvious oedipal format, including envious wishes directed towards my husband. As this episode also occurred prior to my coauthor's and my elaboration of the concepts of early maternal erotic transferences (see chapter 3), both the patient's and my primary focus on these "oedipal" cues obscured their earlier roots, and his wish for gender transformation. In any case, as my insight came too late, the patient abruptly terminated. What we learned from this fugitive patient has nevertheless contributed greatly to these concepts.

MATERNAL EROTIC ENACTMENTS

In the foregoing enactments, each patient "brought this or her body" in the form of a representative object (the lobster, the video, the flower, the wet nail polish, the costume) into the treatment. The

---

[2]Heinrick Racker (1968) used the term "complementary counter-transference" to denote the therapist's experience of projective identification of aspects of the patient that have been split off and projected. The ability to be helpful will ultimately depend on the therapist's capacity to identify with impulse, defense, and internal object.

patients were communicating (if it can be decoded) something they felt very deeply and had been unable to verbalize. These patients believed themselves to be somehow defective. While maternal erotic transferences and countertransferences portray in actions the specifics of that belief, the clinical situation is complicated by the fact that the patient's felt sense of defect may be split off and denied. As Coen (1986) puts it:

> The sense of defect is experienced concretely, as fact, which is emotionally deeply etched. At the same time, the sense of defect is usually vague, poorly defined, not easily verbalizable as to what is wrong. Although there is a profound awareness of something being wrong with oneself, this aspect of the self or body representation is usually split off, unintegrated, exhibitionistically repaired and perfected. (p. 54)

For each of the patients presented, the nature of this defect was experienced as having been present from earliest history, long before words, and was organized, either consciously or unconsciously, at a bodily level. Each patient sought a transformational experience. An aspect of early maternal erotic transferences is the belief that transformation can occur only through physical contact. Sometimes consciously, but more often unconsciously, the patient is convinced that bodily contact with the therapist's corporeal body is the only avenue for relief. We understand this as the patient's seeking in the therapy an experience that has its roots in the healing and holding of the early mother who cares for her infant in a fully physical way. Edith Jacobson (1965) noted that this physical holding function of the mother fosters the development of a body ego.

PREGNANT PAUSES: BIRTH ISSUES IN MET

The next series of vignettes depicts somewhat subtler transference enactments, less disruptively introduced by the patient, and more specifically related to gender and to pregnancy.

Carole, the young woman mentioned earlier who urgently asked me (JKW) to accompany her to a small anteroom to tell me something, had been in psychotherapy for a long time without making any visible demands. Responding to a level of anxiety that I had never seen before in the patient and that seemed of nearly psychotic proportion, I immediately granted her request. In the small room, she asked me to sit cross-legged on the floor. I did. Then Carole told me she was pregnant, and wept with anxiety. I told her that she seemed to want to experience our bodies as very close together in a small room/womb, like twins safely in utero or herself inside me. I suggested that she was afraid that being pregnant might disrupt our relationship. This calmed her down and evidently was a justifiable inference, leading as it did to extended discussions of the meaning of the event. Although it is always difficult to demonstrate what one has avoided, in my own mind I have attributed the absence of postpartum depression to this series of exchanges between us.

Christopher, the man who suddenly and inexplicably did not recognize me (JKW) in my waiting room, had had eye surgery as a very small boy. At that time, with his eyes fully bandaged, he was tended by a nurse whose voice he fell in love with. When the bandages were removed, the reality of the nurse's grossly overweight appearance disrupted his fantasy and he "was crushed." Just at the point in his analysis when powerful early erotic feelings were beginning to emerge, and just as he began to notice my female body and have a complementary experience of maleness, he reenacted his "blindness" by not recognizing me when I came for him in the waiting room. As we discussed this, he revealed that he had often had great difficulty keeping my real shape in mind. For example, once, when I wore a cape, he grew alarmed that I had grown swollen and misshapen, virtually overnight. I was initially alarmed about cognitive or visual impairments and had to satisfy myself that his misperceptions were neither psychotic nor physically based. Over time, I gathered that his distortions represented his fears that I would turn out to be the sweet-voiced but immense and crushing nurse of his childhood. He also saw me as magically impregnated by his erotic thoughts, although at the same time he feared he was a damaged little boy, inadequate to that task. The most primitive, and terrifying, aspect of the fantasy was that my imagined engorgement represented my having cannibalized him, or reengulfed him into my body.

These preoedipal fantasies reflect a developmental period characterized by magical thinking and a longing for transformation in the sensual body of mother. Emerging in an adult analysand, it can resemble an encapsulated somatic psychosis.

In the treatment of an ordinarily garrulous woman, Shelle, who fell completely silent for periods of a week or more, I (HKW) experienced her silence initially as a stalemate, a resistance to talking about what we had been working on in the preceding sessions. Slowly, however, I became aware of her primitive erotic and sensory longings as she wordlessly stroked the textured wallpaper on the wall beside the couch. I actually felt as if she were tracing the curves of my body, the indentations in the surface of my skin, as she wordlessly fingered the paper as if enraptured.

An avowed homosexual, Shelle had been utterly unable until then to access or "touch on" any erotic longings for me while, for two years, she had kept up an animated banter about all her affairs and dreams. She preferred to keep me "enthralled" but at a distance in a verbal, Scheherazade-like encounter that would last indefinitely if possible, rather than make the genuine sensual bodily contact she longed for but that she believed would precipitate my abandoning her as her psychotic mother had done at her birth in a mental hospital. She was indeed aware of her charm and gifts with words and her ability to seduce me with a kind of appealing narrative. When her longings became unbearable, she fell silent and began this wordless stroking of my wallpaper.

Shelle was one of the rare patients who actually brought to treatment an already articulated fantasy of a different birth story and a longing for a different birth mother. She wanted to be able to feel she had been in my womb and would emerge helplessly dependent on me, "on my back, unable to move, remaining as close as possible to your legs." Although a back injury precipitated her request to lie on the floor on her back during sessions, we subsequently understood the enactment as an effort to force me to permit her to experience a fantasied birth from my body. Thus at a certain point in the treatment, she herself, by way of a somatization of serious back pain, had assumed the position of a birthing mother, desperately hoping unconsciously that I would understand that she had selected me to give birth to her.

I was able to make contact with these fantasies because they were so palpably, albeit nonverbally, projected into me through the vehicle of the enactment. Immersed in the countertransference, I felt alternately like the mother who was overwhelmed by this needy and helpless infant and who wanted to get rid of her, and touched by a deeply maternal wish to heal her by rebirthing her and holding her for as long as she needed to be held.

HERALDING THE EMERGENCE
OF PREVERBAL BODILY TRANSFERENCES

In this chapter, we have briefly introduced the typical kinds of enactments that herald the emergence of primitive preverbal bodily transferences. These occur either when the patient is unable to make use of the "narrative space" to explore his or her feelings in words, often because the very feelings themselves come from a "time before words" (as for example, in the case of the man with the video or Shelle's fingering the wallpaper); or when the analyst has been unable, for whatever reason, to provide the security of the "narrative space" (such as when Maureen's therapist moved her office). In the next three chapters we elaborate our understanding of maternal erotic transferences and specify how each patient has a different idea about what kind of physical contact will lead to transformation. We arrived at our understanding of maternal erotic transferences largely through analysis of our own corresponding countertransferences. In chapter 4 we delineate the various defensive strategies that undermine treatment and entrench perverse narratives.

II
Maternal Erotic Transferences and Countertransferences

3

The Maternal Erotic Transference

All things considered, it seems to me that the analyst's bisexuality must be well integrated to enable the development of the baby, made by the analyst and the analysand in their work together, the baby which represents the analysand himself, recreated. (Chasseguet-Smirgel, 1984, p. 175)

FREUD AND THE FEMININE PSYCHE

In his declaration of female psychology as a "dark continent," Freud (1933) acknowledged the limitations of his own understanding of the feminine psyche. He invited female analysts to consult their own internal lives and their experiences with their female patients in order to gain understanding of female psychology. In developing our narratives about the maternal erotic transference and countertransference, we have indeed taken him up on his invitation to explore the "dark continent," as that is an apt description of the primordial swamps and uncharted territories we describe.

We wish at the same time, however, to call attention to the phobic, racist, and sexist implications in Freud's choice of the phrase. "Dark continent," referring to Victorian Europe's Africa, carries the implication of danger, disease, and colonial exploitation. These dark connotations are inseparable from the development of psychoanalysis; they are not to be dismissed as a simple semantic or poetic choice. Freud's "radical distrust of maternal influence" (Keller, 1985) lends an enduring tilt to psychoanalytic theory and practice.

33

According to Freud (1933), erotism was stimulated in females primarily by their longing for the strength, excitement, and power of the phallus to fill the void left by their castration. In our opinion, the construct of ubiquitous penis envy is the single best example of analysis' being temporarily blinded by the prevailing view. Early critics of Freud's phallocentric views challenged penis envy by elaborating the complementary presence in males of breast and womb envy (Horney, 1926; Fliegel, 1982; Chehrazi, 1986).

The classical paradigm of transference was that it was oedipal. When it was erotic, typically female patients to male analysts, it was viewed as disruptive and needing to be "managed" (see Introduction). This early paradigm of erotic transference has had to be radically amended. Sensual bonding between mother and baby, what we call "body loveprinting," and its appearances and permutations in the analytic dyad pique much interest. Infant research, making possible newer understanding of preoedipal development, has dramatically challenged the classical view of the internal life of the infant. Further impetus has come from feminist scholarship and interest in gender countertransference. Important developments in the philosophy of science and postmodern literary criticism have been applied to theory and clinical work. Questioning basic assumptions has opened the doors and windows, so to speak, on the nature of transference in general and the erotic transference in particular. It is within this intellectual atmosphere of challenge and response that we elaborate our narrative.

CONCEPTUALIZATION OF
THE MATERNAL EROTIC TRANSFERENCE

It is our view that maternal transferences, anchored in preoedipal matrices, are not merely precursors of oedipal, genital erogeneity but are erotic in their own right. These phenomena are indispensable aspects of subjectivity, self-esteem, and the continuous narrative of emotional development.

The early sensual bond between mother and baby, when marked by reciprocity and attunement, makes separateness tolerable and engenders baby's "love affair with the world" (Mahler, Pine, and Bergman, 1975). That love affair becomes the basis of loving relations and all erotism after the separation-individuation phase and into the oedipal and postoedipal period. When we use the word "erotic" we are talking about the gamut of feelings— from tender, sensual, and romantic to anal erotic, sadistic, aggressive, and masochistic—that stem from that original mother–baby bond. The feelings pertain to bodily contact and arise in the transference.

Ours is the broadest possible view of maternal erotic transferences. It includes all manner of sensual bodily fantasies in relation to the analyst's body. We locate the origins of erotic experience in the preverbal arena, when the mother's and baby's contacts are really about dealing with body fluids. The infant, having once been literally encapsulated in mother's womb in amniotic fluid, experiences closeness to mother postnatally through contact with skin and bodily fluids, through her caretaking in relation to milk, drool, urine, feces, mucus, spit, tears, and perspiration. A mother's contact with and ministrations to her baby in dealings with these fluids may optimally create a slippery, sticky sensual adhesion in the relationship; it is, so to speak, the medium for bonding. This sensuality, experienced by both parties, is key in their relationship.

It is precisely these physically encoded and generally repressed memories of the mother's voluptuous body that may be both longed for and feared by the adult in treatment. Maternal erotic transferences and countertransferences re-create this primal, preverbal, sensual-erotic contact between mother and infant, and often have a kind of juicy as well as gooey and messy dimension.

While fluids conduct contact, there is a rhythm to the wetness and dryness in mother–infant contact, and a suitable balance of neither too much wetness nor too little must be maintained. Wet or full diapers must be changed for dry ones so that the baby is not left helplessly swamped. In an optimally functioning mother–infant dyad, the baby is given an appropriate amount of milk, bathed regularly, and "patted dry." Similarly, the analyst is aware of metaphorically maintaining a fluid balance by creating and justifying a viable narrative space for each patient.

All the sensual precursors to adult sexuality are subsumed and consciously or unconsciously rekindled within later genitally focused erotic experience. The seminal and vaginal fluids of genital erotic contact in adult love play are the symbolic extension of these earliest sensual fluid connections between mother and infant. Thus, taking issue with the classical views of transference, which distinguish maternal transferences from oedipal erotic transferences, we contend that maternal transferences are not only libidinal in themselves, but also aggressive and that they underlie and make a direct contribution to genital sexuality. Thus we emphasize what psychoanalytic research has affirmed about infancy, namely, that the early experience of mothering and being mothered is distinctively erotic.

Maternal erotic transferences may first manifest in the analytic setting in concrete fantasies about the real parts of the therapist's body. We often know we are in its midst when the patient's dreams and communications are characterized more by powerful sensory imagery. Bodily concerns take center stage and are expressed in fantasies of nursing, putting together, getting inside, pouring, patting, and making, as in making a baby, messing, making pee and stool, smearing, poking, exposing, drooling. The therapist may become aware of a range of his or her own somatic responses to the material, including "melting" or sleepy feelings akin to the letdown reflex during nursing, or skin sensations indicative that the relationship is being communicated and experienced on a preverbal bodily level. The therapist may experience an impulse to pick up, bathe or clean, bundle up, or rock the patient rather than make verbal interpretations.

These primitive fantasies may be inhibited, sometimes for both therapist and patient, by the shame and difficulty of putting into words these essentially bodily experienced and bodily expressed phenomena and by "erotic terror," panic driven by early erotic transferences. Given the ambivalence associated with dyadic union, the transference can oscillate between blissful and terrifying and is often fought against or fled because it is experienced as humiliating or, worse, engulfing. We think this may account for many treatment interruptions and failures. Here and in subsequent chapters, we explore the ways in which the transference is inhibited and how, if ignored, it can lead to treatment failure.

We emphasize that the MET is a positive and necessary transforming phenomenon in psychoanalytic treatment. Analysts of either gender who have access to their own maternal erotic countertransferences in response to their patients' matching transferences may make possible their patients' acceptance of and immersion in the maternal erotic transference—with its loving and sadomasochistic permutations—thus fostering a sense of wholeness.

FOUR STRANDS IN THE NARRATIVE OF DESIRE

In an effort to distinguish maternal erotic transference more sharply from other transference manifestations, we shall recount four interrelated narratives, which are clinically derived and developmentally based. We discuss them first in relation to their developmental origins and then as they manifest in early maternal erotic transference phenomena. They include 1) what we describe as the birth of desire and body-based aspects of the self; 2) anal erotism and permutations of desire; 3) the sensual matrix in the formation of object relations; and 4) erotic desire as a transitional opportunity fostering the solidification of gender identity. Full understanding entails the differentiation of these broad narrative strands notably from one another, but also within the context of other transference phenomena.

Birth of Desire: Body-Based Aspects of Self

Of the four interweaving threads of the preoedipal maternal erotic transference, the first and most encompassing is the rich sensory/bodily attachment reminiscent of the sensual reciprocity between the baby and the mother[1] from birth. This narrational theme has its origin in the rich sensuality of the earliest mother–baby relationship.

Far from needing the "autistic" isolation postulated by classical theory, infant research confirms that infants actively seek sensory stimulation. The beginning of relating is evident in babies as young as three days: they show distinct sensory preferences for their mothers and select by smell the breast pads of their own mothers over those of other nursing mothers (Stern, 1985). Much attention has been given to the sensual bonding of feeding, bathing, cooing, and holding during the first year of life (Emde, 1976; Lichtenberg, 1981, 1983; Call, Galenson, and Tyson, 1983). This sensual, erotic attachment proceeds developmentally and includes reciprocal visual, tactile, olfactory, taste, and auditory behaviors, cues, and fantasies.

Primitive precursors of object relations are evident on sonograms of intrauterine life (Piontelli, 1989). In Piontelli's studies, fetuses actively related to the uterine wall and sought out the umbilicus sometimes playfully, sometimes harshly, sometimes peacefully. The womb functions as a container, a "rumpus room," a nest; the umbilicus becomes a

---

[1]"Mother" refers to the biological mother, mothering person, or caretaker, whoever is the primary object of basic attachment and care; it may also refer to the maternal aptitude and mothering aspect of the father as nurturer. Similarly, maternal transferences are described primarily in relation to the body of the female analyst but may also manifest in relation to the fantasied female body of the male analyst.

familiar plaything. Both womb and cord are omnipresent aspects of the most fundamental meaning of "other."

Sanville quotes Joan Erikson (1988) writing of the prenatal origins of creativity in the early mother–infant sensual surround. She maintains that

> part of the biological purpose of the bodily activity of the foetus is to increase the sensations (themselves necessary . . . for the very development of the brain). . . . Hearing is already functioning in utero, and light and dark can be distinguished. After birth, visual experiences can lead to a veritable "orgasm of delight." (cited in Sanville, 1991a, p. 431)

As these earliest interactions make their way into the analytic relationship, typically in wordless, pregnant silences, they provide access to the nonverbal, primitive precursors of emotional relating and underlie the transformational possibilities of regression.

Anal Erotism: Permutations of Desire

In the Introduction, we spoke of the metaphor of the rose growing from its roots in the fecund earth into the bloom of mature love. We also referred to our interest in the mother–baby sensual bond as it pertains to issues of anal erogeneity. It is this earthy, primitive soil of anal erotism we now till. The second narrative thread weaving through maternal erotic transferences centers on positive and negative fantasy re-creations of the developmental period of anal erotism. In it, the evolution of a patient's early object relations can be traced and reworked in fantasies of anal containment and expulsion, anal spoiling and valuation, and anal birth.

Although we do not believe these phenomena to be necessarily limited to any group, the patients who first illuminated our particular perspective on these issues shared certain characteristics. They were intelligent, verbal, and successful in work; although free of overt perversion, they were particularly conflicted or uncertain about physical sexual characteristics. Some had had very early intrusive toilet training, including enemas. They presented themselves for treatment exhibiting obsessive-compulsive defenses against both their earliest erotic longings and their later sadomasochistic impulses. From the beginning, they exerted a powerful, sometimes even stultifying, control over the analytic situation.

While some consciously craved the analyst's words and felt deprived of them, they nevertheless filled up the hours and allowed the analyst little opportunity for intervention. In many important ways, these patients resembled those described by Shengold (1985) as subject to defensive anal narcissistic regression. Safety, for such patients, resides in the ability to transform "life's intensities and precious people . . . into the indifferent and the trivial . . . [depriving] both . . . self and the analyst of variety, vibrancy and value"(p. 48).

We wondered if the obsessional defenses against erotism we saw in high relief in these patients existed over a broader clinical spectrum. While we found some cogency in obsessiveness as a defensive construction, our clinical focus stresses creative and reparative aspects of anal erotism, and we believe it is, in varying degrees and permutations, ubiquitous. For example, for some patients, attention to their anal functions through toileting and enemas, though sometimes perverse, intrusive, or harmful, represented their primary sensory tie to their maternal caretakers.

The anal erotism uncovered in the treatment of a surprising number of patients who had experienced enemas in early childhood first captured our interest. We saw that these ego-flooding experiences not only had been painful, humiliating, and overwhelmingly confusing to them as young children but also had been erotic. For these patients, anal erogeneity was a way into their earliest sensual-relational experience.

For some patients, anal interests centering on toileting are redolent of fantasies of cloacal birth. In the latter case, the fantasies of making a baby are not articulated oedipal, triadic fantasies reflecting genital strivings but, rather, are the more primitive fantasies typical of the preoedipal period, such as fantasies of babies made from mud, food, or feces. These aspects of maternal erotic transferences may manifest in fantasies of "making something special" for the mommy/analyst or bringing dreams into treatment like fecal babies to be proudly admired.

For others, the equation "feces equals baby" is a painful fact of their infantile self-experience. They believe themselves to have been a "shitty" baby whom mother wished to flush away. Transference manifestations of this aspect of MET often surround patients' core belief that they are not worth anything, that they do not deserve the analyst's attention. Conversely, patients may dispense with the analyst's "creative interpretations" as useless fecal babies to be forgotten or flushed away as waste product without value.

The Sensual Matrix in the Formation of Object Relations

A third element of the MET for both male and female patients can be understood as the patient's need to rework a primitive fractured narrative into an integrated view of the mother/therapist as a living whole object.

This third transformational aspect of the maternal erotic transference is adaptive and represents a creative attempt to make the mother/therapist into a living, more dimensional whole person. In this sense, the transference offers a narrative of the development of object relations from part-object phenomenon to whole-object relatedness. At this point in the transference, it is the baby who is making the mother into a whole object, and the mother/analyst is often dreamed of as a container—a car, a pool, a room, a tray, a box. These are concrete transference manifestations in that they appear to be to the real parts of the body of the therapist—fluids, spaces, breasts, limbs.

This integration is prerequisite to the capacity to tolerate separateness and discover a relationship to Mother as Other. Under successful developmental conditions, this integration would have been accomplished by the mother's earlier sensual ministrations to the baby, whereby her continuity and consistency would have helped the baby to experience a sense of wholeness. When this developmental need has not been realized, patients may enter psychotherapy or psychoanalysis to deal with it among other issues.

The process of integrating parts into a cohesive whole also reflects the child's developing ego capacity to integrate disparate experiences, both loving and hating, perceived as directed toward and coming from the mother. Related to this integrative task is the task of internalizing self- and object images built up, influenced, and colored by libidinal and aggressive impulses (Kernberg, 1975). Thus we are talking about a developmental achievement that can be understood not only from an object relations viewpoint, but also from a drive-model and an ego-psychological perspective.[2] Our point here, is that this third thread of the maternal erotic transference, the making of a whole object, is determined (1) by the patient's need to replay and rework successfully the cognitive capability for object constancy and whole-object relatedness and (2) by a growing ability to tolerate and integrate ambivalence in the arena of object relations, so that the primitive defense of splitting does not perpetuate fracturing of the object. To return to the metaphor of the rose, this narrative thread refers to the dawning recognition and assimilation of the fact that the rose has thorns and bugs, as well as petals and an intoxicating scent; it also flourishes and then dies.

Clinical phenomena in the MET that alert us to the presence of a need for transformation often appear in the form of fractured imagery. Patients may reveal perceptions such as seeing the therapist's body as discontinuous, "smushed," or "broken up." One patient said, "I just had an image of your face. It looks like Picasso's cubist period painting, with the parts all jumbled, the eyes off center, the nose askew." Another patient, in an unresolved ambivalent state with her mother, said, "God, I just had an image of her, but her head was like a light bulb—I dropped it on the stairs and it was in shards—but not all separate . . . it moves in and out of patterns." Thus this aspect of the MET commonly manifests in material pertaining to parts—parts of the therapist's body, parts in verbal rapid-fire, the themes of which become a blur. The patient reveals an effort to smash or drop or take the analyst to pieces and also to integrate associational parts by putting Humpty Dumpty together and thereby metaphorically transforming the

---

[2] Melanie Klein (cited in Segal, 1964) articulated the ego's most primitive defense, "splitting," used prior to this integration, as an entirely intrapsychic process whereby, "quite early, the ego has a relationship to two objects; the primary object, the breast, being at this stage split into two parts, the ideal breast and the persecutory one" (p. 26).

Guntrip (1969), taking issue with Klein's totally intrapsychic explanation for splitting, argued for the inclusion of aspects of the "real relationship" in the encounter. He proposed that persecutory anxiety arises in the first place as a result of an actually bad environment: "Anger and aggression arise as an attempt to master fear by removing its cause . . . [but] lead to the discovery of helplessness. . . . This powerfully reinforces the splitting process . . . set in motion by the fear . . . [of] the bad outer world" (p. 146).

therapist from part- to whole object. The consistency of the therapist in relation to this material fosters in the patient a sense of the wholeness of the therapist and of the self.

It appears to us that at times in these transferences, our patients—otherwise intellectual and verbally articulate—dramatically switch their narrative "voices" from typical verbal descriptions and resort to primitive, concrete bodily communications. Galenson (1985) has noted "sudden and massive regressions which characterize the transference . . . [and] reflect the pattern of the preoedipal shifts during childhood and infancy from expression through physiological channels to the more advanced levels in psychological functions" (p. 82). To illustrate, the patient we discuss at length in this chapter would suddenly report the feeling of feces dripping down her legs or would imagine feces running down her analyst's legs.

As we consulted each other about these puzzling "eruptions" into the analytic treatment, we became aware of a number of dreams whose major focus was an effortless, continuous motion, with body fluids invoked as a lubricant. In the clinical hours, we noticed that our patients tended to take up and put down topics rapidly, making the themes hard for us to pick up. The purpose seemed to be to touch as much as possible in a given hour, not necessarily to work with it, but simply to touch it.

We understood this phenomenon as having a parallel in early motor development: babies learning to walk use their hands in the period of cruising to touch and go. In treatment, this release and reengagement manifests as a dizzying succession of verbal images. Over time, as topics and themes are returned to, the touched-on pieces must be put together into an integrated whole, a task that appears to mirror the process of making the therapist/mother into an integrated whole object. Once there is an internal picture of the mother as a living, whole object, colored by both loving and hurtful associations, greater separateness can be tolerated, and ultimately the mother of the outside world can be apprehended as the beloved Other. This object-related achievement further develops the capacity for intersubjectivity that is essential for loving.

The Solidification of Gender Identity Through Erotic Experience

A fourth narrative theme of the MET is that it occurs in relation to the vicissitudes of psychosexual stages from the earliest sensual relations between mother and baby to the genital-sexual erotism of the oedipal triangle. The emergent desire of the maternal erotic transference provides both a transitional and a transformational opportunity for patients. Work within this aspect of the maternal erotic transference can be gender verifying. Experience in the maternal erotic transference oscillates between preoedipal and oedipal phenomena. In this sense, it "bridges" between them in such a way that the consolidation of gender with respect to both preoedipal and oedipal issues can be reworked.

For male patients, the narrative line alternates between advances and retreats from oedipal, sometimes chivalrous, and occasionally aggressive courting of the mother/therapist as love object; shifts to fear of oedipal defeat or success; and circles back to the baby boy–mommy closeness. This closeness is fraught with the dangers of imagined loss of the masculine self through merger with the preoedipal mother, and the oedipal courting returns. (See chapter 8 for an elaboration of this dance and its attendant dangers with respect to patients who are particularly threatened by, yet drawn to, closeness to the mother's body.) When the boy-in-the-adult-male analysand fantasizes that an intolerably high price will be extracted for the security and bliss of maternal reunion, he fears the loss of his masculinity, sacrificed in the at-onement with the female body. Thus his fear, or erotic terror, rekindled in treatment, typically leads to flight or the reinstatement of triadic fantasies and rekindled sexual romantic overtures toward the female therapist.

Male patients' early maternal erotic transferences appear to be inhibited by patients and their analysts alike (Lester, 1985; Shengold, 1985; Chasseguet-Smirgel, 1986; Goldberger and Evans, 1985; Gornick, 1986; Kulish, 1986; Lane, 1986). Consultations with male colleagues confirm that phenomena relating to the early maternal erotic transferences may also occur regularly not only with female but with male analysts and, in our view, can be worked with by analysts of either sex who are comfortable with their own maternal selves.

For female patients, this gender-consolidating narrative thread of MET includes the little girl's oedipal disappointment, as she turns her romantic attention defensively back to her mother and relates to her in a different way than she did previously. As she guards against the loss of her father's love, attendant narcissistic humiliation, and perhaps rekindled issues of body integration, she seeks her mother's soothing and reparative love. She may also or alternatively identify defensively with father in an attempt to deny her defeat at his hands. In the treatment, such identifications gain expression in extratransferential passionate encounters with available males; these encounters mask a longing for or a defense against (or both) physical contact with the analyst's maternally voluptuous body. For the female analysand, the narcissistic deflation incurred in transference fantasies of oedipal defeat fuels the early maternal transference to her analyst, as she seeks her mother's love as a healing salve for her wounded sense of femininity.³ Girls' intensely erotic vaginal and anal sensations, begun in infancy (Plaut and Hutchinson, 1986) and associated with early anatomical curiosity and early sphincter control, are important in erotic feelings toward their mothers in separation-individuation experiences and in feminine gender identification. In our view, an abiding identification with an adequate mother and identificatory access to her sensual body is the missing link for many women who feel themselves defective in their femininity.

This identification occurs during a period of what may appear to be homosexual interest in the female analyst. This interest may alarm both participants if they are not aware of the transitory developmental aspects of this process. There is, unfortunately, a paucity of reports of positive work with early homoerotic maternal transferences. McDougall (1986a, b), an exception in the literature, has written a rare and detailed narrative of a case that delineates her discovery of her own homoerotic countertransference feelings toward a female patient; that awareness allowed her to gain access to her patient's erotic transference. She did not name it then, but in subsequent conversations she has acknowledged that she was talking about an aspect of what we call the maternal erotic transference. With characteristic candor, McDougall also revealed that in neither of her own complete classical analyses with male analysts was this phenomenon explored.

A Continuum from Erotic to Erotized

As is typical of the classical view of erotic transference, Blum (1973) uses the term *erotized* to describe a transference that has gone awry, in which erotic preoccupation with the analyst is used defensively by the patient to avoid the analytic work. Others, for example

---

³For this felicitous rephrasing of our notion of the daughter's retreat to her mother, we are indebted to Dr. Elizabeth Berlese.

Bollas (1992), describe *sexualized* transferences as those which permit no meaning to be explored. The patient's very insistence on physical contact with the analyst precludes subjectivity and analytic exploration. Although it is obvious that some enactments will be more disruptive and problematic than others, we do not make a primary distinction between erotic and erotized or sexualized transferences. Rather, we view erotic phenomena as manifesting in treatment along a continuum from deeply repressed and only hinted at in derivatives, to obvious, outright enactments. Some of these transferences are accompanied by a strong defensive component that requires interpretation; others appear as attempts at concrete enactments that must be managed before yielding to interpretation; others can be worked with in the conventional analytic process of transference with associations and interpretations; and some reflect the bridging phenomenon between body and mind characteristic of the development of subjectivity. "Narrative attunement" on the part of the therapist, as described in chapter 1, fosters transformation and the development of subjectivity. We consider it basic that erotic transferences include a reparative wish, which is very often the clinical key to understanding and defusing the situation (Sanville, 1987, 1991b).

In summary, with these four narrative threads we have proposed a broad view of maternal erotic transferences (MET) to include all manner of sensual bodily fantasies in relation to the analyst that offer creative, transformational opportunities in the development of object relations, gender identity, and the capacity for separateness and for mutuality. For us, the potential for erotic transference is universal and stirs rich transference issues that, if understood, can be a "gold mine" instead of a "mine field" (Person, 1985).

CLINICAL ILLUSTRATION

The First Narrative Version in an Oedipal Overlay

Margot, a 55-year-old scientist, was seen in psychoanalysis (by HKW) four times a week for six years. She had been given enemas as a child but, atypically, did not focus on them as a humiliating intrusion. Rather, she seemed to have stored them as unusual and stimulating contacts with her mother. In this way, her material opened up an understanding of the exciting side of anal erotism between mother and daughter that was often overshadowed by attention to battles for control, sadistic invasions, and humiliations.

Margot came to treatment because she was worried about her inability to have what she called a vaginal orgasm with her lover. His concerns about this "lack" had struck a core anxiety of hers—not yet articulated—that she was not genuinely feminine. Margot's longed-for father[4] was a socially adept businessman, but he was, apparently, relatively absent emotionally. However, he showered Margot's voluptuous mother with affection in front of their three children. Margot's mother, a conventional though distracted mother, was apparently pro forma in raising the children. She was absorbed in her own looks and her singing and, considering herself above being a "milk machine," resented breast feeding. Acting on the pediatric advice of the day, mother placed Margot's arms and hands in splints when she was an infant to restrain her from sucking her thumbs. Margot's maternal grandmother lived with the family six months each year and reportedly joined with mother in accomplishing the feat of toilet training Margot at nine months. There was apparently no tolerance for the messy, earthy pleasures of intermingled roots and soil; Margot was to be hurriedly cultivated into a pristine and perfect rose, clipped and put forth for show.

As a child, Margot felt that her considerably older adolescent sister, Lily, got closer to their mother by keeping mother titillated with stories of her budding romances. Lily later stunned the family and its social circle by becoming an unwed mother. By contrast, Margot was the consummate good little girl, pleasing everyone and challenging no one. An extremely pretty child, she was treated as the family's "little doll." These observations and Margot's responses to them constituted an important feature of the narrative Margot had constructed for herself prior to analysis, namely, that although others may indulge, for Margot sexuality was bad and to be restrained. Watching her sister's and her mother's flirtatiousness, and determining early that she would never have the breasts to rival either of them, led to the construction of another key narrative line. Margot, at age 7, forsook her femininity and began her focus on her studies.

She pursued scholarship, refused makeup, and at 17 went to a university to study. Her willowy beauty became almost alien to her.

---

[4] Throughout, the "fathers" and others referred to in the patients' narratives are described as they appeared at that time in the treatment to both patient and analyst. Where the analyst had doubts about the description, or where the patient's narrative evolved, it is noted.

Like Sylvia Plath's, another sad and beautiful intellect of her generation, Margot's first jobs after she graduated, before marriage and graduate school, were as cover girl, model, and fashion editor. The irony here is that while she adopted a false self as a "model" of femaleness to show others, she actually felt a core sense of inadequacy as a female.

During the early phase of the analysis, Margot's relationship with her lover, Phil, took center stage. Whereas she was the distinguished scientist, writing and lecturing internationally, he was her opposite. Phil was passionate, chaotic, foundering, and alcoholic. Having retired from his business to paint paintings that never found a market, he proudly followed and supported her career. Margot's first husband had told her on their wedding night that he actually had no particular interest in sex. While she had unconsciously experienced this revelation as a personal disaster and a reenactment of her oedipal defeat—yet another confirmation of her feminine inadequacy—consciously she had accepted it, ostensibly sharing her husband's avowed preference for the life of the mind. During their long marriage, she had enjoyed a warm intellectual but dispassionate closeness. By contrast, Phil's insatiable passion for lovemaking opened a deliriously sensual side of her she had denied her whole life.

At the outset of her analysis, Margot presented her conflicts entirely in oedipal terms, as centering on the longed-for doting relationship with a father who always had his heart elsewhere, on mother. At the beginning of treatment, she focused on her obsession with her small breasts and her fear that they would not hold Phil's amorous attention, and on her jealousy toward any woman he looked at or talked to. Phil fed the fires as he painted voluptuous women and told her of his sexual fantasies about younger women.

At the beginning, Margot seemed to approach me either as a sexual rival, in the hope that I would be the good mother who would share her sexual secrets and who would help her "get it right with a man," or with polite respect. During a period of preanalytic evaluation, I, in turn, anticipated that this would perhaps be a rare "classical" analysis in its focus on neurotic conflicts around oedipal issues. Margot was a remarkably articulate, introspective, attractive, and high-functioning woman. My presumption of a "classical" narrative tack, triggered by the patient's composure and "classicism," as well as by my wish to experience a "truly classical analysis," illustrates aptly the ways in which both coauthors of the analytic narrative become invested in a particular tone or version of the stories and thereby may limit the scope of the therapy.

Vaginal Orgasms and Fecal Babies

In her first session on the couch, Margot delivered a reverberating blow to my bubble of classical containment. Inadvertently conveying why she was so invested in containment, she also offered a dramatic juxtaposition of primitive anal erotism. She said, "I have always had the idea that if I ever had a vaginal orgasm, my bowels would let go in a total explosion and lack of control." In the next session, she told me the following dream:

> I was taking care of a child. This child was on the toilet and in the toi-
> let bowl there was this huge clot of blood—almost like a piece of liver
> and almost animate. Would the child be able to keep it in the toilet
> bowl? I left but there was a black woman with her.

Margot's dream associations seemed to flow easily. She associated the liver with a memory of a high school sorority initiation rite that was simultaneously frightening, exhilarating, sadistic, and sexual as the older girls forced the younger girls to eat raw liver. Further associations included the idea of the liver and the blood clot as a miscarriage and a childhood memory of seeing her mother naked in the bathroom when she was a little girl. "All I remember are her large, drooping breasts." She also recalled a number of other childhood encounters in the bathroom in which her mother, following the pediatric advice of the day, had administered enemas to her.

Margot's first dream revealed that contact between us stirred fear and excitement at being alone together, producing something; she was eager to "root about in the mother/baby relational matrix, in the humus where roots and earth and worms and moisture are mingled." The dream revealed her pent-up absorption with toileting, messes, deadness, and flooding, as in the enemas. The corollary to her fantasy of creating something with me was the unconscious belief that she was an unwanted turd. Her dream also rekindled fantasies and fears of miscarriage; perhaps I would "drop her" from the analysis. Perhaps the black woman was a split-off, dark version of her mother, who, she feared, had wanted to abort her. The dream also suggested the inability of a mother to give birth to a healthy female/self.

(Variations of this idea of being an aborted or stillborn baby have appeared in so many of our analyses of both men and women that we have dedicated the next chapter to discussing it, so we will not elaborate that aspect at this point.)

Embedded in Margot's first dream was a fantasy we came to understand later: if she could be good enough and lovable enough, then she and I, her mother/analyst, could make a new baby who would be real, not a doll or a picture-perfect rosebud. Her wish was that I would be able to be the toilet/container/mother who could hold and not flush away all the bits and pieces she might explode into. Would we be able to reanimate this baby Margot? Could we make the liver alive instead of inanimate? These concerns illustrate the third aspect of MET, namely, the patient's immersion in primitive fantasies about making babies with the mother/analyst and specifically making a new, more animated baby than the patient felt herself to have been.

Shortly after beginning analysis, in a precipitous move away from me that characterized many to come, Margot announced that she and her lover had decided to get married in a few weeks. My comment on the abruptness of the decision led her to confirm that she was afraid I would intrude on her and take away her passionate pleasures. Her lover, however, soon had an affair with another woman, and Margot recognized that her sudden decision to marry him was an enactment of her simultaneous fear of and wish for growing intimacy with me. Even recognizing this, she still treated me from a courteous distance. She still wanted to leapfrog over the painful experience of feeling robbed of an erotic contact with me as her early mother, an experience she had not yet even acknowledged she desired. She also feared that such a contact, like the enemas, would be messy.

Thus, for the first year the oedipal erotic narrative configuration masked preoedipal libidinal longings. We explored the way in which, in her sessions, she kept herself "mother's pristine doll," maintaining a discreet distance from me, but could only vicariously enjoy her own denied, sensuous messes through Phil. In another early session, she recalled that as a child she had urinated in the backyard of her house. Her older sister, Lily, had observed her and tattled. In the analysis as in that incident, she felt deep shame and humiliation about her bodily functions and her anal sensations. She felt that she had come to the consulting room to make a humiliating mess. In her transference, she wanted to hide her bodily functions from me as though I were her older sister whom she admired but who toyed with her and kept her at a distance. She hated to have my neighbors see her parking her car on her way to her sessions for fear that they, like Lilly, would know what she was doing.

Emergence of Margot's Preoedipal Maternal Longings

Throughout the analysis, Margot was preoccupied with her small breasts. Behind her wish for large sexual breasts with which to woo father (a wish that emerged considerably later) was her longing for her mother's feeding breasts.[5] She recognized her great pain that because she was the last-born child, her mother's feeding breasts were depleted of nourishment and had been withheld from her. Her mother's sexual breasts, however, were tantalizingly full and available to father. This she could see in her memories of the many open displays of physical affection between her parents at the dinner hour. She seemed to feel that she could not ask anyone directly for what she wanted. She was genuinely heartbroken to realize that her mother's attentions toward her had only been halfhearted, but that her mother had been passionately absorbed in her father. Margot seemed to want my love but felt she had to act out and disguise it even from herself by marriage plans and other precipitous "terminations," which, as it emerged in the transference, seemed to signal deepening of her erotic longing for both father and mother.

Once, after an interpretation that apparently touched her deeply, she had a dream in which she was in a medieval church, being offered communion by a woman. In her spontaneous associations to the dream, she stated that she had been "confirmed as a child." Analysis of this dream revealed constructions of her preexisting narrative version of her life in her family, as well as the newly emerging version of her love story in relation to me.

We understood this dream to be a reflection of her longing to be in communion with a woman in a fused, almost perfect Madonna-and-child image associated with the medieval church. Associating to a stained glass window in my consulting room, she recognized that these longings were increasingly directed toward me. The Victorian

---

[5] Subsequent clinical experience has verified a widespread splitting of breasts into feeding-related and sexual in the narratives of women who have a diffuse gender identity. Unification is a major step in the development of a mature female identity.

stained-glass window, which the couch faces, depicts a medieval castle with a scarlet-garbed, androgynous figure in the foreground. We further understood the dream to suggest her sense that she had felt confirmed to remain always a pristine little doll with whom everyone played. She also associated to her later decision to renounce this pretty doll and become an invulnerable, competent male. She came to understand how, "reading" her defeat as the oedipal rival in her childhood narrative, she had defensively celebrated her flat chest, become like father, and embarked on a career in a male-dominated field. Although she had become a cover girl in college and a model, she chose to dress plainly and develop her intellect, seeing these as mutually exclusive roles.

Rhyme Time

Margot brought an incredible profusion of dreams to her analysis. We will paraphrase parts of one detailed dream that signaled the emergence of the maternal erotic transference and countertransference. The manifest and latent content signal this emergence, together with my immediate physical response and subsequent dream response to it. Margot's associative reference in the dream to "rhyming with Wrye" also illustrates the reparative delight a patient can experience in the conarrative process. This poesy is akin to the "aesthetic moment" Bollas (1987) describes as "part of the unthought known . . . an existential recollection of the time when communicating took place primarily through this illusion of deep rapport of subject and object" (p. 32). This dream occurred the weekend after she finally broke up with her lover, Phil.

> I did not have time to wait for a prominent male colleague to buy lipstick at an old fashioned drug store. Instead, I went on to a university where three performances were to be played in medieval or early Renaissance costumes. I marveled at how many people were involved. I saw my colleague again, this time with his girlfriend, and they told me they'd been using my name to register in hotels. I wanted to go home, but I then saw a woman with whom I felt like singing rhymes.

When she finished telling the dream, she was uncharacteristically silent for about seven minutes and I began to realize that I felt, strangely, very sleepy. Then she said "I can't think . . . Oh, I experienced the sensation of a bowel movement running down my legs." After we explored the dream and the slippery, sleepy feeling apparently experienced by both of us, several themes emerged: issues around dyads, coupling, making babies; exhibitionism and performances of the false self yearning for relief through empathy; erotic anality, orality, and skin sensations characteristic of maternal erotic transferences.

She associated the large, old-fashioned drug store to therapy in the office in my 1920s home; to her mother's medicinal prescriptions; the splints on her hands and arms; and the early toilet training that symbolically had robbed her of the opportunity to experience real empathic contact around her body and its functioning. She further associated to the later enemas that paradoxically brought her rare moments of shameful but erotic contact with her mother. Her male colleague in the dream, a particularly dominant and competitive figure, had appeared in many of her dreams as the masculine self she had adopted to cover her damaged feminine self. A male trying to buy the lipstick also suggested Margot's gender and oral/anal/genital confusion. Each of these associations illustrates one or another aspect of the MET.

I silently wondered in the session if Margot was trying to purchase through therapy the feminine identification with her mother and with mother's sensual body from which she felt alienated. Did the lipstick kept in her mother's "purse" represent to her a hidden nipple/enema hose/phallus? Did the lipstick also suggest the feces that Margot as a toddler, wanting to make a baby with mother, gave to her? Margot openly wondered if it suggested that she had concluded as a toddler that she had to get on without sharing in feminine pleasures with mother and that she could not wait for father's sexual advances. She wondered if this early, sad sense of unconscious erotic resignation had driven her to seek sublimation in academia, the university performances in the dream.

We agreed that the performances touched on her precocious performance as a false doll self. Her male colleague and his girlfriend's impersonation of her at hotels evoked for both Margot and me her father's and mother's exhibitionistic sexual drama that had preempted Margot's emerging sexuality. The medieval or early Renaissance production suggested the preoedipal/oedipal drama in her early middle childhood and also implied her wish for rebirth in analysis in her own "middle ages."

Margot identified the woman with the rhymes as me and her second analysis. (She had sought analysis 20 years earlier with a male analyst.) She described the current analysis as more accessible to her, less "technical" than her first, and she associated to the pleasure of making "Wrye/rhymes" as the pleasure of matching and "mating" in the analytic hour. The amazing number of people in this outdoor drama seemed to her to be all the people brought "out into the open air" on the analytic stage. That she wanted to but could not go home with her mate related to her sad acknowledgment that she had been widowed by her previous husband, her parents were dead, her love affair was over, and she could not stay at home with me. She realized that she would have to experience both the lifelong depression she had masked and her current depressive feelings about middle age, loss, and separateness.

A few days later, in a kind of "rhyming" synchrony, I dreamed a "companion" dream of my own that seemed to be related to Margot's and that opened up, through associations to the dream, previously unelaborated erotic feelings for my deceased mother. This dream, like Margot's, included the scarlet-robed medieval or early Renaissance figure of the stained glass door and its ambiguous gender. Associations seemed again to go to that middle period between the preoedipal and early oedipal pageant—oedipal frustration and the return to mother: fantasies of shiny presents and party favors that suggested the fecal gifts made together with or given by the toddler to mother as symbolic babies.

We believe such countertransferential regressions, whether in dreams or associations, make available to an analyst a level of emotional responsiveness that can be used for empathic access to a patient's early maternal erotic concerns. My own dizzying array of associations to the pieces of the dream were an important clue that primitive themes were emerging. Technically, it is critically important to tolerate and sort through such themes, rather than bring them to the patient's awareness. In our experience, an analyst's comfort with and capacity to metabolize such countertransference phenomena are crucial to enabling a patient to work though the parallel transference.

In the period that followed my awareness of my own early maternal erotic longings, Margot struggled against her emerging erotic wishes toward me. One dream revealed her fear that I would teasingly expose a breast to her and then tell her it was for my lover and that Margot could not have it because she had been weaned. In line with our positing that as this transference emerges it is to the real body of the analyst, it seemed that Margot wanted the "real thing" at that time and not some "as if" analytic substitute. She realized that part of her depression was that she felt she had to give up hope of finding with a man what she had missed with her mother; as she said, "I put all my eggs in one basket," namely mine.

An Attempted Solution: Splinting

In another dream, Margot tried to put together an internal solution that had the fantasied mother and father fused, not preoccupied with each other, but fully available to her. In this dream a young mother was going to get a penis for her baby to use as a pacifier. Margot said, "I thought that would be a very good idea as long as no one would see it," revealing both her fantasy of the penis as a "pacifier" in place of the breast and her shame about wanting it. She quickly understood that for her Phil's penis had been not only her father's withheld penis, but also a sweet replacement for her mother's unavailable breast. In the dream, she ordered a present for this baby but later felt it was inappropriate. It was an expensive, complicated metal gift that was uncomfortable for the baby; at this point it represented her analysis. Her analysis at that moment was the complicated metal contraption; analytic restraint felt like the splints her mother had put on her arms to keep her from sucking.

Accordingly, she saw me alternately as a cool, scholarly Freudian father, an alien machine, an enema syringe, and a phallic mother who excited and sadistically penetrated her. She felt shame and humiliation at having been exposed, although she realized that her mother had simply followed doctor's orders and probably had believed that the enemas were for Margot's benefit. She worried that I would follow my analytic training in the same unempathic way. This worry also connected to Margot's recognition that she had gone through her own life "by the book," being gracious in her professional role, hosting parties, and so forth.

Only at that point in the analysis, and for the first time in her life, did she experience a true empathic connection, with a young colleague who had come highly touted to interview for a position and then been bypassed. Margot was astonished by her awareness of the contrast between her usual routine courtesy and the genuine empathy she felt for his exposure, shame, and humiliation. The difference between her real self and her false self was revealed: a doll can only go through the motions of being a mother. With considerable grief, she recognized that she had been unable to empathize genuinely with her own children, and this lack had caused them all psychic pain and still did.

Again she threatened to interrupt analysis, although her conscious reason for proposing an abrupt termination at this point was to accept a prestigious research invitation elsewhere. This enactment threat seemed to signal unconsciously yet another intensification of the transference and to represent Margot's attempt to press me to declare my loving concern. I wondered aloud whether her sudden termination plan was grounded in her fear of giving up the fantasy of being the self-sufficient male or whether it had to do with the need to impel me to argue "passionately" for her to stay, in a way her own mother had never done. On reflection, Margot acknowledged both. As is characteristic of the maternal erotic transference, for such a highly verbal woman, her most poignant communications were often expressed as "passionate" nonverbal actions.

Alas, Alice! The Analysis Was All Ass

Margot then dreamed she visited "Aunt Alice in the Holiday Inn," a tall, cylindrical hotel in the city. She was awed by the sumptuousness, curved walls, and beauty of Aunt Alice's suite on the tenth floor. With its four bathrooms and evocation of a pleasure palace, it offered Alice an invitation to enjoy anal erotism. Margot hoped that she could visit there often. Rooms in a round building are pie shaped, which led to associations to Margot's earlier dream, which we had come to understand as reflecting her feeling of getting only pieces of the pie/breast. Pie-shaped pieces may suggest the oedipal triangle, but for Margot her hungers made it the "edible triangle."

As mentioned earlier, our conception of MET includes a fluid countertransference regression. I found myself "slipping" into Margot's associations of a pumpkin pie, made from a fluid that looked very much like baby diarrhea. Also, associating to a filled diaper, I re-created the experience of being in the warm amniotic fluid and also feeling the fluid that brings mother's care and attention when she changes the diaper and holds and pats the baby. Although highly intellectualized analysands may regularly call forth a ponderous, ruminative countertransference, that was not the case here. This was a countertransference experience very different from coolly wondering about the meaning of the "anal material." While I slipped into my own associations, Margot carried on with hers. She associated the four bathrooms to the four weekly analytic sessions where she was able to come and spill. The room in the hotel was curved, reminding her of my consulting room. The tall, cylindrical building suggested father's phallus. Margot's fantasies were of being *inside* the phallus, not penetrated by it; thus she conflated ideas of the phallus as a containing womb and as a signifier of father's sexual powers (Ross, 1982).

In the dream, she was on the tenth floor—age ten perhaps, another transitional phase, this time between childhood and adolescence, the "late Middle Ages and the early Renaissance" of rekindled sexual oedipal fantasies. The transitional age also suggests that the MET is involved in reworking the transition between anal and phallic oedipal issues. The tenth floor may also suggest the top of the building and her preoccupation with the transition from middle age to old age.

"Aunt Alice" may refer to fused symbols for "falling down the rabbit hole," "phallus," "all ass," and "analysis." If so, it typifies a primary developmental characteristic of the preoedipal period, the combined attempt to make confusing and disparate part objects and body parts into a whole. It also may represent the effort to deny triangulation by fusing mother and father into one available parental object. In other words, on the way to the Oedipus complex, there is a visit to Aunt Alice at the Holiday Inn. This way station, or "bridge," illustrates the oscillation between dyad and triad, between oedipal and preoedipal, that is characteristic of the fourth aspect of MET mentioned at the outset of this chapter. The way station represents an erotic container in which father's phallus is fused with mother's body. Aunt Alice's resolution may also refer to Margot's gratitude toward me in the transference as the surrogate mother, the aunt, who offers another way.

The Room/Womb/Narrative Space
For the Emergence of Maternal Erotic Transferences

Margot's extreme lack of experienced pleasure and closeness to her mother and her concomitant gender confusion are characteristics of the maternal erotic transference. Her longing for an erotic, sensual relationship was expressed in her analysis in concrete, nonverbal actions, including hypomanic episodes of sensual flooding. Before the longing emerged in the transference, it was acted out in her immersion in an affair with a lover who was her opposite—messy, out of control, spontaneously sensual. As her awareness of her erotic longings for her analyst/mother became conscious, her seductive efforts to please, to be compliant, and to accept my competence were punctuated by excited confusion. This rather seductive drama was reminiscent of the intensely shameful, yet exciting, enemas that had brought her into close contact with mother, revealed in her many fantasies of both of us having feces streaming down our legs.

For Margot, her father and mother's open displays of affection had left her feeling painfully small and inadequate to compete for inclusion in the primal scene, so she had taken herself out of the competition. Until the emergence of this transference, she had successfully denied that she even had much interest in a passionate attachment to her mother. After a long, depressive mourning for the early losses, her awakened sensual longings emerged. As they were recognized and contained, she apparently felt her erotic feelings were accepted, and the transference flowered.

Her languorous immersion in the maternal erotic transference resulted in fewer "productions" and more blissful silences, a relaxation of her demeanor and her dizzying schedule, and a flowering of her relationship to her children. She bought a new wardrobe. After a long "winter" during which she felt she could never feel anything but a distant pining for mother, new fantasies emerged of a love affair with a man. In a dream, she wondered whether or not to wear pantyhose to a wedding—suggestive of her wish to be no longer socially compliant and to be able figuratively to bring the anal enema hose, with all its messy pleasures, to her new romances. The maternal erotic transference ushered in a long period of working through oedipal material, this time enriched by grounding in the earlier preoedipal longings and presaging termination of the analysis.

THE ORIGINS OF DESIRE IN THE
SEARCH FOR TRANSFORMATION

In the pursuit of the mother/analyst as an object of transformation, the patient returns to an identification with, and an immersion in, the early mother's body. It is in this search for transformation in the "primordial swamp of the dark continent" that desire is born.[6]

In our view, the medium for communicating these earliest pre-verbal transferences are bodily feelings and sensations. These "body juices" (such as Margot's feces running down her leg while she was in a sleepy symbiotic mood; or Maureen's smelly package, the lobster emanating odiferous juices inside her therapist's refrigerator; or Caleb's imagery of the dank, wet, sump of cat-birth under his house (see chapter 5) precede words as the narrative medium. These bodily sensations are not symbolic of sexual contact; they *are* the contact. Akin to Marshall McLuhan's "the medium is the message" and W. B. Yeats's query in "Sailing to Byzantium," "How can we tell the dancer from the dance?" bodily feelings are the stuff of these archaic transferences.

The relation is very much to the body of the analyst, but not as a differentiated "other" body. Rather, the "body" is experienced as the analyst's whole room, its contents, refrigerators, video players, all unconsciously equivalent to the analyst/mother's voluptuous body. By "voluptuous" we mean to evoke the sensually rich and full body of the birthing, nursing mother. It is in this transference immersion in the body of the mother that transformations occur.

In this space, the narratives of desire are sounded in bodily sensations before they gain expression in words and articulated in songs of love. Related to this use of the analytic space or narrative space in this way is the primitive notion of "wet and dry space," which refers to the "feel" of the space in different archaic transferences (see chapter 7).

Using selected material from Margot's analysis, we have illustrated the four main narrative constructs of the maternal erotic transference and its potential for transformation. We have seen in

---

[6] This quest attempts to re-create the earliest experience of the transformational environmental mother, who is less an object than a process, who is able, through her bodily ministrations to the infant, to "alter self experience" (Bollas, 1987) Bollas asserts that adults periodically seek reunion with this "transformational object." The quest is not to possess the object; rather the object is pursued in order to surrender to it as a medium that alters the self (p. 14). The subject-as-supplicant now feels himself to be the recipient of envirosomatic caring, identified with metamorphoses of the self. We agree, and we believe we add another dimension to this transformational aspect by locating it in the interplay with concrete sensual bodily sensations and fantasies reawakened in the early maternal erotic transference.

this case how MET fosters the emergence of an enlivened subjectivity, as Margot moved from being a perfect but deanimated little doll-object to a subject of desire; how anal erotism provided a creative opportunity for enlivening a formerly tidy but deadened obsessional system; how Margot moved from existence in a split good/bad universe of self and other to a life in which she could play and tolerate ambiguity and maintain a cohesive sense of her whole self as a composite of loving and hurtful impulses; and, finally, how she became able to embrace her disavowed femininity.

In the next chapter, we elaborate on the derailments of self and the damaged capacity for love and desire that surround profoundly negative birth stories. Building on such unconscious beliefs as Margot revealed about herself as being the result of an unwanted pregnancy and as being a "miscarried miscarriage" (revealed in her dream of herself as a little girl sitting on a toilet with a piece of bloody liver), we will look at fantasies of stillbirth and abortion that can profoundly deform the self. We will take up the maternal erotic transference as an opportunity for reconstructing some patients' "cursed birth stories" and rewriting them in the matrix of a transformational encounter in the maternal erotic transference.

4

The Maternal Erotic Countertransference

> Countertransference, while never a warmly received member of the family of psychodynamic concepts, has always been exceedingly useful. (Natterson, 1991, p. 73)

Freud's well-known metaphors of the analyst as surgeon and as reflecting mirror suggest the elimination of the analyst's emotional response as a goal of analytic work. The classical outlook on countertransference was that it was a kind of glitch in the analyst's system, evidence of imperfect training analysis. This early view of countertransference delayed its reporting and elaboration and thus seriously hampered the study and experience essential to demonstrate its usefulness and limitations. The neglect of preoedipal and maternal transferences, also deeply rooted in Freud's phallocentric bias, fostered a strange silence about mothers and their desires.

The classical model has been notably unsuccessful for treating patients whose primary issues are in the area of what Balint (1968) called "the basic fault" or who have narcissistic deficits. We posit that, strictly applied, the model blocks one's access to patients' primitive bodily states by limiting one's own bodily resonance to inchoate material. We broaden the concept of erotic transference to include the preoedipal, the maternal, and the primitive and emphasize its aggressive elements, as well as its tender ones. In the light of this broadened perspective, the therapeutic situation must undergo considerable alteration with regard both to its dangers and to its opportunities.

MATERNAL EROTIC COUNTERTRANSFERENCE:
MINE FIELD OR GOLD MINE?

Although our position on maternal erotic countertransference is closer to Person's (1985) notion of erotic transference as a gold mine rather than a mine field, we are mindful that even gold mines are susceptible to sudden collapse and the sometime uncovering of fool's gold. This is dangerous territory to enter and requires a great deal of the analyst. A continuing analytic relationship is a kaleidoscopic endeavor: transference–countertransference shifts are limitless, and the consequent reflections of the pattern undergo radical change. For the interaction to remain alive and fruitful, the analyst must be able to tolerate the uncertainty inherent in unceasing realignments of self, object, and content.

Until recently, the few published descriptions of erotic counter-transference portrayed female patients and male analysts in oedipal engagements. As mentioned earlier, Kumin (1985) focuses on the need of the analyst to refrain from erotic desire for the patient lest he create a threat to the treatment. We know well the crucial importance of self-restraint and maintaining neutrality. Certainly, misreading and mishandling of oedipal and preoedipal erotic transferences and countertransferences lead to pressing problems and deserve serious consideration in the literature.

We must emphasize that as we talk about preverbal, body-based transferences and countertransferences, while encouraging resonance, indulgence, and play in fantasy, we insist that, however urgent the patient's desire for actual bodily contact, the work remain exclusively within the domain of fantasy and words. In fact, central to our thesis is the creation of a narrative space for inchoate material, permitting the translation of preverbal bodily feelings into some kind of narrative coherence in order to foster therapeutic transformations. This applies equally to bodily experienced transference phenomena and to bodily based countertransferences. Carpy (1989), pointing out the danger of the analyst's acting out powerful feelings, notes that the first task is often simply to recognize these feelings, which can be difficult, and then to attempt to tolerate the feelings without acting them out.

In our experience, patients experiencing the preoedipal maternal erotic transferences outlined in chapters 2 and 3 evoke in the analyst powerful and primitive wishes and defenses that may include manic, depressive, obsessional, schizoid, or paranoid elements. Herein lies a paradox: in the preoedipal maternally erotic transference–countertransference situation, the problem may be less one of behaving oneself than of allowing oneself to participate. Where even speech can be erotized yet nevertheless experienced as strangely inadequate, what the patient longs for is contact with the analyst's voluptuous body or with bodily products. Both participants may face the longing for and terror engendered by the wish to be one being in the same skin, and each has to deal with this wish in his or her own way.

If we cannot think about such a reaction in ourselves, we either act out by indulging the patient with actual mothering (with verbal or nonverbal sympathetic gestures) or we may become so frightened of doing this that we freeze and are not even able to acknowledge the patient's wish to be mothered (Brenman Pick, 1985, p. 159) When erotic countertransferences remain unconscious, they greatly impoverish, and even threaten to derail, the analytic process. If and when they become conscious to the therapist and are worked through in self-analysis or consultation, they can enable the patient's corresponding maternal erotic transference to unfold and be understood .

In this chapter, we continue to develop the notion that it is the analyst's difficulty in dealing with erotic countertransference feelings, particularly those fused with aggression, that inhibits their experience and expression within the analysis.

Countertransference reactions to maternal erotic transferences heretofore have not been described in the literature. There was even early speculation that women analysts engendered neither erotic transferences nor paternal transferences. Similarly, female homosexual countertransference has rarely been studied. McDougall (1986a) is among the few pathfinders in this area. Bernstein (1991) cautions, but only in passing, that while it may be easy for female therapists to identify with "how bad mother was," this posture really may mask more threatening homoerotic feelings. We would add that this resistance is shared by both analysand and analyst.

Moreover, the real differences in the ways men and women analyze have not been extensively described by the analytic community. Perhaps the assumption that the gender of the analyst "makes no difference" was somehow an attempted cultural correction of this neglect; perhaps the analytic community was ready to grant that a woman who was thoroughly analyzed could overcome her limitations and conduct analysis like a man. This void where mother should be, this manqué, has cast a great shadow over theory, particularly in the notion that it is the father who is the symbol of the word. (We also look at this in chapter 5, in the course of investigating male and female stories of birth and the commonality of male appropriation of the mother's function.) Chasseguet-Smirgel (1984) expressed our position well when she wrote, "Maternal aptitude on the analyst's part (in men as well as in women) forms the basis of the analytic framework, which defines, so to speak, the outline of the womb" (p. 170).

In our view, typical defensive aspects of the maternal erotic countertransference relate to precautions against archaic, perverse, and magical wishes centering on the analyst's and the patient's bodies. If and when these wishes become conscious to the therapist, they can, like any other unconscious countertransference, be worked through in self-analysis or consultation. Then they can enable the patient's corresponding maternal erotic transference to unfold, be understood, and woven among the narrative strands of the patient's narration of desire. We agree with Carpy (1989) and Brenman Pick (1985)—and here's the rub—that it is not possible to experience a countertransference fully without minimally enacting it in the treatment.

FOUR PERMUTATIONS OF
MATERNAL EROTIC COUNTERTRANSFERENCE

Looking at erotic countertransference from the point of view of our own experiences of the typical defensive constellations employed by analysts when faced with primitive erotic material, we have posited four interwoven permutations of the maternal erotic countertransference, each often colored by culturally and biologically based gender considerations. These constellations illuminate the narration of each patient's desire. They comprise narrative strands that seem to coalesce around issues of fusion, schizoid or obsessional distancing, and grandiose or manic treatment agendas. They include archaic loving and hurtful impulses and perverse wishes, as well as defenses against them.

We group these maternal erotic countertransference (MEC) constellations differently from MET, which, as will be recalled, in chapter 3 we grouped around four narrative strands: 1) the birth of desire and body-based aspects of the self; 2) anal erotism and permutations of desire; 3) the sensual matrix in the formation of object relations; and 4) erotic desire as a transitional opportunity fostering the solidification of gender identity. We realize that transference and counter-transference, even when they seem to correspond, do not actually match or mimic each other.

Grandiose Fantasies

Grandiose fantasies often emerge as feelings on the part of the ana-lyst that the patient will be completely made over or reborn through the treatment. The analyst may see the patient as lacking in certain supplies or experiences that the analyst feels impelled to furnish. This countertransference constellation is typified by such manic responses as the fantasy that one will cure a patient with one's "magi-cal" breast. Reacting to a patient's distancing or denial of erotic responses, the analyst may feel compelled to be excessively mater-nally seductive, to invite the apprehensive patient into a "warm bath" of cooing words that only soothe rather than interpret and advance treatment.

Anaclitic/Depressive Countertransference

A depressive response is revealed in the analyst's unwillingness to "let go" of a patient. Preferring to hold on to a view of the patient as infantilized, depleted, and needy, the analyst refuses to see the patient's vitality and readiness to separate. Conversely, the patient, seeking clinging or fusion, may attempt to regress. The analyst's function may be a defensive refusal to be "consumed" and a wish to construct barriers against the patient, to make "father" reappear by making "penetrating" interpretations, or to "clean things up" with crisp insights into "messy" feelings. Chasseguet-Smirgel (1978, 1986) has written of "the male principle," the child's natural wish to get rid of the father in the attempt to perpetuate a seamless oneness with mother and to make a baby with her without the intrusive participa-tion of a father. In this transference–countertransference duet, as the patient seeks fusion, the analyst wards it off to avoid regression, loss of control, depressive feelings, and loss.

Erotic Horror and Schizoid Distancing

Distancing in the maternal erotic countertransference takes the form of fear of the patient's consuming wish to invade the analyst's body, office, and home with needy and messy demands, suffocating smells, and dangerous oral greed. The analyst, now a partner in a "perverse misalliance," may refuse to deal with such erotic material and may respond with disavowal of the patient's wishes and intense distancing from the patient. Typically, perverse misalliances contain a refusal to participate, with attendant lack of interest, deadness, and lack of creativity. Khan's (1979) thesis was that the essence of perversion is the inability to enjoy erotic experience directly. It is typical of perverse relationships that the pervert's participation is as an onlooker, thus corresponding to the pervert's essentially schizoid adjustment.

From a developmental perspective, Mahler and her colleagues (1975) observed toddlers enjoying physically interactive games with their fathers while at the same time recoiling from their mothers. Mahler interpreted this behavior as evidence of an erotized fear of mothers and understood this as a sign of the fear of reengulfment. We posit that this fear and schizoid distancing is recreated in the maternal erotic transference–countertransference duet.

Thus even though these transferences and countertransferences offer a therapeutic gold mine, analyst and patient alike, unconsciously fearing regression, fusion, loss of control, humiliation, and frustration, may defend against conscious erotic awareness, acting as if they were in the midst of a lethal mine field. Failure to recognize and resonate with early maternal erotic transference phenomena, however, surely blocks movement in analysis and can derail it if unresolved.

Therapist Gender and Maternal Erotic Countertransference

In addition to the countertransference constellations mentioned earlier that block creative and transformational work, there are some culturally determined generalizations about therapist gender that may make working with aspects of erotic transferences more difficult for one sex than for the other. Because the conscious ego ideal of most female therapists is more likely to tend toward Mother Theresa than toward Madonna, the pop singer, female therapists may be more comfortable in the preoedipal maternal role of nurturer than as the sexually seductive objects of oedipal erotic transferences. Also, they may be able to give in more easily to regression into boundariless sensory states because their femaleness is not threatened by "at-onement" with the maternal body.

By contrast, whereas male therapists tend to be better able than female therapists to see themselves as the object of oedipal sexual feelings, they may have greater difficulty recognizing early bodily longings and tolerating the regression requisite to working within preoedipal maternal erotic transferences. Their ego ideals are more frequently figures of sexual and intellectual power rather than, say, Mister Rogers.

Regardless of the therapist's gender, when the resistances on both sides of the therapeutic dyad are worked through, and when the patient is not riddled with psychotic anxieties, then the early pre-oedipal maternal erotic transference can surface and even be plea-surable, in the same primal way that playing in a mud puddle or a bath can be enjoyable.

PROJECTIVE IDENTIFICATION AND EROTIC TRANSFERENCE AND COUNTERTRANSFERENCE

Erotic countertransference can also occur in relation to forms of transference that are not primarily erotic, such as those contained in response to projective identification:

> Projective identification is a primitive phenomenon and can therefore involve very powerful feelings which are only able to be dealt with in this way because the patient is unable to put them into words. Particularly with more disturbed and borderline 'patients, the analyst finds himself filled with powerful feelings in the session, and is faced with the problem of how to deal with them. (Carpy, 1989, p. 287)

Ogden (1986) describes projective identification as having three components: the fantasy of expulsion of a part, the interpersonal pres-sure, and the therapist's resonating response. He gives an example of a psychotic adolescent who mocked and harassed the therapist:

> The therapist not only felt angry, but also experienced feelings of disorganization and utter helplessness that at times gave him the panicky feeling that he was drowning. This would be an obvious example. A patient who is unwashed and unpleasantly aromatic is another example (pp. 150–151)

Winnicott (cited in Ogden, 1986) viewed projective identification as "direct communication" in the sense that it is "communication by means of a direct induction of a feeling state in another person that is not predominantly (and often not at all) mediated by verbal sym-bols" (p. 239). In common parlance, the word "chemistry" is invoked to describe and explain the phenomenon. Surprisingly, analytic investigators have given relatively little attention to the fact that projective identification is characteristically manifest, and particularly troublesome, in erotic transferences and countertransferences. As far as we know, the problematic role of this primitive defense within the primitive material of early maternal erotic transferences has not been extensively studied; it is interesting to try to account for this neglect.

Because projective identification is generally nonverbal and often perverse, its erotic component can be the last of which the patient, the therapist, or the supervisor become aware. Even without conscious awareness, however, as derivatives waft upward toward recognition, they typically arouse shame and humiliation in the patient, and anxiety about management in therapist and supervisor, leading to undesirable defensive efforts that may consume the analytic process.

A key aspect to unraveling the enactments of projective identification is the analyst's ability to maintain an "as if" analytic attitude, a state of mind in which her own feelings and thoughts can be understood as symbolic, in the face of the patient's often very strenuous attempts to have thoughts become deeds and facts. That is, the analyst must be able to take in the projection without succumbing to an unmodified regression that would compromise the capacity to think symbolically.

Clearly, it is particularly challenging to deal with information that makes its way to the analyst's notice through projective identification. Further, the wish itself may be of such a primitive and preverbal nature as not to be readily recognizable as erotic, nursing, for instance, or anal penetration with an enema. Supervisees are often timid about bringing such issues openly into supervision. The supervisor, depending on her capacity to empathize with both the analyst's and the patient's emotional positions, can facilitate or hinder the process. Attuned to projective identifications from the patient to the supervisee, and also to parallel process, the supervisor fosters the supervisee's learning to self-observe and self-modulate through these situations, which can be embarassing and difficult to understand and deal with.

Thus, although they are not conventionally experienced initially by either party as directly erotic, maternal erotic transferences and countertransferences can be productively viewed through the template of projective identification. Countertransference constellations that include archaic loving and hurtful impulses and perverse wishes, as well as defenses against them, often are announced through the mechanism of projective identification and counteridentification.

CLINICAL ILLUSTRATIONS OF MATERNAL EROTIC COUNTERTRANSFERENCES

Having described some aspects of our theoretical constructs regarding maternal erotic countertransferences, we want to emphasize that we believe that transference–countertransference is a highly individual matter, typical of a given analytic pair at a certain stage in their ongoing relating and in some sense irreproducible outside their interaction. Recognition of the limitations of any theoretical construct increases the responsibility of the analyst to consider alternative constructions to the traditional transference-centered ways of conceptualizing the clinical situation. We see what we expect to see and have been trained to see, and we may miss newer and richer possibilities. We conceive of the MET/MEC as an organizing construct. Like all models, it is useful to the extent that it does not preempt or exclude other models. We do not suggest that these countertransference models are found in pure form; more than one form is often evident in a particular case, as can be seen in the following vignettes.

Sam: A "Baby in a Gift Basket at the Analyst's Door"

Sam, a 35-year-old-engineer, entered treatment after many years of giving himself repeatedly and masochistically to a series of women who appeared to offer salvation but refused to be sexual with him. He was quite overweight and appeared blurred in outline so that it was possible to see him as a large infant, although in reality he was a large and powerful man, noted for intellectual achievement, and especially good at contact sports. Sam's father had died suddenly when Sam was an infant. Sam's homoerotic impulses were bound up in his lifelong search for a "father figure." Although his mother remarried several times, her marriages never lasted more than a year. During childhood, when there was no husband in her bed, Sam slept with his mother. He had two younger half sisters, whom he sensed his mother favored; but as he perceived she held no expectations for their success, he felt it was his job to carry on his father's family's prominent name and banner. He felt himself destined for greatness as his ancestors had been, but he had very little sense of how greatness was to come. He was terribly unhappy at his failure to have even begun a family of his own or to progress in his career.

In adult life, his relationship with his mother remained both erotically tempting and frightening, as he experienced her as intensely infantilizing and seductive. When she traveled, he often looked after her house but was absolutely unwilling to spend the night there, even in her absence. Masculine authority also frightened and attracted him; he developed a symphony of passive-aggressive responses to authority figures but never crossed the line into outright rebellion.

From the beginning of treatment, I (JKW) was aware of countertransference in thinking of him as a large baby who had been left on my doorstep. I recognized my ambivalence about receiving this "gift basket" but defensively dealt with it by succumbing to a magical countertransference wish to make him over. I found myself colluding with the "baby," wishing to give him a new start, to "make him a man," while denying that he was already a man. My wish to transform him was accompanied by a vague sense of being distant from him, not exclusively attributable to either of us.

His first dreams of treatment were about the terror of the ocean flooding the land. Then innumerable dreams contained manifest references to food. Food preparation and consumption was an intense source of gratification to Sam, but in many dreams, the food became spoiled because someone was "being sexual instead of minding the stove." When women in his dreams began to appear separated from their feeding function, Sam gleefully threw them from small boats. Typically, before he dealt with any woman in an erotic context, he would shrink her to child size. Kissing began to occur in his dreams. In happy dreams it referred to fusion, in angry dreams, to cannibalism. Treatment was well advanced when he had the following dream:

> I came into the session and you directed me to lie on the couch, where you proceeded to operate on my abdomen. You made a series of triangular cuts into my belly, and attached a vacuum-like tool to each, painlessly removing the excess fat. I was very pleased by this, and felt infinitely more masculine when it was over.

At about this time in the treatment, I had a dream. Frequently, when we dream about a specific patient it is a signal that unconsciously we are struggling to become aware of some issue relating to the treatment or to the countertransference. I dreamed that I had finally agreed to Sam's expressed wish to be nursed, but not on the couch and only through my dress. In the dream, this felt like a reasonable solution, serving decorum and modesty, honoring the analysis, and healing the patient. The dream seems to reflect a straightforward example of the therapist's matching the patient's early erotic transference wish with countertransference impulses for renaissance obtained at a magical breast. This is also an example where the patient's preoedipal longing to be nursed, and the analyst's wish to gratify it, covered more threatening oedipal material.

Study of these dreams made me aware that I had not noticed how radically the patient's appearance had altered over time. He had lost a lot of weight and did indeed, as he claimed, resemble a particularly attractive public figure. Instead, I had continued to conceptualize and experience him as an insatiable nursling. In this case, recognition of the deeply erotic nature of the early feeding wishes and impulses opened the path to more oedipal genital material.

In the following weeks, as I remained more aware of Sam's emerging masculine presence, he began to produce the first frankly oedipal and phallic dreams of the analysis. The following is an example:

> I was on a pistol range on the property of an old man my girlfriend was living with. I had my special pistol with me. Another guy was with me. I brought out my gun, a fine Browning automatic. It was an odd shape. It had a dual hand hold on either side of the barrel. The other guy is impressed with it. It's outstanding. The target is a projection screen. You shoot into the target, and you can almost see the bullets when this gun fires. It's more like bolts of electricity. Its a real electric experience. I feel ten feet tall!

Although there are obvious homosexual references in this dream, Sam's associations and subsequent behavior were toward ending masturbation as his preferred sexual activity and beginning more adult sexuality. It also emerged in his associations that this gun had double handles on it because both the analyst and the patient were to remain in charge of it and because the dyad itself was recognized as powerfully charged.

This dream occurred at the beginning of Sam's first "experiment in dating," during which he had as many sexual partners as possible. Feeling that the world of women was open to him, he was determined to "have every woman in town." For a long time he seemed driven to "earn notches" in his gun. Eventually, he came to consider this behavior excessive, aggressive, and related to displaced feelings toward me. Subsequently, he settled into a long-term relationship with a suitable and sexual woman. He felt, at last, that his adolescence had passed, and he was a full-fledged man.

Roger: Perverse Distancing and Swollen Impregnation

Roger described his experience of the analytic interaction as a kind of a war dance, with sword parries and retreats into a fortified cave. A 46-year-old professional, he had grudgingly sought treatment when a number of important relationships collapsed under the weight of his hostility. Analysis soon revealed his pervasive unconscious fantasy that anal intercourse was the goal of every relationship: do it or be done to.

Roger had an internal voice he dubbed the Mocker, a kind of father or older brother whose function was to provide him with constant companionship and to keep up a steady description of the flaws of all humanity. Accused as a boy of being sarcastic ("People thought I had nails for breakfast"), as an adult Roger was the object of endless, bitterly contested business disputes. In the early part of the analysis he rarely confronted me.[1] Instead, his sessions were filled with circumlocutions and long, vague ramblings delivered in a singularly monotonous manner. Using this manner of speech, which he called "low and slow," he delivered droning catalogues of "shit kicking" during which he seemed utterly to disregard my presence in the room. When he did notice me, he described me as a totem pole—a stick—wooden heads—a shrinker. His perverse deanimation of me as a nurturing presence generally elicited a defensive, obsessionally distancing countertransference. I counted the minutes slowly ticking by in the sessions and found myself gleefully wanting to "nail him" with particularly trenchant interpretations punctuated with lists of adjectives, such as, "Your pleasure in shit-kicking that clerk in the store seemed to make him treat you as an annoying, demanding, pushy client whom he chose to ignore."

The patient's sexual life was consciously fragmented and split up. There were nameless women catalogued for convenience. He delighted in his own demeaning and novel meaning of the term "bag lady" by maintaining his utter disregard for the personhood of his

---

[1]Neither of our initials is included here because "Roger" is, for reasons of confidentiality as well as illustration, a composite of three of our cases.

sexual partners; he wished they would figuratively keep their heads in a bag during sex. His material matched his fantasy that the best mother would be "one who would come with a small can" for the boy "to pee in, so he needn't disrupt his game."

Roger orchestrated all his relationships and was remarkably effective at forcing people into positions where they would behave in the desired way. I experienced many hours of being stuck and trapped and filled with deadening material. I often felt dismantled, drained of vitality, initiative, sensuality, and ideas. Struggling to remain emotionally involved in his treatment and in control of my own rage, I was pulled between my own countertransference schizoid distancing and occasional seductive wishes to gain the upper hand by treating him as a little baby in dire need of my nurturing. I experienced his transference projections as alternating between the "bag lady," the "pee can mother," the grandmother (a singularly upright, intrusive, and relentlessly sexless maternal figure), and the father, who was usually absent but henpecked and mildly sadistic when present.

Roger reported at length having uncharacteristically, and needlessly, lied to his lover to minimize the number of times a week he was in analysis. There was reason to expect that the lie would be revealed and that, at the very least, he would be embarrassed. He considered exposure preferable to the deep shame he would have revealed by indicating the extent of his "dependency."

The lie struck me very forcibly, and I was determined to reexamine my emotional position. I realized that I found it difficult to think of him as sexually attractive, although he told me he had recently been described as "looking like a movie star." I recognized that my inhibition of erotic resonance had at least two sources. First, the patient's hateful and demeaning behavior toward women made any erotic considerations seem tantamount to the masochistic surrender he required of his lovers. He constantly let me know how replaceable I was by any of a number of his catalogue of "girls." Under the circumstances, I felt that emotional availability would render me extraordinarily vulnerable. In this area of the relationship, I defensively substituted vigilance and maintaining authority for empathy and erotic access. Specifically, I unconsciously feared the humiliation of erotic rejection and the worse humiliation of erotic acceptance, which would entail, it seemed to me, an abject masochistic capitulation.

Second, and harder to identify, was the insidious deadening of the relationship, which resulted in my continuing sensation of being a disjointed puppet with replaceable parts. In this condition, I could not organize an erotic resonance. As I worked with aspects of the countertransference in self-analysis and consultation, I recognized the marked absence of erotic resonance to this man. Following this self-reflection, however, allowing myself to respond to him differently during a session, I experienced an intense physical sensation reminiscent of nursing. It was as if the milk, long delayed, were finally allowed to run. I began to think better, to have new ideas regarding his treatment, and I was able to suggest productive directions. He was subsequently able to bringing forward a fear he had of becoming my slave, in what he termed "a mindless, pink cloud of bliss." Later, we also focused on his shameful wish for loving penetration from father, or me, in father's stead. In these instances he was stating, consciously, the very emotional position I had experienced in relation to him, in which he had turned longing for bodily contact into a kind of sexually deanimating assault.

Now, instead of disregarding me as a presence, Roger began a thorough visual and auditory examination of my being. He became acutely aware of my dress and hair style, my manner of speech, and the previously ignored objects in the office. He believed, erroneously, that there had been tremendous changes in my appearance and in the physical environment. Alternating between rapt attentiveness and obsessional nit-picking, he noticed every mote of dust and gave instructions for correcting "structural anomalies" in the office itself.

In the new atmosphere of investigation and exploration it became possible to deal with such issues as voyeurism and exhibitionism, object- and self-constancy, and anal erotism, all of which had been taken up before but never with emotional currency for the patient.

Analysis of the transference revealed Roger's fear that an embodied, whole woman would loom up with overwhelming sexual power and reveal him as a shitty, helpless baby. Analysis of the countertransference from the erotic point of view resulted in my being able to behave like a woman who, instead of trying to distance herself from him or overwhelm him with her huge, nurturing breasts, or wanting to kill him, was able to contain and nourish him; and he was able to begin the healing process. (Naturally, these changes from preoedipal to oedipal in the transference and countertransference have been much compressed in this composite vignette; it actually involved many years of continuing struggle on the part of the analyst to maintain her analytic attitude.)

Gillian: A Clinical Illustration Of An Analyst's Erotic Horror

The case of Gillian (first mentioned in chapter 2) demonstrates maternal erotic countertransference with a female patient and female analyst (JKW). Work with this patient is presented around countertransference struggles within an erotic context in which early and later oral and anal wishes were clearly present. The homosexual, sadomasochistic aspects of the transference and countertransference were defended against in a matrix of paranoid projections, erotic horror, and perverse distancing. This kind of paranoid/schizoid constellation is developed in more theoretical detail in chapter 6; here we are interested particularly in its impact on the countertransference.

Gillian, an intelligent, energetic professional woman of 63, gave the initial impression of being an old-fashioned schoolteacher, conservative, reliable, and always about to ask a question. Saying "I am the injured party," Gillian entered treatment because of dissatisfaction with her sexual relationship with her uninterested husband. She had suffered from insomnia, anxiety, and depression for as long as she could remember. Additionally she had never risen in her work to a position commensurate with her abilities and diligence.

Something had gone wrong between Gillian and her mother from the beginning. Gillian described herself as "born angry" and related that she had had great difficulty in nursing and had "refused to eat" throughout childhood. Gillian knew that her young mother had been raised, like many southern girls of "good family," by black nurses and must have felt degraded by the task of caring for her own children, as well as frightened by the babies' demands. Gillian herself while still a child was charged with caring for an infant for a while. When the infant cried and cried and she was unable to comfort him, she bit him. When treatment was well advanced, Gillian hypothesized that her own mother might have felt that same urge; she wondered whether babies could sense that but would be confused about who was frightened, who was hungry, and who wished to bite.

As the treatment progressed and the transference and countertransference were engaged, we each felt under threat of destructive invasion by the other. Gillian had many early dreams in which the breast, exemplified by lovely mountainous hills, were torn apart and damaged by unthinking young people on powerful motorcycles. There were also dreams in which mother's milk was discovered to be poisonous to babies.

It gradually emerged that Gillian believed all her body substances to be highly toxic. Issues of bodily contact mediated through wetness (see chapter 8), in this case noxious bodily fluids, predominated in Gillian's psychic economy. Once, when there were no tissues, she took their absence to indicate my wish that she not "cry around on the couch." When there were tissues, she examined the tear stains with great interest and folded and refolded the tissues to hide or expose the tear stains. Often, she wound the wet tissues around her fingers, pulling them together into one mass that she deemed unacceptable for my wastebasket. At the end of the hour, the tissues were always placed into her otherwise immaculate purse.

She had been an "enthusiastic and unrepentant bed wetter." She had called her mother "Vom-ma" (Vomit Mother) in a scornful reaction to her mother's anger at her soiling. It became clear that Gillian had experienced her toilet training as having been invented to hurt, humiliate, and disarm her. The overriding theme of the first six months of treatment was control: over rage, over drinking, over her husband, over herself, over sleep, over bowel movements, which had to be coaxed by external massage. She had been reared in a family that discussed their excretions daily and in great detail. The patient's anal concerns included her intolerance of fecal material within the bowel and toilet habits associated with its removal. Revealing these toilet habits caused her great shame and humiliation. Gillian had suffered from anal parasites in her childhood, and she maintained a fascination with worms. She had been given enemas with some frequency in her childhood and continued them into her adulthood, when she suddenly realized that others did not function this way. Gillian maintained a lifelong preoccupation with parasitic infestations, which I understood in this context to represent the fluctuation between maternal erotic wishes and horror.

Gillian's maternal erotic transference promoted confusion in me about whose erotic and destructive wishes were being activated. My countertransference reaction included the manic, depressive, obsessional, schizoid, and paranoid elements typical of the maternal erotic countertransference. The negative transference fulminated in Gillian's perception of me as an arachnid mother, enslaving and all-powerful. Her perception was echoed in my own unconscious countertransference projection of the patient as a toxic, parasitic infant who seemed bent on, and capable of, dismantling and devouring me. The following is the first of many her dreams of worms in the treatment:

I was looking into an old hollow tree with a white, stringy substance like hair in the hollow of the tree. I noticed scarlet worms in my hair. Someone suggested I comb them out of the hair. Somehow, the worms came out, and instead of being scarlet they were pink and transparent and clinging to my clothes in great masses like spaghetti. I scraped these worms off my clothes and put them into the dead tree, knowing it would kill them. I felt them crawling on my legs. I thought, "They're gonna get on my pussy; it smells bad and they won't like it." I felt the worms on my pussy. I knew if I scraped them off they would leave stubs. I tried to.

This dream encapsulated the transference and countertransference matrix of this case. It was an early indication of my patient's fear that no one would be able to help and that, left to her own devices, she could only make things worse. The worm motif accompanied the treatment throughout and was richly symbolic of many aspects of the patient's experience. Her horrified denial of devouring, greedy, and intrusive wishes was symbolized by worms. In her original narrative, she was destined to remain forever fetid, a stunted rosebush whose roots were trapped in dank soil, invaded and spoiled by a worm-mother who would not help her break through to fresh air to grow separate branches and flowers.

Worms were a key symbol in her lexicon for the relationship between parasitic babies and host mothers. They could enter the body at any point, through any orifice or through the pores of the skin. They could live in hollow trees, often associated with fat women or old women. Gillian's descriptive associations often linked worms to food. She also associated to worms as rectal parasites, amounting to mouths in the anus and linked to an infantile form of intercourse and a symbol for babies invading and destroying the mother. At the same time they paid her homage; they were utterly contained in and dependent on her. The worms also revealed a primitive aspect of the patient's ego and object world, experienced in bits and pieces, and presaged later conflicts within the patient about penises and castration. In some ways, the worms were best understood as bits of projective identification, and were the major players in our later transference–countertransference engagement.

Under the sway of a defensively distancing maternal erotic countertransference, and prior to our developing these constructs of MET and MEC, I consistently emphasized the obsessive-compulsive aspects of the patient and paid less attention to indications of borderline and psychotic phenomena. I thus attempted to deny the worms access to my conscious thinking. Gillian seemed attuned to my avoidance when she noted "someone's" blithe, perhaps slightly manic, suggestion to simply "comb" (or *analyze*) the worms out of her hair.

Gillian thought of me as a spider that observed in secret, waiting for her to become entrapped. She simultaneously idealized and denigrated me as the "Queen of the Worms," the "Woman on Whom the Whole World Feeds," who needed no one herself. At the same time, Gillian saw herself as slaving to support my life; if not for the analysis, Gillian would retire and be free to pursue her own interests. She developed a plan to starve me by retiring from work and abandoning the analysis. When the host starves, the parasite too dies. A starving baby can no longer support and feed the mother it creates, can no longer fill the breast it imagines.

Gillian's sexual fantasies were invariably humiliating to her. They included masturbating with a turd and being required to mutilate her genitals. This activity was always in response to an internalized figure she called the "Bodiless Head," which was all intellect, control, and sadism. As Gillian began to include me as an erotic figure, she saw me as a potential executioner.

Defensive against this sadomasochistic enticement, and below the level of my awareness, I began to view Gillian as a vengeful, invading worm horde that entered the hollowed-out mother in order to be killed. I found myself struggling against a wish to exclude or expel Gillian. Unconsciously responding to this atmosphere in primitive, nonverbal ways, I became suspicious; I was beginning to think of the patient as dangerous and needing to be carefully watched.

During this phase of treatment, Gillian wore a perfume I very much disliked and that grew to seem almost overpoweringly intense as it "invaded" my consulting room. She acknowledged an association to her experience in adolescence of feeling that she and her father signaled each other with anal smells. Her interest in smells reappeared as an interest in flowers. She never missed a chance to smell flowers in the office and brought especially fragrant blossoms from her garden as gifts.

What emerged was a recognition of both the paternal and the maternal aspects of this erotic transference–countertransference matrix (see chapter 9). It evoked the "Bodiless Head," which ordered sacrifice and self-denial but nevertheless protected her from the fragmentation of maternal erotic diffusion. In short, it was better to turn to a torturing father figure than to risk the disintegration of herself into her analyst.

The transference alternated between anal and oral aspects of erotism. Gillian was unrelenting in her contempt for men, and I found myself increasingly uneasy with her disdain, although her remarks were irresistibly clever. As I retreated from emotional contact, I was unconsciously recoiling from the threat of invasive erotic overtures. I consciously focused on the "clinically interesting" aspects of the case and experienced myself as an echo of the patient's fear of a distant, watchful, uninterested analyst.

This patient's maternal erotic countertransference was intensified and exacerbated by the transient psychotic aspects of her maternal transferences. Self-analysis of the countertransferential bind was also delayed by her masochistic acceptance of my "penetrating" interpretations of her hatred; when the worms came at me, I redirected them to her. In her terror that no one would pay attention to her or be willing to join with her, she invited sadistic assault and was remarkably successful in achieving it. We eventually were led to a recognition of Gillian's active vacillation between the courting of the anally erotic father and the seduction of a "vampire mother," both as a defense against her fear of abandonment by uninterested parents.

As I slowly came to understand these obstacles, Gillian spoke a little, and with great shame, of a physical desire for me, and a more typical maternal erotic transference ensued.

While on vacation during the third year of treatment, Gillian was involved in an accident for which she bore more than a little blame and that resulted in her husband's being severely injured. As a result, he became in real life very like the impotent infant she had imagined him to be. After her return to treatment, it emerged that she was enraged with me for not "seeing this coming," for not warning her and thus preventing the accident from occurring. She threatened to quit the analysis. Although she did not, there was damage to be dealt with.

I consciously interpreted but unconsciously accepted Gillian's reproach as valid. This reaction, I now believe, was related to my having failed for so long to recognize the nature and quality of Gillian's maternal erotic transference. I had been pulled into a defensive maternal erotic countertransference that allowed me to distance myself from a feared invasion by her worm hordes. For this I unconsciously felt guilty.

At the time, I consciously felt I had failed to exhibit the required omnipotence, and I became increasingly avoidant of contact with the patient. I became aware of a growing reluctance to see her first thing in the morning. I became alert to and then increasingly incensed by the abundance of Gillian's perfume in the elevator. I took to walking up the stairs to avoid this repugnant experience, which became increasingly one of being surrounded by and trapped in something malignant, menacing, and suffocating. I felt invaded by the patient's habit of using the public restroom before and after each session, leaving me no opportunity to do so without seeming to invade her privacy. I felt annoyed by the way Gillian looked at me when entering my office. At times, Gillian's eyes appeared to have an unnatural glitter and intensity. I felt as if Gillian were asking for things that could never be given and, if they could be given, could never be retrieved.

Gillian's hands were like creatures alive, perpetually wringing, moving. Her efforts to still them took the form of entrapping the one within the other and remaining constantly alert to its wish to escape. This gesture too seemed momentous to me, and strangely invading. Gillian intensified her old habit of coming into the office with wet nail polish, and I began to worry about her smearing the couch. She did not. She held the wet hand, always the right hand, with the fingers spread and the hand itself motionless, about six inches above her abdomen. She was largely silent. When she did speak, it was to express considerable misgivings about my intentions toward her. She experienced me as menacing, maligning, trying to trap her "in her own shit" and "rub her nose" in her evil nature.

Illustrative of our discussion of projective identification at the beginning of this chapter, Gillian projected into and introjected from me a sense of being haunted by a powerfully evil, utterly necessary witch of a mother. Specifically, Gillian and I believed she had ruined me by putting poison into my body and that she faced death and murder.

The most primitive aspects of the maternal erotic countertransference had remained largely unconscious; indeed, these concepts had not yet been formulated. It was, in fact, the force of the emotional turmoil evoked by Margot (see chapter 3) and by Gillian that ultimately required HKW and me to undertake that intensive process of understanding together. I realized only retrospectively that I had not been fully aware of the intensity of my feelings. Instead, I had conceptualized the clinical situation as stagnated around a gradual increase in the patient's "resistance," an error easily understood given a deepening degree of work. It was some weeks before I consciously acknowledged having grown to dislike the patient and to dread being with her. It was considerably longer before I became aware that I was horrified by the extent of the patient's masochistic impulses and was doing all I could to keep these feelings "outside."

At this point, I "accidentally" purchased the very same perfume I had found so objectionable on the patient. Chagrined and amused, I set about understanding this event. Although I was concerned at the lack of differentiation it bespoke, I also saw it as important information about the transference–countertransference situation and of my wish to repair the damage between us. If I could find a way to immerse myself in what was objectionable about the patient, this breakthrough might end the "cold war."

The focus of this chapter is not the working through of the maternal erotic transference and countertransference, and I will not fully elaborate how this occurred with Gillian. Suffice to say that, along with an emotional recognition of the countertransference, I became able to accept, tolerate, and productively use new ideas to reconvene the analysis. My increased receptivity had its effect on Gillian, who began to mourn for her aborted babies, literal and figurative, and for the parents she so needed and wished she had had. A long period of painful depression was ultimately productive, as indicated by the following dream, which also was a harbinger of termination.

> I dreamt of plants growing in a cavern in rows of buildings and also inside the house. I was watering them, outside and inside, and I knew this would cause no damage.

WEAVING THE STRANDS OF MATERNAL EROTIC TRANSFERENCES AND COUNTERTRANSFERENCES WITH THE CLINICAL MATERIAL

As noted, considerable attention has been paid to the creative uses of countertransference in general, but not specifically to early maternal erotic issues. In chapter 3, we grouped MET around the birth of desire and body-based aspects of the self, anal erotism and permutations of desire, the sensual matrix in the formation of object relations, and erotic desire as a transitional opportunity fostering the solidification of gender identity. As mentioned prior to the clinical illustrations, we have grouped countertransference constellations (MEC) differently, in recognition that transference and countertransference, even when they seem to correspond, do not actually match or mimic each other. The four principal countertransference threads, coalesced around issues of fusion, schizoid distancing, grandiose treatment agendas, and gender issues can now be reviewed in relation to the preceding clinical material.

Countertransference Issues Relating to Fusion and Separation

The first countertransference constellation, as shown in the case of Sam, relates to the analyst's wish to be overly close to and protective of the patient. It may arise in the analyst's impulses to infantilize the patient to perpetuate a mother–baby fusion. The therapist's own fantasies and dreams may include intimate physical contacts with the patient's body: birthing, nursing, toileting, dressing and undressing— acts of parenting. Specific genital contact is seldom part of these preoedipal erotic fantasies. This contact-seeking may be a countertransference reply to the patient's longings for attachment (see chapter 3, particularly in the case of Margot). When unchecked, both therapist and patient may so exclusively seek to maintain "at-one-ment," avoiding conflict and separateness, that other purposes of the treatment, such as the growth and development of the patient, may be abandoned.

Changing the Birth Story: The Grandiosity of the "Author"

A second countertransference constellation expresses itself as the analyst's grandiose impulse to rebirth and remake the patient and may apply particularly to patients who have bad birth stories (see next chapter). The analyst's wish is literally to start from scratch and make of the patient a different person, to provide for the patient a new history. The "renaissance maternal erotic countertransference" is a basic reply to the basic fault. It may stem from the analyst's grandiose, possibly manic, internal reply to the patient's desperate plea to be made over as well as from the analyst's retaliatory or obsessional need to control the differentiation. The core fantasy is that intimate physical contact or sexual union between analyst and patient will heal the patient. This countertransference constellation is typified by such manic responses as the fantasy that one will cure a patient within one's "perfect womb" or with one's "magical breast." We may also feel inclined to be maternally seductive, to invite the apprehensive patient into a "warm bath" of softly beckoning words, which serve only to soothe rather than interpret and advance treatment. We have already spoken to the analyst's need for patience and understanding of the need for rebirthing by those patients with faulted births; here we are talking about an excessive countertransference response that may lead to arrogant treatment agendas that, in turn, will only result in further pain and disappointment for the patient.

In both of these countertransference predicaments, the analyst may come to rely exclusively on providing a holding environment, which is likely to result in a dearth of interpretive activity, especially transference interpretations. The countertransference collusion results in infantilizing patients, failure to maintain appropriate boundaries, and failure to notice patient development. Additionally, to the extent that this collusion represents manic reparation on the analyst's part, the patient's continued complaint may be perceived as an attack on the analyst's essential goodness and result in the analyst's frustration and narcissistic or paranoid anger. The result of this impasse is seen in the continuous elaboration of dependency needs to the exclusion of aggressive and erotic concerns. Although it may be defensive, we do not consider this form of countertransference to be essentially aggressive.

On the other hand, the analyst may respond as if to "rejection" by the patient's beginning to differentiate, as the mother of the adolescent recalls the "good old days" of dependence and idealization. Optimally, as the analyst is taken in or internalized by the patient, the person of the analyst ultimately suffers the same fate as Winnicott (1952) describes for the transitional object—to be consigned lovingly to limbo. When this happens, as part of the analytic process, the patient has the possibility to create a whole, living, autonomous internal object to take away from treatment. The analyst, however, experiencing abandonment, may resist this differentiation and internalization process, for it signals the end of the fusion. She may repay by becoming obsessionally controlling or perversely picayune.

Issues Relating to Erotic Horror and Perverse Distancing

Contrasting with fusional longings and grandiose rebirthing agendas are two forms in which the aggression attendant separation and differentiation issues is prominent and threatens to call up a corresponding aggression in the analyst. The patient's longing to experience fusion by "entering" the body of the analyst may engage the analyst's defensive, paranoid refusal to be invaded, "lapped up," or consumed by the patient's wishes to breach the skin barrier. The analyst, refusing to participate, may instead engage in distant intellectualizing about the patient's issues and austerely exaggerate the enforcement of the frame and the benefits of nongratification. We consider this form of withdrawal to contain significant destructive impulses, although they are rendered passively. This countertransference is illustrated in the work with Gillian and Roger and in the cases of Leonard (chapter 6) and Michael (chapter 8).

The patient, whose MET struggle is to make of the analyst a whole, alive internal object, picks the analyst metaphorically to pieces, sometimes in verbal rapid-fire, to study each piece in detail. This dissection usually takes place later in treatment and may be misapprehended by the analyst and experienced as an aggressive intrusion into her person or private life; it may summon up the analyst's angry or frightened countertransference. The patient, experimenting with distance and autonomy, is not only rending the analyst to bits, but—focusing on minute aspects of the analyst's person—is busy internally reassembling those bits. The analyst must tolerate any feelings of being cut to pieces. Both participants may believe that this intensely voyeuristic process is destructive. The analyst must refrain from countertransference impulses toward retaliation, especially in the form of "penetrating" interpretations.

This typical maternal erotic distancing countertransference may also result from the analyst's fear of perverse sexual impulses; such a fear may culminate in the unfortunate inability to participate in an emotionally alive interaction. This is seen when the analyst colludes with or phobically avoids the patient's sexual impulses, particularly the patient's perverse wishes. When "erotic horror" predominates, the analyst, reacting with unconscious dread, may fall dull or silent, in defense against erotic feelings or those nascent impulses in the patient. The attendant deadness can destroy the analyst's creative use of countertransference. Similarly, the analyst may unconsciously structure the situation so as to protect herself from such unflattering or noxious projections as the incestuous arachnid or vampire mother.

Another side of this countertransference bind occurs when analyst and patient engage in a defense against maternal erotic regression by enlisting the aid of the forbidding oedipal father. One or the other may feel compelled defensively to raise the specter of father by becoming uncharacteristically authoritarian. The analyst may find herself inexplicably making potent, "penetrating" interpretations, seeking specifically male resources, and in general behaving in ways that interfere with the patient's use of the analyst as an early object.

Gender Issues Relating to MEC

We have already mentioned that we believe it likely that patient's maternal erotic transferences in their pregenital forms often go unrecognized and unacknowledged by some male analysts in defense against regressive immersion in the boundariless erotic fusion. Kumin (1985) refers to the natural resistance to experiencing the kind of inevitable shame and humiliation that is rekindled in an erotic transference. No person wants to reexperience the horror of being the small, inadequate loser in the contest to dispossess the same-sex parent and enjoy exclusive sexual union with the opposite-sex parent. Kumin also refers to the horror of discovering one's separateness and exposing one's vulnerability to romantic humiliation.

Kumin speaks, however, from the traditional viewpoint of the male analyst in an oedipal transference–countertransference situation where participation could literally mean sexual involvement. Why this cautionary note? Certainly, sexual acting out appears to be significantly more common among male than among female analysts, and this phenomenon certainly warrants caution. To the extent that the male ego ideal tends to be measured by demonstrations of sexual potency, and to the extent that oedipal issues are constellated around sexual genital fantasies that are closer to notions of romantic love, the very "normalcy" of the situation might allow it to masquerade as ego syntonic. To that extent, both superego reminders and careful study are very much to the point.

From our vantage point as female analysts, however, we posit quite a different take. We feel that in the preoedipal transference–countertransference situation the countertransference problem is less related to "behaving oneself" than to allowing oneself to participate. Involvement in preoedipal erotic experience is not about genital sexual intercourse; it is far more diffuse and relates more to fantasies about feeding, bathing, and diapering and perverse variations of these wishes than to genital intercourse. What the patient longs for is contact with the early mother's voluptuous body (represented by the analyst's body) or with bodily products. Both participants may face the longing for, and terror of, being one in the same skin, but it is rarely accessible to conscious thought. Our experience is that the greatest threat to the therapeutic experience when the erotism is preoedipal, preverbal, and essentially pregenital is not to experience or recognize it.

The greatest danger to analyst and patient alike is they may fail to recognize early erotism. The analyst must be able to experience an array of primitive, sensual bodily states engendered by the patient without recoiling in anxiety. She must be able to tolerate the anxiety that primitive erotic feelings will flood and pull her away from a pre-ferred analytic composure and erode professional boundaries. Typ-ically the feared breaches are not sexual but, rather, are such lapses in maintaining the frame of a session as being overly solicitous or casual, "spilling over" the allotted time, or revealing personal infor-mation. Moreover, as the ego ideal for females (especially analysts), in contrast to that of males, is more identified with caretaking and nurturing than with seductiveness, female analysts tend to behave in a more matronly than vampish way. Positive images surround Florence Nightingale types, and there is general derogation of the sexually seductive woman; thus female analysts tend by nature to feel inhibited from seeing themselves or being seen by their patients as sexually seductive.

Male and female analysts' fears of regression and fusion may lead them to move into overanalysis of oedipal genital issues in the ser-vice of avoiding messy, boundaryless early preoedipal erotism. Fur-ther, conscious erotic awareness is often unrecognized precisely because it does not present as an organized genital sexual excitation, but rather tends to surface in sometimes diffuse, primitive bodily feelings that carry both positive and negative valence. Finally, such schizoid and sadomasochistic defenses against preoedipal annihila-tion anxiety and the MET as discussed in chapters 6 and 7 may result in psychic paralysis and deadlocks.

TREATMENT CONSIDERATIONS— TOO LITTLE OR TOO MUCH?

It can be seen that the maternal erotic countertransference (MEC) may at times approach the perverse in the various senses we have described. We have discussed instances in which MEC represented a perpetuation of symbiosis; an attempt by mother/analyst and baby/analysand to rid the room of father so that the mother–baby fusion could flourish; a grandiose magical fantasy of making a new baby/analysand; or a refusal to participate, with its attendant lack of interest, deadness, and lack of creativity.

Grandiose wishes for magical rebirth, compulsive seizure of control, and horror-inspired perverse voyeuristic stances all deny and block the flowering of the maternal erotic transference. Among the many ways the analyst's unconscious resistances may find their way into the treatment are the analyst's overactive and premature interpretations of erotic longings, interpretations that, paradoxically, inhibit their development in the patient. On the other hand, the too-easy acceptance of a patient's protestations of lack of erotic interest may signal the analyst's insecurities regarding sexual attractiveness, resistance to containing the transference, or both. Some countertransference defensive maneuvers relate to fears of and wishes for active sexual oedipal engagement with patients. These wishes elicit all the superego prohibitions so familiar from the oedipal period. A typical response to the heat of this conflict is to douse the fire and become deadened. The task at hand, then, is to tolerate the "heat" without fanning the flames and allow the erotic transference to unfold. When the countertransference reaches consciousness and can be well modulated, it can be very useful in the long and arduous analytic process.

We emphasize two keys to releasing an analyst from the deadlock of paralyzing countertransferences. First is the analyst's ability to view herself or himself as the erotically sensual preoedipal mother (as opposed to the genitally sexual oedipal mother or father). Second is the analyst's ability to experience, contain, and make accessible to analysis the patient's potential erotism in its earliest forms, which by necessity include its perverse aspects. It is necessary to exchange the magical wish for radical change for the commitment to assist in the patient's gradual growth and transformation. By creatively holding in mind a positive picture of the evolving patient, the analyst contains the hope for the treatment. The emergence, recognition, and working through of these countertransferences fosters the patient's narration of desire.

5 _____

The Birth of Desire

Transforming Birth Narratives
Within Maternal Erotic Transferences

Rosenfeld and Ochberg (1992) have emphasized the critical importance of what they call "life stories" and the central role such stories
can have in self-understanding and ongoing development:

> Personal stories are not merely a way of telling someone (or oneself)
> about one's life; they are the means by which identities may be fash-
> ioned. It is this formative—and sometimes deformative—power of
> life stories that makes them important. (p. 1)

Many people believe—and this is the single most important fact of
their existence—that they are somehow fundamentally defective, that
they were not "born right." It is very difficult for such a person to tell
the analyst much about the defect, beyond the fact of it. Over time,
the listening therapist pieces together a narrative of this defect. Balint
(1968), who developed the idea of the "basic fault," put it this way:

> The patient says he feels there is a fault within him, a fault that must
> be put right. And it is felt to be a fault, not a complex, not a conflict,
> not a situation. Second, there is the feeling that the cause of this fault
> is that someone has either failed the patient or defaulted on him; and
> third, a great anxiety invariably surrounds this area, usually expressed
> as a desperate demand that this time the analyst should not—in fact,
> must not—fail him. (p. 21)

THE NARRATIVE OF A FAULTY BIRTH

The "fault" the patient feels is experienced as present from birth,
long before words, and is organized, at least in part, at the level of

89

the body. The patient's theme, more or less formulated, is that she
has not actually, or entirely, or properly been born. A variation on the
theme of "stillbirth" is that she died, sometimes destroying her
mother in the process. Sometimes the person feels invisible. There is
a pervasive sense of waiting for real life to begin. This theme, which
devolves from the basic belief that one has been born dead, the null and
valueless produce of a ruined mother, may be seen in the recurrent
dream motif that one hauls around a lifeless second self.

Such a person comes to analysis in dire need of being seen, recognized, and thereby called back into life. The clinical picture includes anhedonic or masochistic psychic organization and may even
reveal, as in the case of Rosie described in this chapter, an encapsulated psychosis. To ask such a person what she desires is unproductive; she alternates between not knowing what to want (or even how
to want) and imagining she needs everything, including life itself. A
person in this plight does not desire one thing or another; instead,
she desperately seeks an experience of transformation. *The patient's
wish for a transformational experience, organized in relation to the
body of the analyst, is what impels maternal erotic transferences to
develop.*

Although such wishes and beliefs may be understood by the therapist as symbolic, to the patient they are concrete, real, and urgent.
The patient's life depends on it. We have found that the early maternal erotic transference, with its strong verification of the capacity for
desire, may reactivate the patient's "birthright" to feel alive.

SOME BIRTH STORIES: A MOTHER'S CURSE

Particularly significant is the theme of the action of birth in clinical
narratives of the story of the basic fault and the basic healing that
must take place. Birth is not a psychic reality for everyone for whom
it is physical fact. If, as Winnicott says, "there is no such thing as a
baby without the eyes and the ears of the mother glued to the
pram," it follows that for some neonates the unquestioned claim to
being may miscarry or abort. Such a baby is only marginally alive,
awaiting the humanization of the ego, the "going on being" that
comes from being held and handled, mirrored and enjoyed.

Winnicott's statement refers to a fundamentally inseparable configuration: a mother who recognizes, craves, and envelops the equally
and likewise enthralled infant. The good-enough environment is

defined by a wanted baby, a desirable baby, freed from the womb yet embraced within the human habitat.

But how does this happen? How does ego development proceed to the point where one reliably believes in one's own existence? And how does the parent and later the analyst facilitate this transformation? And when does it fail to occur?

In this section we examine some ways in which the first words said about a baby often hold a narrative key to the unfolding life story, which in turn continues to configure ongoing life events. Each of the following descriptions encapsulates a different woman's belief about her mother's first words to her:

"Seven pounds, wet and sticky, eyes shut, face screwed up, features barely formed, arms and legs flailing. And my mother said, 'How peculiar! She looks just like E.' and no one said otherwise."

"She's so red. Send her back to the Indians."

"When you were born, you ripped me from one side of my ass to the other."

"Even though I was a good Catholic I tried using a diaphragm, but along you came—God's punishment for not following the way."

The first quote is from Iris, who was to continue to feel doomed by her physical resemblance to a maiden aunt; with anatomy as her destiny, she could be intelligent but not married. This gifted woman, with advanced degrees and qualifications, could barely support herself when she started treatment and was in imminent danger of becoming homeless. As I (JKW) worked with her, we came to understand that poverty and failure linked her to her mother. She brought in this fictionalized account she had found, saying it described her deep belief about the circumstances of her birth:

I, of course, heard her comment. My arms and legs were flailing because I was searching frantically for the key to her navel so I could crawl back in, but it had already dissolved in a pool of blood and mucus. A nurse was clearing it away. I didn't have the vocal cords yet to scream, "Wait, I have to find the key!"

The second patient, a writer named Linda, born to a pretentious woman who felt she had married beneath her, became the vehicle for her mother's social climbing. While attempting to live like the consummate sophisticate, she spent every day longing for and fearing the return to the Indians whence she had been told she had emerged; perhaps they would welcome her. The third, a therapist, was the abused child of a borderline mother and a paranoid schizophrenic father. She went through life apologizing for the unremembered crimes insinuated in her mother's rageful narration of her birth. Christine, the baby who was God's punishment, suffered from chronic depression and unrelenting guilt for never achieving the perfection she demanded of herself. She became a nurse/midwife, hoping to help other babies be "born right."

The following case illustrations describe Iris in detail and then present a detailed analysis of another patient, Rosie.

Iris's Birth Story

Iris, who searched in vain for the key to crawl back into her mother's womb for a second chance, was addicted to men. She prayed to them for salvation, for the mothering she believed she never had. In what follows, she describes her state of narcolepsy as though she were a sleeping princess waiting for a kiss:

> I think I have been spending my life trying to be born. I don't feel I'm from Pluto any more, thanks to you. I don't feel like an intruder from another biosphere, thanks to you. But I'm still not at home in the world. I'm not here yet.
>
> I think I told you I have been diagnosed as having chronic fatigue syndrome. This is very strange because I sleep constantly and I keep dreaming all the time, these tiny dreams, millions of them. The feeling of sleep and dreaming reminds me of when I was in Turkey with N. and we tried some opium. I had two days of being in this state of falling into sleep and wakefulness, and all of it was dreamlike, and I was sometimes seeming to be dreaming even while awake. Then it was fun. I loved him. He was with me. He was having the same experience. But he was more in control and would go down and get us food, etc. Then we would dream and talk to each other about our dreams. Now I just dream alone and fight a heroic fight, almost an unwinnable battle, to get out of bed and dress and take the express bus to work so that I can be demeaned and underpaid for another week.
>
> And, meanwhile, these wonderful, revelatory dreams are waiting to come out. They're always just below the surface. Interesting. Some

people when stressed might get ulcers or back pain. I get this sort of terribly active non-stop narcolepsy. If someone saw me, they'd think I was lying there all weekend, half dead. But on the contrary, there are houses on fire, children trying to be born, men giving birth, blood spouting from a man's head when he takes off his hat.

This poignant and exceptionally clear description speaks to the ultimate futility of trying to find in a lover, or a drug, a substitute for the missed experience of mothering. No prince would be able to awaken this sleeping beauty; her mother's curse reached a full 50 years into her life. Freud noted that artists "possess in their art a master key to open with ease all female hearts, whereas we stand helpless at the strange designs of the lock and have first to torment ourselves to discover a suitable key to it" (cited in Gay, 1988, p. 318). For Iris, her art was never adequate to secure her place with the mother she pursued.

Rosie's Birth Story

Rosie, a lovely young artist, was the last of "too many children" born to religious parents. Her father, a biologist, was described as sadistic, her mother as childlike and dependent. In the course of the treatment, however, these descriptions were to be reversed. When I (JKW) first met Rosie in my waiting room, she was seated on the lap of her boyfriend, and she spent many of the initial couple-counseling sessions tightly wound around his body. The couple's presenting complaint was that although they loved each other they were not sexual. Rosie was, however, sexual with other men, and that confession precipitated the crisis that resulted in counseling. After the couple separated, Rosie decided to continue in individual psychotherapy, although it was frequently interrupted by her art exhibitions. When she was in town, we generally met three times a week. Long separations were sometimes bridged by telephone consultations.

Rosie looked like a frightened, big-eyed child in the body of a woman. She quickly formed a very intense link to me, which she likened to her obsessive love for her mother. Early in her life, she had been "wild, an animal," inarticulate and perpetually frightened in her tribe of older siblings. Animals were her principal source of company and comfort into adult life. She read and wrote poetry, some of which had been published. She had obtained an advanced degree in art.

Sometimes she was silent and very hard to contact. Sometimes it was as if her thoughts flew everywhere in the room, a piece at a time. I had the feeling I was supposed to gather them up and organize them. Sometimes she felt her words to be sharp objects inside her head; sometimes she saw them as she spoke them. She seemed sometimes to be hallucinating. Although she could generally be called back into the room, she could not always say where she had been. It was a source of wonder and delight to her that I noticed her "absences." This gave her the first hope she experienced in our relationship.

Life and Death with Rosie

Rosie generally felt herself to be oscillating between life and death, dream and reality, sleep and wakefulness. She expressed the fear that one day she would "wake up dead." For some people, the only way to maintain a cohesive self-experience is the renunciation of desire. For Rosie, ceaseless thought, unending activity, constant, preferably sexual companionship, and nonstop questioning was the only way to feel even intermittently alive. It was her plan to make herself feel real and alive by finding out everything about me that could be learned through the senses. She even noticed the minute shifts in my eye muscles that accompany refocusing and took them as a sign of interest or lack of interest in what she was saying. She also thought that it was necessary to keep me constantly in her mind in order to ensure my continuing existence. She "ate me up" with her eyes and then apologized for it.

As our relationship developed, Rosie revealed a ravenous desire to know about every aspect of my being. Nothing was too mundane for her to want to know. She asked about the color of my floors at home, the floor plan of my house, what I had just been doing when she called, what kind of bras I favored. She asked me for tampons, needle and thread, and Band-Aids. She inquired about my sex life, what I preferred, what I had done the night before and with whom. Did I have a boyfriend as well as a husband? Once, she called me on a Sunday and heard in the background the sound of a football game on TV; she was thrilled because her visiting father was also listening to that game.

Having previously experienced the deeply intrusive quality of some maternal erotic transferences, I was partially prepared to deal with these themes, although Rosie's intensity and persistence added a new dimension. In general, for a long period in the treatment, I was unable to feel truly comfortable with answering, reframing, interpreting her questions or even with not answering them. As Rosie became increasingly aware of my discomfort and began to question me about those feelings, I experienced an accelerating self-consciousness. Sometimes I retreated into a watchful distance; sometimes I offered a piece of information; sometimes I was impatient and annoyed. What seemed ultimately productive in the treatment was our agreement that her questions, while experienced by her as a way of making contact, were sometimes experienced by me, and by others in her life, as intrusive. Craving to be "ravished" in just such a way, she found this very difficult to comprehend.

I struggled to understand the intensity of my reaction, both within our developing constructions of maternal erotic countertransference and within the broader tenets of psychoanalytic theory. I identified the relevant theoretical issue: to what extent was my departure from the analytic blank screen justified by the patient's pathology and unique personality configuration? I conceptualized a conventional superego conflict and weighed the cost of causing pain to the patient against the cost of straying from "standard technique." This concept proved insufficient to illuminate my discomfort. Ultimately my internal plight was most fruitfully explained by an unconscious clash between gratifying exhibitionistic/narcissistic wishes to tell this eager child all she wished to know, and my fears of the embarrassing self-disclosure that honest responses to some of her questions would entail. Rosie wanted to know everything about me, even things I did not want anyone to know about me—some things I did not particularly want to know about myself. Bringing this realization to awareness and working with the content did much to resolve this extremely disquieting aspect of the countertransference. (Chapter 4 presents more detail and suggestions for working with such anxiety-producing and problematic maternal erotic countertransferences.) I also was able to see that Rosie demanded for herself and from me a relationship shared with no one else, not even my husband or child.

Working through to this point also yielded a new understanding of Rosie. In essence, I realized she was trying to psychoanalyze herself by proxy, through analyzing me. It was as if Rosie believed that since she was dead and I was alive she might discover the key to living by knowing everything inside me. But this was not her only plan. Rosie used anything she could think of in her rapacious wish to engage her real life.

She brought not only dreams to her sessions, but also drawings and sculpture. At one point, she brought in materials to make a doll: pieces of fabric her mother had worn and small objects she associated with me. She wanted me to draw a face on the doll. She brought in a clay-modeled child's hand and arm, lifelike even to the fingernails. It was so real looking it might have been removed from a sleeping child. Much later it emerged that she had a recurrent fantasy of a child whose arm had been amputated. Her participation in all these events was total, and she generally left them with the feeling that something real had been accomplished. For a long time, these sessions felt more like play therapy with a terrified child than anything else, and interpretation was secondary to the urgent need to not frighten her away.

Early in the treatment, Rosie had been intermittently anorexic, self-mutilating, and psychotically preoccupied with her body functions. These preoccupation's we traced to her early experiences of being hospitalized and operated on for a congenital digestive deformity. She actually believed she had died then, and again at age 12, when her best friend suddenly "dropped" her. She told me that the day she found out about the rejection, a part of her stomach suddenly "dropped out," pushing itself out against her abdominal skin in the shower. Terrified, she was able to "push it back in." She had never told anyone about it before. In this particular session, she drew a picture of a bleeding child. I put tape on the cut, and she was very satisfied that she had been heard.

She developed an intense fear of contracting AIDS. This particular preoccupation was a new edition of her childhood belief that she had cancer, a belief that at times amounted to a somatic delusion, accompanied by extreme states of anxiety. Rosie was afraid of magical means of transmission. She was convinced she was dying of AIDS because she had spoken to her HIV positive friend on the telephone. The slightest symptom became proof of the delusion. If she chanced to see the letters AIDS written in the newspaper, she would "have it" for the next few days, until she could somehow move past it. She phobically avoided routine medical care for fear a blood test would be ordered and this would be a death sentence. She watched my face anxiously for signs that I believed in her illnesses. If she could convince herself that I was calm her terror was sometimes relieved. She often described the experience of calming herself in the light of our mutual gaze.

The Course of Development: Skin Themes

French analyst Didier Anzieu (1989) describes in detail the pre-oral needs and capacities of the human infant, particularly the importance of the skin, which denotes the boundary between the psychic outside and inside and is also a symbol of containment for the good sensual experiences the baby begins to collect as memory. Winnicott (1962) also stressed that body ego, on which ego is built, is in part defined by the skin. Skin and hair in all manifestations were prominent themes in Rosie's repertoire. She associated unpleasant sensations on the back of her neck as presaging a threatening take-over of her thoughts and insides, especially by her mother. Disgusted by pieces of hair that fell from her scalp, she stored several of them in a large vase in my office. Over time, they became less disgusting to her. She intermittently scratched her skin, sometimes in a desperate effort to feel, sometimes with the idea in mind that she needed to make an escape hatch for unbearable emotions. Once she scratched my initials into her arm, branding herself as belonging to me. Several years into the treatment, after I had to interrupt her sessions to have surgery, she begged me to show her the scar or, failing that, to describe it and its location on my body and draw it for her. She wanted to know of other scars, and she wanted me to see her scars. Both of us having scars made us "sisters in the skin."

She drew pictures of her dreams for us to study and sometimes invited my participation. We used three different surfaces for this purpose: white paper, a chalkboard, and a magic-marker surface according to the degree of permanence she wished for the picture and the amount of color it required. All these surfaces were approximations of a skin she yearned to create for herself: the more she was able to develop these concrete yet symbolic themes, the more she was able to feel herself cohesive and alive. Rosie described her overwhelming anxiety this way: "Your skin crawls and you crawl after it. Then it crawls the other way and so do you." Rosie was always in search of her skin.

She was also preoccupied with drawing maps. She drew and redrew the floor plan of her parental house, delineating the placement of everyone's room. Many dreams rearranged this placement, putting her closer to her parents than she ever was able to be.

Rosie did not experience her skin as a reliable container for her self. Over time, I understood that in her relentless focus on me she was actively constructing a shared skin for us. This was why it was vital that my gaze never waver; I must never "drop her" from my mind. In her continuous and anxious map-making, she was trying to locate separate entities within our shared skin. As she grew more secure in her immersion within my constructed womb, she became far less anxious about physical illness.

Fire and Water: Trials and Baptisms

In Rosie's discourse, fire and water were the giver and taker of life, the symbols of the parental matrix. Rosie's mother had reportedly been lax in protecting her from the sun, and Rosie recalled painful summer sunburns, with dead skin that her mother delighted in peeling from her shoulders. Rosie had once held a beloved cat over the barbecue, singeing it. Because she was unable to contact any feeling about the event, she was unsure why she had done it. The memory was split off from affect, stored separately as a "dead event." It, like so much of her life, had an aura of unreality. This sort of splitting resulted in a prominent discontinuity of self-experience. One of Rosie's recurrent fantasies involved her being humiliated in a shower and peed on.

There was, throughout the treatment, some question in my mind of possible sexual impropriety with a male family member. Rosie would address this possibility in only a very limited way. She accepted it theoretically as the explanation that made the most sense of what she remembered and knew. She felt that this explanation pulled together otherwise disconnected and senseless pieces of dreams, fantasies, and memory fragments, but that it was impossible because she *did not remember it.* Rosie could not accept that something so important could be forgotten. This disparity troubled her a great deal until she hit upon the solution that she had been molested in a former life, the dreams and memory fragments being remnants and evidence of a prior life.

Although I did not overtly challenge this new "religious" solution to her anxiety, I thought it imperative to help her to acknowledge and understand her split-off sadistic impulses. This interpretive line provoked a major "trial by fire" for the relationship. Rosie felt as though I were shoving these evil intentions into her, trying to kill her, making her die. For a long time she could scarcely tolerate my presence, but the long years of working together and the trust we had developed eventually prevailed. In the end, my quiet insistence that hate is part of being human seemed to allow her greater leeway in understanding her own motivations and enabling to deal with her frightening sadistic and masochistic fantasies.

Dreams: Transformations of Stillbirth

Like Iris, Rosie felt her dreams were meaningful and important; often they were more "real" to her than waking life. Rosie had come to me to be transformed and that goal was primary for her. She also believed that in the course of her being transformed I would likely be destroyed. She, like Margot in chapter 3 and Gillian in chapter 4, held the notion that either the mother or the baby must die in order for birth to be accomplished. Rosie told me repeatedly about dead babies, babies needing to be rescued, and about the vehicles of baptism, "by fire or by water."

In the majority of her dreams someone was transformed into something or someone else. In many dreams, helping someone turned out to be dangerous for the helper. For example: "There was an orphan with old baggy clothes. She wanted food. I brought her into my car, and she turned into a mean, awful old man." In another dream: "Someone was trying to kill you. You were going to make a speech. People were chasing us. You and I became like the same person. There were men with guns and they wanted to kill you for helping me."

The person to be helped often fared no better, and assistance often proved unsuccessful. This theme was illustrated by a series of dreams that typified the failure of early attachments. In those dreams a person in a precarious situation tried to hold on to something, only to be disappointed and "dropped." For example, in a dream when she reached out desperately to grab on to something to keep from falling from a great height, her hand grasped a cloud. In another dream, someone tried to rescue a baby, who slipped through her fingers and drowned. In the saddest dream of this series, described in more detail below, even a successful rescue effort left everyone dead.

The ocean is roped off for people to swim. Babies are playing. You and I are at the edge, holding on to the rope. The ocean tide comes in. Parents are trying to save their babies. Its dark. You and I decide to go in. I say we have to hold hands. We are looking for babies. I think all the babies are saved. We see zombielike parents, moving in the water, holding dead babies.

The next series of dreams illustrates Rosie's rapidly shifting object relations as they were elicited in the transference. As she moved from an idealizing transference into a terrifying, perverse erotic transference, she saw me as the mother who "killed me in order to save my life." In her dreams I changed rapidly from beloved rescuer to a persecuting all-powerful monster. The following dream included a husband for me, an unusual event in her dreaming, and therefore anticipated more oedipal transference material.

> I came to see you. Your husband came to get us. I slid into the waiting room. You had all these personal books, things you stole. You lost your mind, started to call me by the wrong name. You had my whole life in your hands. "You're a little ogre," you said. "We're gonna have sessions in the basement." We went through five layers of curtains, and your clothes came off. You had a grotesque body with three breasts, and you were pregnant with all these heads and all these naked bodies. It had to do with AIDS research. Thirty of them, all probes with cancers all over them. I was freaked. You said "I'm gestating." Out of your belly was a face, a jewel, me, but dead.

It took many weeks to translate the symbols in the dream. This dream encompassed Rosie's psychotic narrative of birth as it was expressed in the maternal erotic transference. She saw me as the totally powerful mother who held all the things which had been lost or stolen from her. I held her life in my hands and could not remember her name; she was my little ogre. After going through many levels of skin, symbolized by the curtains that came off, my grotesque maternal body was at last revealed. I was seen to gestate all over my skin. All the naked bodies attached to me were connected with AIDS, the major somatic delusion she manifested in treatment. Rosie herself was the face on my belly, my jewel, born dead.

Rosie's treatment continued for many years after this very critical dream. During that time, Rosie made significant improvements in virtually all aspects of her life. Her work continued to bring her success. She was able to live with a man she loved in a fairly stable relationship. She formed and maintained friendships and felt that her life, which had always been episodic, was now a continuous enterprise. She began thinking about becoming pregnant herself. At the same time, the intensity of her relationship with me gradually diminished, and she was progressively able to tolerate separations. At one point, she thought of asking something about me but decided that she would prefer not to know. She could tolerate the idea that people were entitled to some mystery after all.

The New Narrative of Birth

Of those aspects of the therapeutic encounter that seemed to be most beneficial to Rosie, two nonverbal features emerge as critical: gaze and the skin. Within the analytic frame, Rosie and I were continuously fascinated with each other, and this mutual absorption was to contribute in no small part to the development of her ego. Although there are obvious theoretical difficulties in moving from the literature on infant development to the clinical situation, perhaps Boothby's (1991) description will convey the sense we had of each other and the effect this fascination seemed to have.

> We are to think here of the infant whose wide-eyed gaze, fixed on the face of its mother, seems to deliver it momentarily, as if by magic, from the chaos of movements that characterize most of its waking life. Fascination is absolutely essential to the phenomenon of the constitution of the ego. The uncoordinated incoherent diversity of the [infant's] primitive fragmentation gains its unity in so far as it is fascinated. (p. 31)

A fascinated baby, then, is a baby on the pathway toward ego development, a baby using something in the mother's gaze to transform uncoordinated longings and sensations into desire. This is the "location of cultural experience" (Winnicott, 1967). It is within this gaze that the baby begins to construct itself and create its selfhood. In the course of normal development, when all goes well, a mother actually and literally transforms the infant's world.

Ordinary interpretive analytic work, which makes the unconscious accessible to consciousness, was a secondary aspect of what helped Rosie. It was much more important to help her organize a meaning system linked to a belief in her own existence. The major interpretive work that I believe was essential for her led to her recognition of and tolerance for her own oral-sadistic impulses. The other substantial interpretive work I did was with myself, within the countertransference, enabling me to deal with her desperate need to be inside of me so that rebirth could take place.

When her treatment had progressed to the point where we were considering termination, she wrote this poem while waiting for me to arrive at my office. It denoted her exquisite attunement to my presence and affirmed our separate existence.

> I hear the obscure one coming
> the sweet of her keys
> the chaos her body causes
> when the air moves before
> around and then after her.
> Her little feet scratching the
> porcelain floor.
> They echo.
> What a jambled delightful
> human dervishing mess,

MALE STORIES OF BIRTH

Our preliminary investigation suggests that the format of birth stories is gender related, which underlies their significance in gender formation and solidification. While writing this chapter, we realized that although we had routinely collected many female birth stories typified in the quotations at the beginning of this chapter, birth stories from our male patients were rare. Trying to account for this, we considered the degree of regression necessary to entertain in fantasy the period of total encapsulation within the body of the mother. Perhaps the notion of having been "of woman born" poses a threat to masculine identity. Keller (1985) offers a dynamic, feminist explanation for this observation. She argues that denying the fact of birth from a woman's body serves important narcissistic needs for males in our culture. She describes a culturally endorsed male appropriation of the act of birth, following a paternal developmental line and uninterrupted by maternal influence.

> In identifying himself with the race of fathers who can give birth, the young boy can simultaneously assert his independence and safeguard the earlier and conflicting wish for identification with the mother; in presuming to father himself, he satisfies his wish for omnipotent self-sufficiency. (p.41)

This explanation extends what we describe as "erotic terror" (see chapter 7), which relates to the male panic at, and defenses against, the fantasy of engulfment into the overwhelmingly sensual body of the early mother. We postulate that men experience this engulfment in the body of a female as a threat to an unstable sense of masculinity and therefore to existence. Mother, by her very material presence in the world, is a threat to male *qua* male existence. We were able to collect some narratives that we considered to be birth-story equivalents. Here we present two brief examples of frightening screen memories related by male patients who had no information at all about their own birth stories. Both memories concern the abject helplessness of infant animals before a powerful, marauding male. In an early world from which the protecting mother has been erased, all that is left is the infant, ripe for killing by the plundering male animals he wishes and fears to be.

A 35-year-old physician named Damon was struggling to understand his intense reaction formation against aggression, prominent in his devout vegetarianism and animal-rights activism. Following a dream in which the innocent-looking vegetables he was eating turned out to be seafood, he retrieved the following memory. He recalled that at the age of six or seven he had found a nest of baby rabbits, considered enemies on his family farm. He very painfully revealed that in a "murderous moment," which was to haunt him the next 30 years of his life, he had "stomped the life out of them."

The second patient, Caleb, to whom we shall return in later chapters, recalled an incident, a kind of anal birth, screen memory/ nightmare, from his early childhood in which he found a batch of decapitated kittens in an "icky hole" under the house (described in more detail in chapter 8). The kitten's birth in a dark, disgusting place from the body of the mother who offered no protection served as his own birth metaphor.

For different psychodynamic causes, neither man was able to conceptualize a "good birth" from the body of his mother. Damon, a heterosexual man without overt disturbance in gender, was ruled by the depressive fear of spoiling or killing his mother with his rage and envy. Caleb, a homosexual man, was more in the grip of early paranoia than of depression, and was terribly frightened of "phallic women." For both men, memories of helpless animals being killed by powerful males are screen memories for the encoding of the self seen simultaneously as helpless and omnipotent. The inability to identify with the encompassing and potent womb of his mother leaves a male child traumatically isolated, helpless, not entirely born, or briefly born and then "killed" by envious males intent upon destroying "womblings."

Desire, which refers to the representation of wishes within the human psyche, is not adequately encompassed by the concepts of instinct and drive, which denote the impelled and mindless enactment of inevitable biological forces. By contrast, desire specifies the quintessential human manifestation of these forces, enriched and contextualized with meaning. Appetite, yearnings, craving, and longings are better words to describe desire because they evoke the narrative instances of innate human intentions.

The capacity for desire, as we defined it in the Introduction, is a developmental achievement ranging beyond mere instinctual behavior. Desiring includes at least a rudimentary presence of self and other, which manifests clinically in believing one has been well and truly born. For many patients, this seems to require a sense of the goodness of the mother's womb and her mind, her "internal spaces." A mother who is perceived as damaged or absent cannot transform the basic fault and does not provide a safe environment in which to meet and know the primitive father, a discussion pursued in chapter 9.

III
Perversions: Derangements of Desire

6

Perverse Narratives

The Threat of New Narratives of Desire

Patients who are most terrified of experiencing primitive body sensations and longings associate them to a loss of control, loss of gender identity, and fear of annihilation of the separate self. Although unconsciously longing for the passionate intensity of a blissful fusion with the body of the analyst, they experience near panic at the prospect of losing body boundaries. They may also dread that close body contact will unleash rage that will destroy the self, the other, and the very world. Accordingly, defenses erected against the impending disaster of erotic desire are typically extremely complicated. We consider these defenses perverse because they are connected to the distortion of desire, they limit development, and they may not be altered in any way.

For such patients, creating a "narrative flow," or "word linking," signifies a degree of intimacy that is initially intolerable. Hence, they feel they must not engage in the "mutual story making" that analysis offers. Before illustrating these perverse narratives with clinical examples, we will discuss one of its underlying features, the "deadlock," which is key to this chapter and to chapters 7 and 8.

THEORETICAL AND DEVELOPMENTAL CONSIDERATIONS

The Dynamics of Deadlock

In "Mourning and Melancholia," Freud (1917) described a situation in which a disappointing object is clung to and no new object relationship can be established. Fairbairn (1943) emphasized the child's attempts to protect what is gratifying and control what is not gratifying in the relationship with the parent by establishing compensatory internal object relations:

> It is above all the need of the child for his parents, however bad they may appear to him, that compels him to internalize bad objects; and it is because this need remains attached to them in the unconscious that he cannot bring himself to part with them. (p. 332)

Objects, the internalized correlates of the actual parent, must be constructed in ways that make it possible for the dependent child to feel some measure of attachment to those people on whom he depends. To coordinate this activity, a child frequently creates a series of fantasies. These fantasies, aimed at making life endurable, reach consciousness through a kind of "normalizing narrative" (Welles, 1993) function. For example, a terribly withdrawn or absent parent may be thought of as quietly following every move the child makes, only waiting for the right time to appear. Or an abusive parent may be seen as acting in the child's best interest, to take the "badness" out of the child. Sometimes these narratives are of the child's design; sometimes they may be contributed by a parent or a sibling. What they have in common is that the parental object is a "good" object, seeking, through punishment and pain, to perfect the child.

It is a dreary and oft-repeated psychoanalytic observation that some people cling to impossible relationships with greater tenacity than to good ones. If they manage to extricate themselves from the abusive interactions they describe, they soon reconstitute them with other partners. Psychoanalysts have long understood these relationships as yielding a perverse unconscious satisfaction. Their underlying construction features the self and object in a deadly suffocating embrace. "Deadlock," a term coined by Welles (1989), describes a paralyzing unconscious object situation.

Such interpersonal relationships derive from and represent consuming, antitransformational, unconscious object relationships. In such relationships, fantasy is used to compensate for the lack of important self- and object functions; that is, managing rage and grandiosity, dealing with the fear of death, and, above all, compensating for the inability to be alone. Sadly, a person enmeshed in a deadlocked internal object relation may actually believe he or she is seeking a healing transformation obtainable no other way. The problem in these scenarios, however, is that they are antitransformational, perverse, rather than health giving. They are perverse because the object relational fantasies involve erotic tortures. They are intransigent, stalemated, and lacking in the vitality that characterizes genuine, mutual, loving relations. In this sense they are deadlocked and refractory to genuine therapeutic engagement.

The intensity and primitive vitality of the maternal erotic transference threaten to unlock such a deadlock because the transference represents the patient's opening up to involvement with someone other than the deadlocked other. In the generally unconscious fantasy of the patient, death is the only possible outcome of differentiation from the original object. The opening of the self to a relationship with a transformational other signals release from the deadlock and the opportunity to recompose the original perverse narrative. Although it is not immediately visible in the clinical encounter, we have frequently encountered a fantasy of continuing primitive omnipotence that proves extremely resistant to analytic intervention. The highest internal priority for a person in a deadlock is a stasis, or "dead calm," where needs may proliferate but conscious desire does not exist. Nothing is added, particularly pleasure, or removed, particularly pain. In the darkest secret, the object and the self are endlessly torturing each other; perhaps a psychic equivalent for the religious concept of purgatory.

As they are described in patients' narratives and eventually relived in the clinical encounter, these deadlocked relationships range from a static lack of active complaint, to overt fighting, to repeated superficial interaction, which may have a manic quality; the external form of the relationship may vary, but what is essential is *that nothing may change inside.* Consequently, the patients remain unable to develop mature relationships, even while involved in serial "affairs." Instead, the participants are tied together within the object relations drama in a form of combat that is never entirely acknowledged. There is a kind of eternal, slow-motion wrestling match in which the participants forever struggle for position; and without therapeutic intervention, no conclusion is ever achieved.

The analytic situation reveals that such individuals' powerful enmeshment with these unconscious internal objects leaves them functionally removed from current emotional life. If they come to analysis, as they often do because their suffering is considerable, they must insure that minimal change can result. In other words, they come into treatment with a perverse unconscious narrative firmly in place; the type has been set and sent to the printer.

Some patients, sensing that a new and vital relationship with the analyst will result in a form of psychic suicide, matricide, or homicide, oppose the relationship adamantly. In the first long rounds, they maintain an atmosphere of deadness and deanimation that precludes the emergence of early maternal erotic transference. The wall is maintained through a characteristic set of transference and character resistances, including selective inattention to the analyst's interventions, superficial compliance, the repetition of stale responses, and stereotypical behaviors, all of which ensure that nothing surprising can emerge.

In the face of this deadness, the analyst feels paralyzed, crucified, even dead, trapped within countertransference images of jail houses, graveyards, or purgatory. Mysteriously deprived of the ability to engender creative thought, we may struggle for long periods to remain involved. Wrestling to stay alive in this desert often engenders such countertransference enactments as grandiose fantasies of magically rebirthing (described in chapter 4), aimed at "waking up" the patient.

One of the major obstacles to the resolution of clinical deadlock is the patient's fear of permanent disconnection from the object world and the loss of self that would follow from the abandonment of the archaic object. This condition is tantamount to the schizoid organization of internal object relations. The resolution of these deadlocked, schizoid states requires first the elaboration in the transference of the patient's paralyzing fantasies of abandonment and psychic annihilation. The analyst concurrently develops and resolves similar issues in the countertransference. Then the fear of committing psychic matricide or homicide can be understood as a motivation for holding the analyst, as a partner in crime, in subjugation. Finally, a treaty for release is negotiated. Guilt regarding the "death" of the deadlocked other and the creation of new internal objects often makes its appearance in dreams.

In what follows, we discuss perverse narratives of desire (Wrye and Welles, in press) marked by such a deadlocked internal object world and describe its marked difference from transforming and transitional objects. For Leonard, the first of two cases we present, the perverse narrative of his relationship with his internal mother was marked by hatred and denigration of the disappointing parent. For Suta, discussed later in this chapter, the relationship was reversed, and the disappointing other was enshrined in an idealization that could not be questioned. Both narratives emphasize the importance of a careful explication of the self and object position, particularly as this manifests in the matrix of the transference and countertransference.

THE CASE OF LEONARD

Leonard, a "power" in the entertainment industry, remained entrenched in a deadlock, deanimating his analyst (HKW) by repeatedly referring to me as "the girl shrink." He maintained a similarly frustrating emotional distance from his fourth wife, who had threatened to leave him if he did not change. Leonard entered an analytic treatment, which lasted about five years, in order to placate his wife after he had punched her during an argument and had begun to fear losing her. His treatment, which was only partially successful, was incomplete because Leonard moved to another state and, more significantly, because of the deep entrenchment of his defenses against the genuine intimacy that a meaningful therapeutic encounter could foster.

From the outset, Leonard set about to "go through the motions" of therapy but let nothing genuinely touch him. He assumed that his wife would be too gullible to recognize the plan. He took pains to have his wife write the check each month to pay for his treatment; thus she would have proof that he was in therapy and be mollified. He believed that his "shrink" was on his "payroll" and, wanting to keep it that way indefinitely, would be satisfied simply to fill the time and be paid; there would be no need for him to change. He assumed that I, like the prostitutes whom he used routinely and paid well, would not protest.

For a remarkably long time, Leonard resisted the notion of any narrative meaning. He kept any meaningful information about his personal life and his childhood out of the treatment. He preferred instead to recount in boring detail the "inane" and "stupid" behaviors of the clients he felt were daily opposing him, or the outrageous behaviors of this or that driver on the road on the way to his session, or his profound satisfaction in maintaining exactly the same rare and expensive tobacco mixture for 30 years of his adult life. He ordered this unique blend in exactly the same amount year in and year out. He referred to his business dealings surreptitiously, as if they were covert operations: he never named names, locations, or details.

He deliberately omitted reference to anything pending so that I would not develop a scheme to undermine or get the jump on any of his business deals. He felt he was "a piece of work" who had everybody's number. He ruefully revealed, however, that just about everyone around him saw him as "a bastard." He had no friends, just those of us who were "on his payroll" and his wife, who could not afford to leave him.

I experienced the clinical encounter with Leonard as one of mutual deadness. For a very long time, it was difficult even to gain access to his deadlocked internal object world. He maintained that he had no internal world, no dreams, no fantasies. Whatever he wanted, he ordered up on his car phone and he had it: he had no need to fantasize. He liked to obtain sex as one ordered a video—rent it, use it, send it back, and never see it again. He denied memories of childhood: he had "locked that door behind me years ago, when I realized there was nothing there for me." Although I was unable to make contact with anything in Leonard's internal world that could have been described as a struggle, I surmised that it must have been a passionate struggle that had deanimated him so.

"Bagging Ladies/Tossing Out Babies"

Over time, he unwittingly revealed his desperate dependency on maternal replenishment by describing a series of daily sexual encounters with nameless women with "huge boobs." Some of these encounters had taken place prior to treatment and resulted in illegitimate pregnancies, abortions, and disowned births. There were, in the course of our work together, several more liaisons. Leonard was utterly contemptuous of these women and "their" illegitimate children, in contrast to the financial indulgence and idealization he heaped on his only legitimate child, whom he saw as the star in his crown.

In his rageful dependency on deanimated women in his external world, Leonard recreated his internal object relations with his mother. His protracted and frequently deadlocked treatment required considerable restraint on my part. My interpretations of the castaway infants as aspects of himself that he felt no one wanted met only mild interest. Most often, Leonard played a time-passing "game" in which he carefully scanned my demeanor and tone for any evidence that he had "gotten to" me. Beneath that, he searched for any evidence that I held him in the contempt that he believed his overwrought mother had felt for him. If I ever used more than two adjectives describing him in an interpretation, he seized upon them as evidence that I was "worked up" and losing control of myself. When I posited that perhaps this was what he wished for, some evidence that I felt passionately about him, he snorted that I wasn't his type.

Over several years of treatment, although he was appreciative of my analytic constancy and even allowed that I might be "smart" and an exception to the "broad mold," he generally maintained a deadlocked distance and insisted on making no substantive changes in his essentially perverse stance. His need for perverse distancing minimized my meaning to him. My frustrated efforts to understand him did elicit, in various ways, my own maternal erotic countertransferences. At times, I fantasized magically transforming him, giving birth to him as a sweet, innocent baby who could be cherished and mirrored and who, in my care, would open up and discover a miraculously rich inner world like a rosebud bursting into bloom. I was not always so generous. For example, when he intoned my name contemptuously and dismissively, calling me "Mrs. Wrye" instead of "Dr. Wrye" (both divesting me of my training and making clear that some other man owned me and used me), I felt like mentally summoning up all manner of male authorities on the subject of perversion and schizoid phenomena. Sometimes I sought the solace of female collegial consultation or girded myself with recollections of male supervisors who had praised my work.

Leonard resisted both exploring his own early stories of childhood experience and weaving any kind of a narrative of our work together. For a very long time, he remembered nothing that had transpired in the past or earlier sessions except those occasions when he felt he had "gotten to me." Those he seemed pleased never to forget. As he became unwittingly more involved in our work, I suggested that it might help us to move past his need to maintain such a tough exterior if he were to come in more frequently and if he were to use the couch. His use of the couch was brief, only a couple of months, but very illuminating. He became so panicked that I would castrate him while he lay on his back that he sat up. Much later we uncovered his terror about his vulnerability to early maternal erotic longings.

In retrospect I see that my own misguided impulse to imagine that such a person would be amenable to analysis was a countertransference enactment. Frustrated by his unremitting insistence on gaining the upper hand, I wanted to render him susceptible to a potent combination of my magical analytic phallus and my magical analytic breasts, filling him with infusions of mellowing milk as if he were the "sweet baby" to whom I had given life.

The Dried Turd

Through introjective identification and retrieved memories, pieces of Leonard's early encounters with his mother came into the treatment. His early infancy appeared to have been unremarkable. His mother seemed to have been warmly involved in his care. When he was about 20 months old, however, his baby sister was born, and he was banished from the throne. Leonard felt lost between his older sister, who was a star student and a prime athlete, and his baby sister, on whom his mother doted until the child's early accidental death. That sister's birth having occurred at the time approaching his own toilet training, we posited from later memories that a dogged struggle had begun between his mother and him. He withheld his bowel movements to wrest her attention away from his baby sister or his older sibling's academic and athletic achievements. For this, Leonard's mother rewarded him with physical punishment. He became encopretic, and she raged. Once, when he was in first grade, she found a dried bowel movement in his underpants under his bed. She wrapped it in aluminum foil and brought it to his school.

This drama became paradigmatic of his relations with all women. It appeared in the transference in his indefatigable pleasure in rubbing my nose in any "errors" I made. He held on to this narrative construction and remained faithful to his interminably deadlocked struggle with his mother. "Women use you and leave you. Then they demean, humiliate, and punish you." He deemed it wiser to wrest this scenario from his mother and to turn it around on women for the rest of his life. He had "slipped" once when a popular girl in high school captured his heart and then dropped him. He vowed never to "fall in love because then you're not in control."

Leonard's ambivalent relations with babies had tragic consequences. He demonstrated his omnipotence as well as his murderous rage toward his own "unwanted" baby sister by making many unwanted babies. He would use no birth control protection in his numerous illicit affairs, making many babies, demonstrating his prowess; these babies were discarded through abortions or, if the mother insisted on giving birth, through dereliction of support. By contrast, with his one legitimate child he recreated the mythic rapture of the months between himself and his mother, before his sister's birth. Through repetitive births and deaths, Leonard assured this child, and himself, the permanent position of being the "one and only."

In his narrative, there was no adequate father to help him attain manhood, and, having designated me the "girl shrink," he could not find that strength in me. He became a caricature father, making innumerable "dead babies." Leonard's story is one of splitting and projective identification, which he used perversely to bind himself to two particular women. He saw his mistress as his demeaned, encopretic outcast self; he abused and humiliated her. Internally he remained doggedly loyal to her, even though the relationship was patently destructive to both of them. He saw his wife as the ideal-ized, good-angel mother whom he had longed for but who had betrayed him. He had loved watching his wife nurse their baby, and he kept her securely tied to him by economic dependency and by "spoiling" her with gifts.

Over time, he was occasionally able to let down his guard with me. Cautiously, he revealed an emerging hint of an erotic transfer-ence. What he had meant, for instance, when he said I was "not his type" was that he feared he was "not my type." He timidly acknowl-edged his fear that I, like the "first class" popular girl in his school, would prefer someone more cultured, one who was not always en-gaged in messes. In his contentious business dealings, he typically emphasized and evoked "shittiness" in his business opponents. He then felt persecuted by them and had to counterattack. In this way he replayed his internal narrative of childhood endlessly in his adult dealings. He slowly began to recognize what a dead-end defensive drama he had been repeating for decades.

A Countertransference Lullaby

As time went by, I found myself, in the countertransference, wanting to enliven his deadened, puppetlike relationships and bring vitality into our relationship. I fantasied magically weaving for him the sto-ries of our clinical encounters; I imagined myself singing them to him in lullaby form. I imagined I would sing to him about his loss of his mother when he was so small and needy, of his misguided efforts to regain her attention, and about his terror to relinquish the per-verse songs that had guided his behavior throughout childhood and into the present.

My fantasy of singing to him recreated that aspect of primary maternal preoccupation in which a mother "knows' what her baby needs without thinking about it. Knowing that countertransference may be informative of aspects of the patient's experience, I wondered with my colleague (JKW) what my lullaby fantasy meant. We concluded that it related to my sense that he surrounded himself so much with perverse erotic sexuality that for him body contact was too contaminated at this point to be a mode of healing. Instead, the healing contact he needed would better come through music and song. My countertransference reverie resonated with Anzieu's (1989) notion that a mother's encompassing "sound envelope" precedes visual mirroring and the "skin envelope" in the creation of the loving holding environment: "Hearing the other when the Self is enveloped in harmony (what term but a musical one would do here?), and when in response the child stimulates itself by echoing these sounds, introduces the child to the world of illusion" (p. 168).

Slowly, over time, Leonard relaxed somewhat and became more curious about the possibility that I was genuinely interested in him and had something of value to offer him. He no longer had raging tantrums, gave up terrorizing waitresses in restaurants. He became more patient with employees and clients. He began to mediate rather than litigate disputes.

Unfortunately, his changes were too little too late, for after years of lawsuits and infamous dealings in the entertainment industry, he had backed himself into a lonely corner and ran into insurmountable financial difficulties when an economic recession hit. He was unable to find partners to close a crucial deal and was forced to declare bankruptcy, move to another state, and end his treatment.

Leonard's Farewell

In the final moments of his last scheduled session, as he was departing, he took me quite by surprise. He turned back and faced me tearfully. Sobbing intensely in the doorway, he reached out his arms and hugged me warmly and tenderly. This breakthrough of deep feeling, vulnerability, and longing for the comforting maternal breast had certainly been there all along, warded off and enacted outside the transference in his numerous perverse sexualized liaisons. For this very damaged man, the only transformational contact he could uninhibitedly allow was expressed through his final tearful embrace.

Conscious acknowledgment of his longings for contact with my maternal body had been too threatening of loss of control and loss of his core gender identity as a man of power over women; thus he had been unable to tolerate lying supine on the couch in my presence. His longings could be expressed only after five years of treatment, as he was on his way out the door.

In a brief follow-up contact by telephone some months later, Leonard told me that the last session had been a most moving experience, but that it had terrified him by unmasking his vulnerability to a woman who was not just a sex object but who could understand him and the meaning of his erotic behavior. He felt "deeply touched" and changed by the experience and expressed appreciation that I had stayed with him through all his denigration. But he added that his fear was so great he doubted he would ever be able to return to therapy "unless I hit my wife again and have to."

A Final Note

For Leonard, the dried turd of childhood had represented both his earlier longings to win his mother's favor and attention by producing something special (Fraiberg, 1958) and his sense of himself as an unwanted "piece of shit" that mother had tossed off. In the imagery of the rosebush, it represented a dead and rotting root system, poisoned by some unwanted toxin, the lethal atmosphere between boy and mother. The dried turd also represented the counterfeit coin of the realm in their deadlocked struggle. Leonard thought of his penis as a dried turd and used it as a means of sadistic control over women. He preferred to make them feel like the needy ones who longed for his sexual attention and his financial favors, while he maintained the illusion of himself as indifferent and totally in control.

His castration anxiety was apparent in his panic at not being the macho king and in his fear of becoming the passive woman, lying on her back. He feared the analytic couch, which would render him vulnerable to castration by me, leaving him a demeaned female. Erotic terror made the use of the analytic couch impossible for him. A dead baby, needing to be "sung to life," sadly he could rarely hear the song in therapy because his defenses were so entrenched. I wondered to what extent his defensiveness also masked threatening homoerotic passive longings for the father he felt never took an interest in him (see chapter 9).

As we discussed in chapter 5, patients who believe themselves to be unwanted pieces of shit, who believe that their mothers would have preferred to abort them and flush them down the toilet, are particularly traumatized by the prospect of regressing to early infantile states of utter vulnerability represented by early maternal erotic transferences. Yet, immersion in maternal erotic transferences represents one of the few keys to free them from the hate-filled object relations deadlocks that paralyze them. Such transferences can enliven them to the possibility of relinquishing their counterfeit protective selves.

GENDER AND MATERNAL EROTIC TRANSFERENCES

For those males whose gender identity is shaky and for whom the early longings are intense, the preoedipal maternal erotic transference threatens not only their schizoid isolation, but also their very gender identity. Female patients seldom approach this degree of "erotic terror. Although frightening to female patients to the extent that they fear losing their separateness, intense bodily feelings toward the early mother do not usually threaten female core gender identity. Male patients by and large experience more pervasive anxiety in the face of early maternal erotic transferences than females.

However, for some women patients whose abhorrence of an intrusive mother figure is elaborated with paranoia of psychotic proportions, the threat of psychic annihilation is spawned by early maternal transferences. Identification and merger with mother may represent among other things, merger with the annihilating archfiend, the desperately needed yet demeaned mother's denigrated body. For female patients whose only imagined escape route was total renunciation of their femininity and identification with the male "other," immersion in the maternal erotic transference may threaten the survival of the whole self. The clinical case of Suta describes one such woman.

THE CASE OF SUTA

Suta, a young woman of paranoid character, brought deeply masked, homoerotic anxieties into analysis. At times these psychotic anxieties threatened to derail her analysis. Her core anxieties related to the fear of her own annihilation that would accompany a transformational erotic encounter with her analyst. She feared that close bodily contact would unleash a killing rage that would destroy her, the other, or both of them. At the same time, like many others we have seen in treatment, she both longed for and feared the passionate intensity and boundary loss that comes with blissful fusion.

Suta's Narrative: "I Must Be Holy"—
A Paranoid Story of Erotic Abnegation

An academician in her late 20s, Suta sought analysis after two earlier attempts at therapy. The first, essentially a counseling situation, had not approached her deep pathology. The second, more dynamic treatment was unfortunately interrupted when the therapist relocated to another state. Two major stresses had led Suta to seek analysis. The first was the death of a close family member, which she seemed to ignore and did not consciously respond to. Second, she felt forced to accede to marriage, either to Dom, her fiancé, or to Paul, her secret lover. Each demanded a public commitment or threatened to terminate the relationship. With Dom, the businessman whom she did marry and with whom she was anorgasmic, she felt asexual, maternal, "dead," safe. With Paul, whose fluid gender boundaries included cross-dressing, she episodically enjoyed sexual "ecstasy." Having to choose between the two men, Suta decompensated, became paralytically depressed, and unable to function at work. She completely disappeared from contact with either man, her family, or her friends for two weeks. At this point, she realized the gravity of her psychological fragility. She knew she needed nothing short of an analysis.

I (HKW) saw her as functioning in a paranoid schizoid mode, unable to tolerate the intensity of a full relationship. Her defenses early in the analysis were powerful intellectualization, splitting, dissociation, and projection. For the first seven years of five-days-per-week analysis, Suta feared the loss of control she associated with lying down on the couch; she remained seated, constantly vigilant, and at some distance from me on the couch.

When Suta entered treatment, she consciously hated her father and idealized her mother. She was also cognizant of the fact that at the onset of puberty she had declared herself "dead to the world," eschewed her femininity totally, and embraced the effort to become a kind of perfect saint in a "man's world." Analysis revealed a core self-loathing; she saw herself as a dirty creature with a "smelly vagina" and maintained a paranoid distance from intimacy.

The eldest of seven children born overseas to a foreign-service family, she had early been given the role of caretaker for her siblings. In an interesting parallel to Leonard, she had enjoyed, she believed, a blissful infancy in a sublime love affair with her mother that was disrupted when she was two by the birth of her first sibling, an "angelic choirboy with strawberry red curls" who became seriously ill and required all the mother's attention. Suta's father, called "The Colonel," was absent most of the time on government business and abusive when present. Her mother enlisted the children's loyalty in a "we-against-him" alliance. Mrs. L conveyed to her children that while sex with this huge and explosive man and child-bearing were both intolerable, she loved babies and it was a woman's religious duty to bear them.

These were the origins in Suta's original perverse narrative, of the denigration of the father, the idealization of the mother, and, at the same time, the renunciation of femininity. In order to maintain her image of her mother as the beautiful Madonna, the fragrant and perfect rose, she took into herself all the anal smells, the worms and snails and the muck, and feelings of being the despicable smelly vagina.

A child's absorption of the unwanted and split-off aspects of the parents often results in the child's emotional illiteracy, denial, and even hatred of internal reality— sometimes, sadly, in hatred of life itself, often of suicidal proportions, as with Suta, Mark, and Caleb in the following chapters. In treatment, this may lead to patients' entrenched belief that their analysts are attempting to drive them insane by insisting on meaningful connection of those elements which must be kept apart. Accordingly, we find that a key aspect to the management of countertransference issues in these cases is being able to tolerate and rework projections, holding bits of meaning in mind while refraining from retaliatory "interpretation." This, in effect, "lends" the patient the expanded analytic space of the analyst's mind for the containment of these intolerable projections.

My countertransference with Suta for all but the last years varied from feeling that I was tenuously and carefully reeling in a large fighting fish, to the specific fear of being murdered in a session by a small pistol I imagined she secreted in her purse. Sometimes I thought of work with her as "romancing the stone." When she was a bit more available, she portrayed me in the transference as one of her mother's close friends, another foreign-service wife with whom she exchanged a banal but pleasant version of the "daily news." These feelings elicited countertransference responses ranging from a kind of perverse schizoid distancing and deadness of my own, to a desire to break through her stony isolation, to "woo" her, or to give in, abandon the analytic endeavor, and accept Suta's distanced yet intriguing posture and engage in stimulating intellectual conversations.

For the most part, I refrained from enacting these countertransference impulses, but doing so was often challenging; an analyst can never be sure of the extent of unconscious acting out. No matter how much she "shrunk" me into a small wooden object or threatened to assault me, I nearly always felt able to maintain some uncontaminated aspect of my psyche that genuinely liked and cared for her, and felt a pained empathy for her isolation and suffering. I always sensed that she was a lovely and passionate woman, even when she denied that she was, both verbally and by her clothing and appearance. The analyst's capacity in the countertransference to find such an erotic resonance is particularly critical with perversely distancing patients such as Leonard and Suta. This resonance supports the containment that permits and helps overcome the paranoid paralysis of deadlocks and fosters transformation of their selves locked in perverse narratives.

Suta remained unable to pursue her passions, both sexually and aesthetically. By marrying the "good man" she had denied herself easier access to her lover. Instead of practicing as an artist, her secret passion, Suta dedicated herself to her "holy mission" in academic research, seeking a breakthrough in environmental protection. She also portrayed herself as stalemated in her research, subordinated to a team of "chauvinistic superiors."

Analysis of her deadlocked internal drama revealed what she came to call "the loyalty rule," referring to her explicit loyalty to her mother and her mother's way of seeing things, including her hatred of father's crudeness and rageful tirades. This view depicted mother and the other children as victims with no recourse other than placating and hiding. Seeing her mother as trapped and victimized, Suta at age 12 renounced her emerging femininity and dedicated her life to rituals of self-purification and to "becoming a saint" who would save the planet and its inhabitants. Remaining loyal to mother's mythos of revulsion at sex, she mostly denied her femininity and sensual life or split it off in the infrequent clandestine meetings with Paul, her secret lover.

Split-Off Homoerotism

After her two-week disappearance from her family and both suitors, Suta made the more conservative choice. She married Dom, the businessman, and began her analysis. Consistent with the paranoid schizoid mode, in which splitting is predominant, Suta kept her occasional trysts with her polymorphously perverse lover completely hidden from Dom, her husband, and for long periodic intervals out of view of the analytic relationship. Brief glimpses revealed her homoerotic longings, concealed even from her own consciousness through her active and almost panicked homophobic rejections of the entreaties of a number of prospective female lovers and through her exclusive choice of male sexual partners. Yet she fantasized that Paul's penis was an udder providing an endless supply of delicious milk. Although she told herself that his cross-dressing represented exclusively his own sexual perversion, which she indulged, it also conveyed her own latent homoerotic longings.

During the first several years of analysis, Suta moved distrustfully in and out of a transference deadlock. She preferred to keep me small and at a safe, intellectualized distance. Like Leonard, she referred to me as her "shrink." Occasionally her transferences assumed psychotic proportions and revealed a passionate intensity, as when she threatened to attack me when I was recovering from shoulder surgery. Feeling particularly concerned about Suta midway in her analysis, I had cut short the recommended postsurgical recuperation period especially to see Suta and one other patient. My visibly bandaged state fostered her representation of me as the debilitated and victimized mother imago. It also reminded her of mother's homecomings from the hospital where yet another sibling had been born. Wanting to destroy her weakened, victimized mother or her abusive father and his too many babies, she threatened to throw a heavy piece of sculpture at me.

Passionate Fury at an Interloper: A Change in the Story

In one session a few years into her analysis, there was a mix-up about her hour due to a time change. When she came to what she thought was her hour and I was with another patient, she banged on the door, barged in, and saw a young, slightly built, red-headed man lying on the couch. Enraged, she demanded that he leave. She threatened to quit analysis, this mixup having demonstrated my unreliability to her.

I urged her to come back for her session later that day and insisted that we explore what had happened and what it had meant to her. Reluctantly, she agreed to see me. I encouraged her to explore her fury at me and the meaning of this accident.

For the first time, she was able to recognize that she had become very attached to me (and her hour) although she had openly denied it to herself and to me. This red-headed "sibling" stirred her fury at her mother and me for displacing her. Several weeks of working through her rage at me dislodged some of the deadlocked "loyalty" to her idealized but abandoning internal mother and allowed her finally to acknowledge that I was deeply important to her. She recognized that I was not just a "technical wizard" and acknowledged her analysis as her "lifeline." At the same time, this realization generated considerable anxiety about betraying the "loyalty rule," which referred to her deadlocked relationship with her internal mother; she feared that she was betraying, even killing, this internal mother, and her "matricidal" anxiety was excruciating for her.

A maternal erotic transference (in the sense that we mean it) had not appeared but was now a possibility. All her conscious sensual pleasure was invested in her own maternal care for her children, particularly nursing them as infants. She delighted in their pleasure in her breasts and her touch. She was completely unaware of any similar longings for my touch. An aspect of her passionate feelings toward me was, however, revealed in the fervent nature of her rage at me as the mother whom she had blissfully and faithfully loved and who had betrayed her by "sex with the beast," in my case, with my husband and in my attention to the red-headed rival baby.

Apparently, the mix-up about her hour had threatened the safety and containment of the analytic and narrative space to the point that Suta felt like quitting analysis. On the other hand, because she had over the preceding few years experienced me as a "good-enough" analyst, the damage could be repaired through analysis and her experience of my attunement to her distress. A significant transformation began to occur in Suta's mythic narrative. Whereas she had held fast to the "story" of her indifference to me as the mother who was too absorbed in a needy, red-haired baby sibling to care about her, now she was able to revise it to include the possibility that there could be a mix-up that did not signal abandonment. Also, she altered her deeply ingrained identification with her father's tirades whenever mother appeared inadequate. In the face of the confusion about her session time, she had launched an assault of major proportions (so threatening that it terrified the diminutive redhead for weeks).

Suta had been "loyal" (Lichtenberg, 1991) to her fantasied construction of me as at best a flattened object and more typically an inconvenience toward whom she had no feeling. The powerful "assault" on that view alerted her to her deeper feelings. It is significant that this learning did have the aura of an attack; many of her most formative memories were encapsulated as assaults. Hence, when I did not turn to mush, as her mother had, and appeared capable of withstanding Suta's attack, she reconsidered the situation. I had not been damaged or destroyed by her rage, nor would I eject her from treatment: rather I assured her I was dedicated to understanding the meaning of the incident and of her outburst. Thus, another internal narrative line could be altered. Suta was able to reconstruct her previous narrative portrayal of herself as father's clone, the nuclear reactor with a hair trigger.

Narrative Transformation

Confirmation of this "transmuting internalization" (Tolpin, 1971) occurred a few weeks later. Suta was in her car with her infant daughter, Cara, and young son, Damian, and got in a minor accident. Typically, regardless of the circumstances, she would have leaped from the car in a fury and threatened revenge, but this time she kept her cool. Though she was very shaken, she listened calmly to the genuine apology of the other driver. When she reported this event in her analytic hour, I said, "I sense something shifting and I wonder if you do too—you could have raged as father would have done. Instead, you listened to the other driver express his own anxiety and sorrow and allowed him to have an 'accident,' as you never allowed yourself. You could respond empathically to him."

Suddenly, she was reminded of a prior incident in which her car was blocking a truck in traffic and the truck driver flew into a terrifying rage at her and chased her car for miles on the highway. She said, "I guess you are saying something about how I experienced that truck driver, how terrifying his rage was to me. I thought he was going to follow me with his truck and run us down and kill us. He seemed out of control, like my dad, and I guess like me when I attack you. I never think my temper hurts anybody because I feel I'm invisible. But you told me how it was when I threatened to throw the sculpture at you after your surgery a couple of years ago. I guess you actually felt like I did that day."

We can understand this therapeutic shift from a number of different perspectives (Wrye, in press). Prominently, it reveals a significant step toward dissolution of the deadlocked enmeshment with her mother, and the construction of a new internal object based on her experience with me. It represents a shift in her identifications from a unidimensional one with the out-of-control, vengeful father to a complex identification with the empathy and calm she experienced in her analyst in response to her attack. Thus we see the shift from the paranoid schizoid to the depressive position, as she became concerned about the safety and well-being of her objects. From another vantage point, to be developed more fully in chapter 9, we see the patient taking heart from her experience of a strong, adequate paternal imago within her female analyst to offset entrapment by a seductive but debilitated mother.

In her own new narration, she was able to tolerate minor mix-ups, maintain some equilibrium, and not jeopardize her most important object ties. When she felt threatened or anxious, the newly constructed story of herself replaced the one she had felt doomed to repeat endlessly and that guaranteed that those she needed most would be kept at bay.

From the perspective of desire, Suta, a violinist, was now rewriting the songs of her desire. Previously, she had felt that the only way she could express passionate feeling was in discordant and thunderous chords conveying her rage. Now, she was learning to compose her songs of desire with occasional pianissimos, harmonious chords, and some melodic line. Parenthetically, it is in incidents like this that analyst and analysand tend to develop the "private language" or ideograms of mother–child intimacy. We could speak in shorthand of the "truck driver" or of "red hairs on couch" with a rich range of evocative and symbolic meaning. These phrases appear like leitmotifs in the songs and narratives of desire.

Blissful Changes in Her Narration of Desire

Once the deadlock was sprung and Suta was able to enter into a mutual mode of narrative construction, she also became more open to exploring her previously denied femininity and her sexuality. At the same time, however, she continued to maintain a distant attitude toward my body. I was still, after all, just her "shrink," and she studiously avoided feelings about my absences.

After I returned from a brief vacation, Suta arrived 30 minutes late to her Monday session. She had called earlier to say that her

newborn had developed a frightening symptom and desperately
needed her. Now, in the brief remainder of the session, she spoke
of being snubbed by another mother in her daughter's nursery
school class and mostly of her exaggerated fears of what could happen to her children—guilt over her own murderous wishes toward
them at times and toward her baby brother who had gotten so
much attention because of his illness.

I felt it was premature to interpret her denied fury at me for leaving, or to mention the parallel between her baby's urgent need for
her and her own feelings of desperate dependency on her mother/
analyst, so I remained quiet.

The next day, Suta arrived on time. Smiling, she exclaimed, "It
smells so good here! I was in my sculpture class, and I drove home
to nurse the baby before I came here. I could have pumped my
breasts, but, I don't know, I wanted to be there in person with
him. I'm so much more in touch with wanting to be with him than
I was with my first two. I guess I know this is the last time I'll be
doing this . . . and when he nurses, he gazes at me, this BIG smile!
With his little fingers, he fondles my breast. It's wonderful! How
you forget. I remember when I was pregnant, I thought, gee, I
remember liking nursing with the other babies, but I can't really
remember it. So this time I want to!" She drifted off, smiling, and
I said, "To really be alive and feeling the bliss."

"Yeah!" she exclaimed. "It does go by so fast! There's no comparison, pumping would have been the smart thing to do, but it was so
worth it! Even the whole ride across town. . . I have so much to tell
you! When you were away, I was supposed to give a lecture. It was a
big deal. I agreed some time ago."

She then described participating on a panel of women profession-
als regarding women's health. To illustrate a point, one of the pan-
elists had held up a picture of an orchid. "It was beautiful! Then I
realized it was *female genitalia*! Amazing! I asked her for a copy for
my daughter, but I realized it was really for me.

"When I got home, I showed it to Cara, because, you remember,
she's been talking about her ugly wee wee. I said, 'Look, Cara! This
is a flower and it looks like your wee wee.' She was so excited and
pleased. She's always running around naked. When Dom got home,
she ran to show him the picture. Saturday, I took a day off and I
went shopping. I got all new, pretty underwear and these scents and
lotions and all. That night, I let Dom eat me for the first time in 12
years! I didn't have an orgasm, but it was *good sex!* I guess I just still

can't allow myself that much pleasure. But it was quite a change."

In the same almost breathless session, she continued:

"A sculptress teaching my art class wanted us to do a head in the old style. So I worked on it for hours. I realized I had it! I had the likeness! She came by, and I said, 'Isn't it good when you *get* it?' She said, 'Yeah, it's a real high! That's why we *do* it!' I'd never thought of that high before. She said once it was so powerful for her that she was preoccupied by the sculpture she'd been working on one morning as she was driving, and she lost all track of time and place driving home. She nearly drove off an embankment on the highway! My God! She was that excited and absorbed by her art!

"You've told me in the past that there seemed to be something in my delight in sculpting, something about me and mother—my searching for her face—oneness, at-onement . . . I've heard you mention it before, but this time I could really *feel* it".[1]

She went on, "There's been so much! And at work, I finally feel the guys respect me. I was telling Dom, I used to be so scared when Dr. Wrye goes away. Usually, in the past, I'd never tell you, but I'd completely fall apart. I was really scared. But this time, I did *really* well. So well, I told him, I can feel the end of my analysis coming up."

As the session ended, I felt that Suta had protected herself from painful feelings about my absence by holding on to our years of analytic contact. She was permitting herself to feel the joy of nursing this third baby, the heretofore denied pleasures of making love with her husband, and sculpting a human face—all as dramatically new ways of experiencing intimate contact. She had stayed in contact with me over the vacation. I felt great happiness for her and a feeling of satisfaction in our work.

In the Bottom of a Gopher Hole, or a "Smelly Vagina"

At the same time, I was aware of a manic quality to the material and, knowing Suta, wondered when and how the unmanaged feelings of abandonment rage would surface. The next day, she said, "I've been thinking about yesterday's session, talking about art class, capturing

---

[1] I had based earlier interpretations on my sense that part of Suta's pleasure in art could be understood by way of Winnicott's (1967) hypothesis that aesthetic experience embodies the baby's pleasure in discovering the beauty of the mother's beloved face and that subsequent cultural experience is located in the reexperiencing of that aesthetic moment.

the likeness of the face of the model, how powerful that was for me, all the wordless pleasure. The 'bliss' you called it; it's like wordless, visceral pleasure. Probably my kids won't remember this either from nursing, but there's a powerful visceral memory I think I'm finally feeling."

I offered, "I wonder if you're touching on the powerful closeness you felt with mother, which you've longed for and feared ever since. Perhaps it's like your art teacher who spoke of almost driving off the highway. This "at-onement" and loss of yourself could be lethal, and it could be taken away—painfully, not in your control—as it was by your mother when she went to the hospital for each new baby, or by me when I take myself away from you."

Her demeanor changed. She responded, *"You?* I didn't even think once of you. I didn't miss you. I was doing so well. I was so happy. I guess I obliterated you. (long pause) We've been having trouble with gophers in the garden. I didn't want to poison them or trap them and kill them. I was talking about it with my neighbor, and he said you need to take some fish and leave it out in the sun in a plastic bag for three days. When it's totally rotten, put it in the gopher hole and bury it. They'll leave your yard. I put rotten fish in the gopher holes to make them go away. God! Is that what I did with you? I buried you like rotten fish in a gopher hole!!"

I said, "Perhaps when I left on vacation, you also had such ugly hateful thoughts about my leaving and fears of falling apart without me that you felt it would be better to get rid of me. Maybe you felt I left you forgotten, so you sort of 'left me to rot' and then you buried me in a smelly, dark, shitty place."

"Yeah!" she said.

We explored this for a while, and then there was a silence. Thinking about the rotten fish, I associated to her preoccupation with her smelly vagina. Silently, I wondered about the meaning of her allowing her husband to have oral sex with her just at this time for the first time in years. I said, "We've talked in the past about your own sense of having a smelly vagina and of feeling dirty and ugly inside. I wonder if perhaps you and Cara both feel you are ugly and have ugly wee wees because you feel your secret thoughts are sometimes so ugly and nasty. Perhaps when your mother turned her attention away from you to the new babies, you wanted to bury her in a smelly dark hole. But then you felt dirty inside."

She immediately responded, "God, yes! I see it. I wanted to bury you in that nasty place, and I feel I *am* disgusting. . . . Did you read in the newspaper of those boys in Beverly Hills who murdered their parents?

The Juxtaposition of the Warded-Off Maternal Erotic Transference and Oedipal Erotic Longings

The session ended, confirming the juxtaposition of therapeutic gains with manic denial; it also represented a breakthrough in linking Suta's narrative of self-loathing with abandonment rage. In the following sessions, we explored these themes—her long-denied wishes for her mother's sweet breast; her murderous impulses toward her mother and siblings (and me, in the transference) for displacing her; and her rediscovery of "bliss" in sculpting faces. She was deeply moved by her fury at feeling abandoned and by the realization that her ugly thoughts toward her mother and father and siblings had contributed to her belief that she was disgusting. She recognized that she had displaced this belief in fantasies about her own genitals and then partly projected these feelings about her "smelly vagina" back onto her parents, thus intensifying her perception of them as weak and gross. She began to realize that her fear of orgasm had to do with her fear of losing herself in the body of another and then being out of control and vulnerable to abandonment. She had had to keep me at bay to avoid regressing to her own infantile immersion in her mother and vulnerability to her father.

She also took up the feelings she had about nursing her son. It was her breast milk that "engorged" this baby boy's body and, in her fantasy, his penis. By nursing him, she had gained power over her hated father. She began to retrieve other feelings about her oedipal father. She remembered him when he was young and slim and very handsome. She knew he had had a love affair and wondered if it was because her mother was so sexually inhibited and afraid of more pregnancies.

For the first time, exciting erotic thoughts about her father emerged. She recalled having heard that when she was little he enjoyed playing with her and tossing her high in the air. In fact once he was having such a time with her that he tossed her so high that she actually banged her head on the ceiling. The idea of their both being so playfully out of control was a totally new construct and changed the old narrative considerably. She recognized that she now felt good about being female, loving a man, and being able to bear and nurse his children; she could tolerate being a "good-enough" although not perfect mother. Engagement of the preoed-ipal maternal erotic transference thus facilitated contact with oedipal erotic material.

The Shift from Upright Vigilance to Lying on the Couch

Some months later, more than seven years into her analysis, Suta finally felt safe enough to lie down on the couch. She described this move as crucial to completing her analysis, for it symbolized that she could finally tolerate giving up her vigilant control. Her move to the couch, however, was precipitous. Typical of other moves closer to me, she "couched" it with the announcement that she would be coming only two more weeks because using the couch demonstrated that she was done. I pointed out that she still seemed so terrified of allowing herself to be vulnerable that she had to have one foot out the door. (Her fear of regression was similar to that of Leonard, who only briefly used the couch to lie down and then sometimes very provocatively accentuating his genitals when he wanted to assert that he had the upper hand over his "girl shrink." When he recognized how vulnerable he felt, he sat up.) Shortly thereafter, she acknowl-edged this defensive strategy, and settled into the next phase of her analysis.

Before Words—Sounds, Sights, and Smells

Once, in response to one of my interpretations, Suta hastily retorted that that might be how I felt, but not she. Then she associated to how she knew her mother's moods so perfectly that the two of them had no need for words to communicate. I commented on her pleasure in thinking about how close they were, that their commu-nications could be so nonverbal, that they were so attuned to body feelings. She agreed and said by that, by contrast, our relationship was "just words" and in her experience she had to "discount words, which in my childhood were weapons. Mostly I'd hear, 'You're a piece of shit!'"

Associating to how she had come to see herself as a "piece of shit," she recalled her school uniforms when she was in seventh grade overseas. She recalled wearing the required wool skirt "every day until I began to notice that it smelled. I asked my mother to have it cleaned and she said, 'No, it's OK, just iron it.' I did, and when it got hot, it smelled awful!" Also, this was about the time I decided it was a sin to touch myself, so I didn't. This included in the bathtub, so I didn't wash myself, and my skirt wasn't cleaned and it *smelled!*"

Thus, revelation of her mother's empathic failure to understand her pubescent daughter's needs was confusing in that it was juxtaposed with her idealization of the wordless understanding between herself and her mother. In an effort to sort it out, I said,

"Maybe it feels like our relationship is 'just words, not real.' What would feel really connected would be close, bodily contact. But as a little girl, perhaps you felt you needed to keep a distance because you believed you were disgusting and smelly and shouldn't be touched."

In the next months, Suta explored her immersion in a living purgatory of guilt and recriminations for her dirty smelly insides. She now realized that in her research into world toxins, she was also trying to locate pollution and ritually purge it; and that, while she denied longing for her father's love and approval, she was really trying to win him over by distinguishing herself academically. If that failed, at least she'd become the powerful male herself.

A Maternal Erotic Countertransference Enactment

In one session, when Suta reverted to a series of flat details, I became aware of powerful body sensations. It occurred to me that she was moving away from putting together something very important. In direct contrast to her deanimation, I felt a complementary wellspring of something inside, as if I were "pregnant." Many themes and issues had come together. Very uncharacteristically, I interrupted her. I suggested that she understood that the "real" for her had to be rooted in the sensory body feelings associated with loving contact with her young mother, before her baby brother's birth spoiled her illusion of at-onement. Having worked hard throughout her analysis to block access to her fantasies of contact with my physical body, she complained that our relationship was "just talk." I suggested that she had been using every means at her command to keep from experiencing me as the mommy who could hold her warmly, as she held her babies, the mommy of the milk, tears, pee pee, poop, and all the fluids of mother–baby contact.

I reminded her of her excitement a couple of years earlier on seeing the picture of the vagina that looked like a beautiful flower—and explaining to Cara that this is what her pee pee looks like and how much of a celebration they'd had. The counterfeit and denigrated image of herself as purging the world of pollution, disease, and dirt through research had become embodied in her envious spoiling and compulsive attention to minutiae. Even her efforts to liberate herself from that "false story" and turn to the expressiveness of sculpture, which involved messy clay that she could smear, did not allow her fully to resolve this core and debilitating belief. On some level, she was struggling against allowing herself to feel a connection with me "beyond and before words," a bodily presence as a source of generativity and healing. If she could allow it, she might be playfully spontaneous with me, and enjoy an ambiance that had seemed strikingly absent in our relationship.

These words represented more than I had ever said to her at one time, and I was aware of my "giving birth" in making this encompassing interpretation. I had indulged myself in this outburst. I was conscious that it was a holiday weekend and that if I waited till the following week, we would yet again lose this. Although I had only briefly weighed whether to say this, I told myself, "Carpe Diem!" I wanted to "give her something" to chew on over the long weekend. Suta's fear of spontaneity with me seemed to have summoned this uncontrolled urge to "break through" to her. By the end of this lengthy interpretation, I felt almost breathless, but knowing Suta, I knew I would probably be "in for it." That awareness signaled my own persecutory anxiety and awareness of overactive countertransference.

After the session, I thought about what had happened, and recognized in my own powerful countertransference feelings of excitement, the powerful presence of a maternal erotic countertransference. I had felt constantly "sanitized" by Suta and kept at a distance. I realized that my excitation was in inverse proportion to the degree of Suta's flatness. In fact, with Suta, this sense of being the spark to a flattened, depressed, or schizoid partner had often arisen in me.

In the countertransference, I felt full of love for her, proud of her artistic gifts, which I saw as considerable, and moved by a wish to soothe her and encourage her. She tearfully replied that she felt "very deeply moved, appreciative, understood." I felt she had finally allowed me to touch her and be touched by her. Our contact finally showed all the earmarks of a full-blown maternal erotic transference and countertransference. It had been deadly, messy, full of pokes and punches; now perhaps it could also be sweet, exciting, and creative. A new sense of pleasure in being together emerged.

Narration in Art Instead of Words

Over the years of her analysis, Suta's "narration of desire" was increasingly composed in her sculpture. At the outset, I did not even know of her art, so absorbed was she in her research and in her periodic suicidal despair over her split life and having married "the wrong man." She did not even reveal art as her other "secret passion" until about a year into her analysis, when she brought a "secret-in-the-night" drawing to a session. Reminiscent of Edvard Munch's "The Howl," it depicted a horrified figure fleeing some nightmarish inner vision suggestive of the plague. Drawn in dark hues of greens and purples and blue-black, it showed an anguished, skeletal woman, her hands, like spiders, holding her face. She told me at the time how she was able to express her suicidal despair and secret horrors only in her art. She asked if she could leave the drawing safely with me, as no one must be allowed to see it. Dom would be appalled if he saw her inner vision. After that, she turned her focus back to research, which she saw as more socially acceptable.

About eight years into the analysis, she began sculpting, first on the side and then almost full time, as she struggled to integrate her powerful feelings into her daily life. She brought into the sessions the pieces that were small enough to manage and photographs of the larger ones, wanting through their physicality to make contact in ways she could not with words. These works depicted massive nudes with pendulous breasts. She approached the human body detachedly, taking it as an artistic challenge and avoiding any psychological resonance with feelings evoked by the subjects. She often asked technical questions: Did I think the shoulder should be more defined? What about the drapery there? I interpreted her anxiety about bringing into her sessions the intense sensual feelings that we had talked about and that she now worked to reveal in her sculpture. I also commented that she felt she must still keep these feelings located safely in the clay.

Working Through Counterfeiting, Distancing, and Perversion: The Sublimation of Manic Defenses

Anticipation of termination coincided with Suta's attendance at a professional meeting abroad. She felt overwhelmed with guilt at having participated in hostile gossip about an absent colleague; she believed she had betrayed a new vow not to speak ill of someone who was not present. That night, distraught and repentant, she first prayed, then called out for her long-dead grandmother, who had provided much of her early caretaking when her mother was busy with the new babies. She related:

"I said 'Oh, Gammy! What have I done?!' Suddenly it was like a clap and a hard punch—POW!! This incredible experience! I felt enveloped by Gammy! Like she was coming from some far away place just for me. She was showing me how much she truly cared for me! It was as if I wasn't an adult now, she was enveloping me as an infant. It was so intense! Gammy's been dead for 30 years, yet she was right there and so loving! Never in my life have I felt anything so intense. I thought, 'I have to tell Harriet!' You've waited so long for me to get in touch with my lost infancy."

In the following session, she rapturously described how her heart was filled with love for the world, her children, and even me. She and her husband celebrated their love with "the greatest sex ever! I realized I had been projecting this nastiness and shit I believed was in me into other people—him, you, all over the place!" She proclaimed, "We had more incredible sex! I do love you. See? I even said it. I'm done!! I want to show the world that through you and my analysis I feel I have a fragrant portal instead of a smelly vagina! I just wanted to thank you. I really don't need you any more. In fact, this is a kind of 'courtesy call' to say good-bye."

It was clear to me that she was, indeed, nearing the end of her analysis, but there was something familiarly guarded about this "story." Although she was appreciative of her analysis, she was using idealization to push me away. Her passionate encounter with her dead grandmother seemed like a resurrection of a good internal object long kept at bay by the paranoid struggle between her internal fighting parents.

Gammy also represented a safer contact than the passionate encounter she had long been keeping under wraps in relation to her analyst, who was quite alive and had been intensely engaged with her for the previous nine years. My vacations still left her feeling vulnerable, and the mere mention of termination had engendered tremendous anxiety about separation and loss. Now her grandmother could come from the afterlife to comfort her at any time of the day or night, at home or abroad. There was other confirming evidence of the manic aspect of this precipitous "termination" that would bypass dealing with death and actual current loss.

I mirrored her joy and her sense that she was approaching the end of her analysis. I valued her appreciation but felt it might have some of the flavor of her initial idealization of mother. I questioned her seeming lack of access to more complex and intense feelings about separating from me. And I returned to questions of the meaning, in the light of this epiphany, of her recent dedication to a faith, which, though far more tolerant and open minded than her parents' religion, appeared to consume all her attention. Suta became absolutely enraged, sat up, and, screaming at me, hurtled a pillow from the couch right at me. I sat in stunned silence. The session ended. As I tried to recover my composure, I felt confirmed in my suspicion that she had been skirting something powerful.

Contact with a Core Erotic Horror

It occurred to me that by hurling the pillow at me Suta had made of our analytic encounter the mirror opposite of the blissful and miraculous encounter with Gammy: "Suddenly it was like a clap and a hard punch. POW!!" she had said. For her, the experience with Gammy had felt very exciting, but to me the hard punch of the thrown pillow ("Pow!") suggested the ragefully sadistic side of her experience of intense intimacy. She had split off and projected her erotic terror into me. I felt acutely the terror of intense close contact between us that she assiduously denied. For about three days, she skirted the incident and went back to the old "neighborly chatting" until I felt centered enough to interpret what I felt might have happened. When I drew a parallel between my experience of being socked by her to hers with Gammy, she became angry, though not enraged. She said it couldn't be; I couldn't possibly know her experience. I assured her that while I could not really know her experience and she could not really know mine, I had felt just as stunned and overwhelmed as she seemed to have been, and her words described my experience perfectly. I told her that her rage had been frightening.

Sobered, she acknowledged that in that moment she really had become psychotic—that she had completely annihilated me as a sentient human being, that she had objectified me and was preparing to depart from me as if she had no feelings. She had seen the film *The Prince of Tides* and, recalling the horrific rape scene that is the centerpiece of the story, she had been able to make contact with her terror, the erotic fusion of longing and violence.

"I have this terror of either being raped or being the rapist who completely denies any empathy for the victim," she said. "Even to say 'terror' minimizes it. My terror is so *primal* there aren't even words for it. I do want you—*I want your breast. I want to suck on it.* Even before I'm finished saying it, I feel this horrendous rage come up. I guess it's got to do with separateness. When I feel I can't have all of you all the time, my rage becomes utterly terrifying. [She sobs.] I annihilate you because I love you!"

There was a long silence that I felt signaled contact with her core horror. The terror of intimacy, vulnerability, and longing for the sensual body of the early mother were in her mind equated with psychotic self-annihilation. I felt that this breakthrough indeed signaled the final phase of the analysis, in which we would work through her terror of loss of control and her associated wish to deny separation. Further, she seemed ready to relinquish a defensive religiosity in favor of a more genuinely integrated spirituality.

Suta's New Narration of Desire

Slowly and fitfully over the course of the almost 10-year analysis, Suta relinquished mother's stultifying narrative imposed on her by the loyalty rule. With the dissolution of the rigid idealization of her mother and denigration of her father, the deadlock was resolved and made way for a sensual and artistic passion and the capacity to tolerate separateness. She gave up the wish to be the powerful man, with a penetrating penis/sword and a male's access to the maternal body, and relinquished the attendant polymorphously perverse homoerotic fantasies of her secret lover. She recognized that the shared perversion had allowed her fantasied merger with her lover's counterfeit female body while denying her own true femininity. It had also allowed her to appropriate rather than appreciate any aspects of phallic potency on her father's or husband's part.

Identifying with the containing strength of the analytic frame, with my ability to contain and detoxify her psychotic projections and attacks, and with my femininity, Suta came to experience her own female body as containing and creative. In her mind, her vagina had shifted from a "smelly vagina" to a "fragrant portal." In this sense, through our relationship in the MET, and within our literary metaphor of rosebush, Suta no longer needed to denigrate her erotic longings by splitting her sensuality into an idealized perfect rose of a mother and leaving herself as the hated muck underground. She could reclaim her own feminine beauty, her primitive anal erotism, her loving and hateful impulses—her own "worms and snails"—and enjoy herself as a whole healthy, rosy bush (pun intended).

She also modified her projections of her father as the brutal, hated, unavailable parent and recognized his competence in business and his youthful attractiveness. Thus, working through the deadlock and the preoedipal maternal erotic transference allowed her to enter into and work through oedipal erotic conflicts and finally to appreciate her adult femininity and her husband's generative and pleasure-giving masculinity.

DISCUSSION: CREATING THE NARRATIVE SPACE TO NAME EROTIC TERROR IN A PARANOID-SCHIZOID CHARACTER

Many seriously disturbed patients, unable to play or enter the "playground" (Sanville, 1991a) of maternal erotic transferences and countertransferences, enter treatment instead, like Suta and Leonard, deadlocked in flattened, perverse landscapes characterized by psychotic fragmentation. They bring with them a deadening tie with an internal parental object that they deem essential for survival—initially, and sometimes for long periods of time, precluding meaningful contact with the analyst, who represents a threat to the survival of that draining object. Thus, experience remains flattened and concrete within and outside such analyses. As painfully illustrated by the initially deadlocked transferences of such patients as Leonard and Suta, torturing the analyst is intimately connected to the perverse denigration or idealization of the internal other.

In this chapter, we have taken up the issue of deadlocks in relation to perversion, whose goal is to maintain distance and stasis. We have also illustrated in Suta's case how, after the deadlock is broken, the working through of erotic transferences and countertransferences can promote consolidation and acceptance of core gender identity.

Unconscious terror, based on fear of murderous rage, annihilation anxiety, and erotic timidity, impedes the recognition of erotic resonance in the treatment. Unanalyzed, these forces tend to result in treatment stalemates and object relational deadlocks. They culminate in either prematurely terminated or interminable analyses. Some typical key developmental issues that emerge in the analyses of such patients are:

(1) Impingement, or absence, of appropriate, good-enough hold-ing and mirroring is problematic for the adequate development of the body-ego that underlies gender identity.

(2) Faulty mothering interferes with the child's ability to identify with positive aspects of the mother, leaving the child instead to iden-tify with those self-hating aspects of the mother; mother's body is internalized as a bad object.

(3) A father's emotional unavailability and deprecation of the mother's and daughter's femininity and self-worth foreclose the remaining avenue to positive gender identification.

(4) When a girl's feminine or a boy's masculine gender identity is thus denigrated or disowned, maternal erotic transference elicits far greater anxiety than anticipated in most patients. It is a terror, sometimes of psychotic proportions that is key to the defensive construction of perverse narratives.

In chapter 7 we turn to a related phenomenon in the lexicon of antierotic transferences, the developmental experience of "dead space," which contributes to such terror.

7

A "Horrible Dry Hollow"

Lost in Arid Deadspace

In the previous chapter, we looked at patients who were deeply engaged in struggles with internal objects antithetical to healthy transformation. We focused on the perverse narratives of their object relations dramas as they replayed in the transference and countertransference. In this chapter, we examine clinical material from patients who exist in an abject, objectless state of psychic isolation. The narratives of these patients are replete with bleak images reflecting the absence of adequate psychic space. This chapter tells the story of the metamorphosis of psychic space through narrative changes. Patients in the grip of this kind of psychic deadness feel barren and apathetic. They evidence an absence of desire and an inability to experience erotic resonance or to tolerate an encounter of passionate intensity. They often describe or evoke feelings of dry desolation, like living in a nuclear wasteland. Adult patients who exist in this metaphoric "horrible hollow" often long for immersion in a slippery oneness; at the same time they are so terrified of loss of self in merger that isolation in dry spaces seems provident. Parched isolation, however, is paralyzing and engenders in adults an experience evoked by T. S. Eliot's (1952) poem, "The Hollow Men."

In that poem, written after the decimation of Europe during World War I, Eliot captured the sense of utter emptiness experienced by an entire generation of young men who had fought in that struggle. Their bodies had survived, but their spirits had been destroyed in the deadening horror of the war. In Eliot's haunting poem, the men describe themselves as hollow men who are stuffed with straw. They lean emptily on one another. Whispering meaninglessly together, they

137

liken their voices to the scratchings of rodents' feet on broken glass in the basement. They are shapeless, without form, without color. Paralyzed, they gesture without motion.

The developmental history of patients evidencing such clinical phenomena reveals very early and profound disturbances around issues of separation. Every infant's perceptions of self–other boundaries are shaped by its experiences of its body in physical space, intrapsychic space, and interpersonal space. For those infants who are reared under auspicious circumstances, when psychological separation is successfully navigated and a reliable mother internalized, a feeling of well-being in physical space ensues; space can be hailed as freeing, regenerative, and welcome. It's safe, often even joyful to "come out and play."

By dark contrast, for those less fortunate in negotiating separation-individuation issues, space can be experienced as a "black hole" (Grotstein, 1990a,b). It can be experienced as annihilating deadness—a barren, "horrible hollow" in which one is potentially "lost in space," disconnected, or "spaced out." Those whose infancy lacked the experience of safe space between the self and mother feel traumatically uncontained and vulnerable to fragmentation, as exemplified in the male birth stories cited in chapter 5. As adults, they often experience themselves as existing in some kind of deadspace.

In treatment, they must first become aware of and gain some comfort with the notion of the separateness of their bodies and minds before they can tolerate the physical intensity of early maternal erotic transferences. The intensity of analytic contact for such patients typically stirs primitive annihilation anxiety; their overwhelming body feelings are associated with intimate contact with the analyst. In the analyses of such persons, we must traverse a long and arduous road before they can be "present enough" to begin to engage in what might be called a "narration of desire."

BODIES IN SPACE

Concepts of spatial experience are valuable in describing aspects of separateness and togetherness in all relationships, and they are important in understanding why some patients can, and others cannot, use the "narrative space" of the analytic setting. "Space," as in "deadspace," has several levels of meaning and experience of space.

These levels relate both to concrete, external, physical dimensions and to their internal psychological and symbolic dimensions.

First, and primarily, we use the term to represent the actual physical distance between the bodies of the mother and the newborn infant; it is the physical space between persons. We also refer to it as the transitional space necessary for the development of a cohesive sense of self and self-in-relation-to-other. In this sense, it has both physical and temporal determinants. This meaning derives from Winnicott's (1952) concept of transitional space, which, like his concept of transitional phenomena, is marked by paradox and often relates to preverbal, concrete, inchoate experience. Winnicott describes transitional space as neither inside (intrapsychic) nor outside (interpersonal) but somewhere in between.

Finally, we refer to space as it is constructed and experienced in the analytic situation. In analysis, the meanings of spatial experiences between analysand and analyst represent extremely important literal and metaphoric nonverbal constituents of the analysis itself: the analytic room, with its physical as well as temporal space, continuity, sameness; the reliable presence of the analyst and the analyst's regard for the patient's space—all components that constitute the analytic space/frame.

DEADSPACE: THE ANALYTIC SPACE/FRAME AS A DESERT

Some very disturbed patients begin treatment unable to enter into the analyst's verbal-symbolic framework (Goldberg, 1989). Unable to communicate by means of and understand symbolic language, they cannot enter into the world of consensual meaning. Such patients often begin by concretely attacking the therapeutic frame, missing sessions, refusing to pay, threatening to quit, and the like. These enactments stem from the patients' hatred of internal and external reality and the belief that the analyst's wish to understand them is tantamount to an attempt to drive them insane or destroy them.

At times, these patients provoke struggles over whether anything can have representational meaning at all. Such patients often fight tirelessly to obstruct understanding of the symbolic meaning of their acts. The analyst must, for long periods of time, be able to tolerate and contain the feelings of hollowness, deadness, and sometimes toxicity that such patients evoke. The task is to establish a consensual space/frame before any other analysis can take place. This space/ frame is achieved slowly and over time by maintaining reliable boundaries and empathic consistency.

For such alienated and distrustful patients, the notion of space as an inviting playground in the presence of the other is utterly incomprehensible. They may compulsively attempt to fill it with activity and things to stave off the terrible void, but their activity has a dead quality. Such patients, as though in a metaphoric parched wasteland, communicate their experience of what we have come to call "deadspace" (Wrye, 1993a).

In their presence, in that deadspace, we may find ourselves stuck with them; we feel dead, our creativity dismantled. In painful "noncontact" with such patients, I (HKW), experiencing such barren transferences, have felt like a broken wagon axle or a pile of bones left on some desert trail.

HELLO THE HOLLOW

The phrase "Hello the Hollow" not only refers to the psychically hollow feelings evoked by T.S. Eliot's "hollow men" but also has personal referents as well. The juxtaposition of "hello" with "hollow" came to me when I recalled a childhood incident that exemplified for me the transformation of fright at facing a "horrible hollow" into a playful experience of safety. It represents a typical childhood transformation of anxious fright into calm and then play. I grew up spending summers with my family in a remote cabin in the mountains. One of my favorite haunts was a huge granite outcropping called Echo Rock where we'd search for Indian arrowheads, grinding holes, and beads. As the youngest, I was sometimes the target of teasing by the older children. I remembered once being taken to the edge of a huge chasm on Echo Rock and shown a cave that my cousins told me was haunted by the ghosts of Indians who had been buried there. A five-year-old, I was suitably terrified of ghosts and afraid of the chasm and ran all the way home. Later, my father accompanied me to the spot and transformed that frightening gorge into a safe place. The huge granite rock had been named because shouting into this chasm produced a magnificent echo, so my father called out "Hello!" It came sonorously back as "hello . . . hello . . . hollow . . . hollow . . . hello!" He made it into a game, and my fear of the ghosts of dead bodies dissipated, to be replaced by play as I joined in the echoing. Thus a frightening deadspace, in the presence of a reliable other, was transformed into a playspace. In analysis, such transformations likewise occur.

FROM DEADSPACE TO PLAYSPACE

If we can recognize and tolerate our own countertransference dread of deanimation, then we can provide in our own waking or dreaming minds an internal space that can contain, detoxify, and hold such fragmented patients. The importance of the analytic time/space/frame to patients and analysts alike in the transformation from deadspace to playspace cannot be overestimated. Analytic empathy and giving words to our patients' spatial experience often bring considerable relief. Interpreting the genesis of paranoid isolation is ultimately critical in facilitating patients' transformation from perverse distancing to a capacity for desire. Premature interpretation, however, is quickly absorbed in the sand of the desert and converted to useless intellectual exercise.

Prior to interpretation is the uninterpreted, nonverbal experience of analytic space in which silence does not signal annihilation or abandonment but slowly becomes tolerable. The analyst's calm survival and containment of psychotic breakthroughs or violent assaults, as with patients like Rosie, Leonard, or Suta sets the stage for interpretive work and the analysis comes to represent a beloved narrative space for creative linking.

Thus, not only can the analysis provide a narrative space/frame, but the analyst functions actively as a kind of holding tank for the patient's projections and as a vehicle for healing and detoxification. The analyst must be able to provide a reliable, noncorrosive container for such patients' fragmented dissociated self-experiences. Over time, and with interpretations and constancy, patients' experiences of a "horrible hollow," or deadspace, can be first neutralized and then transformed into a safe playspace (Sanville, 1991a). The analytic frame thus can be internalized, fostering intrapsychic space for imagination, contact, and creativity.

WET AND DRY SPACE[1]

The transformation of deadspace to playspace can often be experienced in the transference–countertransference atmosphere as a shift

---

[1]See Wrye (1993a) for the development of this concept.

from a quality of dryness or toxicity to a fluidity. The fluids evoked seem to shift from polluted to clean. (Recall from chapter 4 Gillian's initially noxious and then pleasant perfume, and, from chapter 6, the transformation of Suta's experience of having a "smelly vagina" to having a "fragrant portal.") This fluid dimension in the transference has its origins in the phenomena of the early maternal erotic exchanges between mother and baby, often involving fluids—milk, urine, tears. It also relates to the growing child's curious and playful investigations of inside and outside, volumes and spaces, explored through containers: pouring, filling, spilling, emptying.

Wetness and dryness represent a particular sensory dimension of spatial experience. It was through my clinical observations of children engaged in play therapy that I (HKW) first began to think about wetness and dryness as metaphors for issues of separation, individuation, and linking. Children often use water both consciously and unconsciously to represent body fluids which can be sensually enjoyed or experienced as messy or nasty. Through water play, they experiment with boundaries, pouring and spilling fluids, from inside containers to outside. They also play with and explore kinesthetically their subjective experiences of bodily contact through fluids. Playing with water and clay can evoke, for example, the comfort of bathing; a warm, sticky, sensual adhesion; or anxieties of drowning.

Children's—and adults'—pleasure in or distaste for wetness has, I submit, its foundations in early postnatal experiences. The infant, having once been literally encapsulated in mother's womb in amniotic fluid, experiences closeness to mother postnatally through contact with her skin and the variety of body fluids. Through her optimal regulation of wet and dry, mother can create a sensual adhesion in which the infant feels contained. Thus begins the infant's "love affair with the world" (Mahler et al., 1975).

A number of negative scenarios can destroy that love affair. If the contact is intrusive, mother and baby can remain "stuck together" in a wetly suffocating, symbiotic fusion, allowing no space to come between them. Experiences of drowning and psychic annihilation ensue. Or, if a mother regards her infant's fluid productions as hated messes, she may communicate that her baby is toxic and contaminating. Or, if there is excessive maternal absence and unreliable contact, the infant may feel left "high and dry," "lost in space." In either extreme, these scenarios may result in psychosis.

Transferences and countertransferences in analysis are colored by feelings about these primal body fluids and their role as sensual conductors. Although it is beyond the scope of this chapter to explore fully patients' infantile experiences with wetness and dryness, we do posit a "fluid dimension" as a transference paradigm. It is often present and may be helpful to clinicians in accessing primitive areas of preverbal experience. It also provides another avenue of understanding patients' later sexuality in that adult genital sexual contact through seminal and vaginal fluids recreates these earliest sensual erotic connections between mother and infant.

CLINICAL ILLUSTRATIONS

In our experience, transferences and their corresponding countertransferences take on "wetness and dryness" reflecting patients' struggles with issues surrounding separation, intimacy, and contact. We will illustrate with two male patients in various stages of their struggles to move from isolated existence in a psychic deadspace to consensual play in a more sensually alive generative space. Although these two men possessed creative potential and were demonstrably successful in art-related careers, each, at the beginning of treatment, suffered serious disruption in his ability to be creative and playful. Work and relationships were dull, hollow, and unrewarding.

John—The "Straw Man"

John, an engineer-designer in his mid-30s, presented himself for analysis with complaints of feeling "like a straw man, flammable, dry, dead." He felt blocked in his creativity and in his relationships with his boss, wife, and daughters. In my first session with him, I (HKW) experienced him as strikingly disoriented in space, like someone who did not know where solid ground was (which was particularly interesting to me in the light of his work as an engineer-designer). He spoke of having "swept all his feelings under the rug like dust," which matched my impression of barren dryness.

John's early dreams in treatment repeatedly portrayed him as lying on a cliff or a balcony over a bottomless chasm, terrified of falling into the void. He described his childhood pastimes as making tunnels in the tall weeds around his home, "burrowing" as he called it, alone and looking for containment. His "pets" were ants, which he kept in a terrarium; he envied their lives lived completely in tunnels. John's hobby also evokes the earthy underground imagery of the rosebush metaphor from the Introduction. It suggested to me his need to return for transformation to the period before he was born, when he was still "underground." His birth metaphors, if you will, call forth a dangerous yet isolated, dead dryness. His intricate model-building and latency-age drawings frequently included some fortified, cavelike structures. In one frequently drawn fantasy, he depicted himself as a "wolf man," captured by the townspeople and incarcerated in a cave behind thick iron bars to protect the town from his threatened rampages. In these drawings, which he brought to a session, the cave appeared as a black hole.

Analysis revealed that John's mother was apparently depressed and emotionally detached from her baby during his first year owing to the deaths of both her parents during the pregnancy and first year of his infancy. During the first three months of his infancy, and then periodically during his grandmother's terminal illness, infant John was left in the care of a nurse.

The family's constrained emotional style apparently led them to deny their depressive feelings and avoid emotional expression; they preferred to "suffer in silence." This attitude characterized John as well. With his burrowing and fascination with ant tunnels, it was almost as if he longed to return to an intrauterine safe keep; entry into open space left him feeling endangered, isolated, and fragmented. In his treatment, I often felt the impulse to pick him up and soothe him, even to wrap him in blankets and carry him. At other times I would feel awkward, notice my mouth feeling dry, and associate to dusty rocky places. I often had great difficulty feeling connected with him, although he tried in great earnest to "be a good patient."

His use of language was constricted, too. There were awkward, painful pauses as he searched for a word. On occasion, in moments of heightened countertransference, when I felt I could no longer bear his pained loss of access to words, I would supply the obviously missing word. He would sigh in relief as if I had rescued him from the edge of a chasm; such episodes illustrated the use of narrative space as a safekeep in the presence of the beloved other. Over time, when I interpreted my sense that he felt lost in a dry lunar space, he expressed great relief at feeling understood. He volunteered that he was beginning to realize that becoming a designer and an engineer had been his effort to "build a space station" to find containment, shape, and structure for himself, to protect himself "from that graphic feeling that there's a black hole, a void with nothing behind it."

Gradually, over several years of analysis of his unconscious rage at his mother's emotional unavailability and his paralyzed rage at his absent father, John gained greater access to his feelings. He began to relinquish his schizoid isolation and to be present with me in the sessions. He said that he was beginning to experience himself in a different way. He related this change specifically to his growing comfort in the analytic space and room, the time frame, the reliability of our sessions, and his response to my interpretations. He would also describe a sleepy, sensual pleasure at times in response to interpretations. It seemed to him that they felt like a warm "word bath" in which he could be soothed, or a longed-for lullaby, as he moved slowly into contact with loving, tender feelings.

Christina's World

In midanalysis, replacing his initially described experience of living on the edge of a terrifying black hole, John began to describe feeling like the figure in Andrew Wyeth's *Christina's World*. Wyeth's famous painting of a huge grassy knoll leading up to background buildings, with the lone, twisted figure of Christina in the foreground, reminded him of his own long isolated vigils in the fields near his childhood home where he silently watched ant colonies and arranged traps for spiders and snakes, which would become his sole companions. He took comfort in elaborating his evolving analytic experience in terms of Wyeth's visually poignant painting, with its evocative narrative suggestion. He said the painting had always evoked feelings of painful isolation in him, that Christina seemed paralyzed in that huge space. Christina seemed to symbolize his crippled maternal introject, paralyzed in depression, as well as an aspect of his crippled masculinity: perhaps his castration by his tough-minded father.

After visiting a major retrospective exhibition of the work of Andrew Wyeth, John thought considerably about Christina and realized that she was not in fact alone. Wyeth's careful observation of her and his empathy for her must have conveyed to her the experience of being in contact with someone who understood and cared about her. Now, although John had felt alone and crippled since childhood, he talked of his newfound pleasure in experiencing my presence with him. He described me as the artist/observer and likened the consulting room to a sensual grassy playspace. This transformational experience had shifted the dry, isolated ant farm world he had inhabited into a livelier, moister, and more fecund earth; the analysis felt like the sort of soil in which a rosebush could produce roses. He said that he felt (as I did), a new "flow" in the sessions.

From Paralysis to Playspace: Mutative Words

Mutative in the work with John was his experiencing containment in the analytic dyad. In his experience of space he moved from feeling isolated, fragmented, and paralyzed to feeling that space was even a playground. His narrative style changed during the course of this therapy as well. Initially, he used awkward, concrete word bits that came forth arduously from him. Later, he was often fluent: he was even, at times, poetic. Initially, it was my role to narrate his experience as I experienced it with him, but over time he began to be able to take on that function for himself.

It was very meaningful to him that during the session when he had struggled to recall the name of the painting and artist somehow I felt I knew which painting he was thinking of and asked him if he might be thinking of Wyeth's *Christina's World*. (I think my own unconscious access to this piece of information was tapped by my intuition that John was identifying Wyeth with Wrye.) John placed this crippled image of himself within me and hoped for transformation. It was, again, as if I had offered him a drink in the desert; he was so relieved that I knew the painting, that it existed in my inner world as well as in his. He spoke of how it had enabled him to go on and elaborate his own very personal response to this painting.

With patients whose isolation is in these preverbal states, words are sometimes felt to be a kind of warm "word bath." Certain particularly comforting words seem to function in the analytic setting like a transitional object. Words once missing and the found help link inside and outside and bridge the space between patient and analyst.

Dreams

Over time, John's dream imagery changed dramatically from dry to wet and from dreams of deadness and terror of falling into a chasm or a black hole, to dreams about sailing on smooth seas, swimming, and playing in the water. Once he dreamed that he and a psychologist were going to swim to Japan together; then he thought he might be going backpacking in some verdant mountains, which he imagined I would enjoy. In this dream, he stood on a cliff overlooking a valley, which he saw as dry and empty. Since there was no water, he wondered how he could swim to Japan with his companion. Then, to his delight, the valley began to fill up like a sea full of water. I took this imagery to reveal the clear transformation from a dry and barren transference to a wet one; it also suggested his internalization of our contact as blissful and oceanic and carried the literal imagery of the ocean as connecting us. It also evokes the Pacific Ocean, which my office overlooks.

This dream revealed emerging fantasies of playing associated with his analysis, especially swimming in an ocean he imagined full of seaweed and fish and climbing in bosomy mountains rich with life. I felt he was transforming his anal burrows into a holding womb and a birth canal from which he could emerge alive and whole. A proliferation of oedipal sexual fantasies followed in which he replaced my husband as my vacation companion.

As John shifted into a maternal erotic transference and opened the way to later triadic oedipal material, I responded with a countertransference dream in which John showed me his new office, which was light, airy, and cheerful and reminded me of a playroom. I awoke from my own dream feeling surprise at the emergence of sensual feelings, pleasure at the intimations of playful creativity, and anticipated relief from the long period of dryness the dreams signaled.

With analysands like John, reliable, nonintrusive transitional analytic or narrative space, together with interpretations over time, slowly transforms deadspace into playspace and dead internal objects into living ones. The early separation-individuation drama that went awry can be replayed and reworked in the safespace of the analytic setting.

Caleb—"Rattlesnake Man"

Caleb entered analysis complaining of feelings of isolation and despair. Though a highly successful museum curator, he saw himself as a workaholic whose life's work was counting and arranging inanimate objects from the past. He depreciatingly described himself as an "asexual homosexual; a pot-bellied nebbish" who felt "alone and unreal" and who distrusted anyone who wanted to get close. He hated his social isolation and knew that his need to protect his house with chain link fencing and guard dogs was to keep anyone from wanting to make contact with him. He had been referred for an analysis and understood that the extent of his own panic and resistance to it were indications of his terror at allowing anyone near him. Yet as bad as the panic

was, he recognized that it was outweighed by his hatred of his paranoid isolation and his lifelong desire to be able to develop intimate
relationships. He also hoped analysis could free his buried creativity.

Since childhood Caleb had lived in an arid, psychologically deadspace. Over time, his access to vital feelings had been rendered
inert; symbolic, metaphoric thinking was denied and connections
dismantled. Like John, his presence evoked a kind of deadness.
Phrases from Dylan Thomas's (1957a) "Poem on His Birthday" convey
Caleb's barren despair:

> Who slaves to his crouched, eternal end
> Under a serpent cloud. . .
> Thirty-five bells sing struck
> On skull and scar where his loves lie wrecked,
> Steered by the falling stars.
> And to-morrow weeps in a blind cage.

My own (HKW) reactions to Caleb were feelings of alienation
and often boredom from his repetitive droning of the injustices
done to him and of his innocence in creating his dreaded and painful victimization. Working with Caleb became the stimulus for my
colleague's (JKW) thinking about deadspace. (In fact, his issues
were so challenging that clinical illustrations of the work appear
not only in this chapter but also in chapters 8 and 9.) Caleb's apa-
thy, utter social isolation, and lengthy analysis evoked considerable
countertransference in me.

As I attempted to stave off psychic entombment with a deadening
patient through engagement in creative work—to avoid feeling completely "buried alive" by my contact with him—I began to write
about the sessions, and consult with my colleague, and we eventually
began to develop the ideas that became the basis of this chapter.
This defensive maneuver allowed me to continue the work. What
began as a defensive attempt, however, grew into a genuine interest
in and affection for Caleb. In his previous relationships, his deadness
and distancing had always finally driven people away. I think, without knowing specifically about my writing, Caleb did sense and
slowly respond to my interest and unwillingness to be daunted by his
perverse distancing. I also believe that the writing was in part my
unconscious effort to weave for myself a narrative "nest" in which
Caleb could be nurtured, a "potential" space for a maternal erotic
transference and countertransference to unfold.

A Venomous Perversion of Pleasure

Early in treatment, Caleb described an incident from his childhood that excruciatingly conveyed for both of us the paranoid tone of the family culture set by the patriarch, his powerfully sadistic maternal grandfather. When Caleb was five or six years old, his grandfather invited him to go for a Sunday drive in the desert near the family ranch. He said it would be fun. They embarked in grandfather's fancy car and drove for miles in the barren "no man's land" countryside. Finally grandfather stopped the car by the side of the lonely highway and put up the hood as a distress signal for help from passing cars. After a while, a black man stopped to offer assistance. Grandfather, indicating that the tools to change a flat tire were in the trunk, led the man to the trunk and opened it. There was a menacing rattle, and grandfather pulled aside a blanket revealing a coiled rattlesnake in the trunk of the car. The black man was so terrified, he passed out. Little Caleb, who was watching, nearly fainted with fright as well. They recovered to discover grandfather laughing at his success with the tremendous joke he had played.

It turned out that grandfather had stuffed a rattlesnake and rigged it with a motor as a prank. His idea of fun was to find hapless persons he could terrify—typically a grandchild or a Good Samaritan. Sadism was so engrained in the man and his family that each child who was exposed to the trick and was upset by it was teased as being unable to "take one a Grampa's little ole jokes." Complete denial of the sadism was maintained in the family as this joke and many others were repeated as "just a little fun." In fact, when Caleb told me about the incident, it was simply as a story about his grandpa. It took us a long time to bring him back to how he had actually felt as a little boy that day—how terrified he was, and how much he had identified with the kind black man victimized by his grandfather's perverse trick. The incident illuminated, in fact, his preference for black men as lovers.

Caleb recounted many such instances of play perverted into sadism, and he was frequently the brunt of such jokes. Once, playing hide and seek, he climbed into a hassock and pulled the lid down over his head. His father saw this as an opportunity to tease his son and sat on the hassock, trapping the terrified boy in this airless tomb. His screams made his father laugh, and he was released only after minutes had passed and he had become mute in his fright.

Not surprisingly, Caleb was doomed to unconscious repetitions of such sadistic and isolating dramas over and over as an adult and, of course, in the transference. He enacted both parts—sometimes as the generous innocent who reached out to others only to be humiliated, deceived, and taken advantage of; other times as the perpetrator feigning good intent, but shaming and punishing another. He was, of course, consciously aligned with the victim in a dangerous world. It was far more difficult for him to recognize his own sadism.

Rattlesnakes and Paranoid Distancing

I recognized his sadism because I was the frequent recipient of it. I would go out of my way to accommodate his scheduling needs, often inconveniencing myself, only to have him cancel or not show up at the last minute. I would struggle hard to make sense of his deanimated communications and offer interpretations to help shed light on his experience, and he would respond as if my offerings were boring, useless to him, or quickly forgettable. When I tried to call his attention to his behavior as demeaning me, he dismissed me. For a long time, he denied any conscious pleasure in twisting me around in this or countless other ways.

At times I felt either rendered inert, or begged to succor and rescue him, the hapless victim. Early in treatment, he elicited from me the "renaissance" countertransference fantasy described in chapter 4, namely, that I could heal him with my magical breast. When I, however, symbolically offered him my lap or my breast through an empathic interpretation, he would ignore it, push it away, or verbally bite it: he would treat me as the persecutory spider woman who must be warded off. When I remained quiet though attentive, he felt I was uncaring or was silently mocking him; when I interpreted his unconscious assaults, however gently, he felt blamed and persecuted; when I attempted to mirror his positive efforts, he either discounted me as an invalid observer or saw me as the exciting but unavailable seductress. Thus, for weeks, even months at a time in the early years of the analysis, we were deadlocked in a paranoid deadspace.

Poisonous Contact: The Death Knell of Erotic Desire

Outside the analysis, Caleb confirmed his long-held convictions that space was hostile, human contact would always be dangerous, and body fluids were poison. In his rare forays into relationships of either a social or business nature, he unwittingly chose partners who were in fact a threat to him; he picked business partners and lawyers who were predictably self-serving, sociopathic, inept, even criminal. For possible sexual partners, even in a climate in which warnings against the dangers of AIDS were overt, he somehow repeatedly chose men who had the disease. He also chose potential partners who were socially and financially marginal, who were themselves victims of abuse, and who inevitably found ways to punish and humiliate him, even though he was ostensibly offering them help.

Within the analysis, Caleb's use of language was highly concrete and frequently blocked. We explored his flattened, concrete thinking as a way of blocking symbolic and metaphoric thinking and any kind of mental linking, which to him represented alternately terrifying intercourse and persecutory contact.

The Burning Casket

In a classic "deadlock" dream (Welles, 1989), Caleb pictured himself as a monk meditating for a year in a closed coffin. At the end of the year, he set fire to himself, refusing to scream or move until the fire had consumed him and he was dead. It was a chilling dream revealing that the internal object he felt locked into was so toxic that he felt he had to be either dead or psychotic, but he could not join the world of human relationships.

This portentous dream was so disturbing to hear that it gave further impetus and then clarity to my own thinking about the phenomenon of deadspace. In Guntrip's (1969) sense, he deadened his object world in a schizoid way to avoid the terror of aliveness, with all its intensity, passion, persecutory anxiety, and pain. In Shengold's (1985, 1988) sense, he used anal narcissistic defenses to destroy vitality and deny longing. Rereading Guntrip's and Shengold's clinical narratives freed me from my own countertransferential deadlocked swings between the impulse to offer him the magically healing breast and the impulse to shut him out owing to my own frustrated feelings of deadness and despair. They helped me to get back on track, so to speak, to maintain the analytic space with more neutral reliability, to interpret his need to keep us both dead, and to function for him as a detoxifying container.

Enlivening the Deadspace and Creating a Therapeutic Encounter

Pivotal in our work was the effort to create a stable analytic frame and a reliable transitional space. As proposed at the outset of this chapter, patients who experience themselves in a deadspace, have never experienced empathic containment and safety. Each time I went away, Caleb reacted to the disruption with feelings of heightened frustration and stalemate on my return, and it took considerable time to reestablish a connection. He tried for a long time to attack the frame by missing or wanting to move appointments and refusing to pay. At the outset, I understood this behavior as a compulsion to repeat the countless disappointments and humiliations he had experienced in a family in which empathy seemed to be unknown. As our analytic relationship deepened, however, I began to interpret these behaviors as revealing his rage at the spaces between us, the boundaries, rules, and everything else that reminded him of our separateness and his lack of control over me.

Caleb began to take in this interpretive theme and make some significant moves in his analysis. Prior to one of my vacations, he acknowledged that he experienced contact with me differently from anyone else he had ever been involved with. He recognized that his encounters had always had a suspicious and perverse quality in which his unconscious intent was either masochistically to suffer or sadistically to humiliate and victimize someone else. He also realized that he had always felt deadened, that his encounters with his parents, grandparents, siblings, and associates were flattening, deanimating, and destructive, so he kept himself inert to avoid future pain and disappointment.

He finally took steps to end a long-time partnership that had increasingly become a great personal financial drain. He had remained immobilized and deadlocked because the business partner, in addition to not serving Caleb's financial interests, also had AIDS. Caleb imagined it was his own toxic hatred that had poisoned his partner. He realized, though, that as long as he stayed in this type of relationship, there was no possibility for him to experience genuine intimacy.

After our first session following my return from vacation, I had a countertransference dream. In working with such patients, who struggle so against linking and communication, I find myself working overtime in a way. I have felt at times that I was dreaming for both of us, as such patients sometimes seem unable to make or hold on to a dream and yet may be on the verge of doing so. Perhaps the fact that the analyst may find herself dreaming for both is a variation of the renaissance countertransference fantasy of healing with a magical breast, described in chapter 4. In this case the body part offered is not the breast, but the sleeping brain. My dreaming may also reflect a response to the patient's unconsciously communicated long-ing to be picked up and held as I had similarly felt pulled to do with John when I offered him the name of Wyeth's painting.

In this countertransference dream, my own mother, who had been dead for nearly a decade, was alive again. Delighted and amazed, I found that in the dream I could ask her questions about what it felt like to return to the land of the living. When I awoke, I recognized my eternal wish that my mother's sudden death could be undone, but I also immediately associated to Caleb, who, I felt, had been living in a coffined world of dead objects. I felt my dream was my counter-transferential hope that he was on the verge of awakening to a living and nurturing relationship with me.

In subsequent sessions, Caleb defended against emerging excite-ment. I suspected that he reacted against the new pleasure he was feeling about his sessions because of his unconscious fear of stirrings of erotic feelings. Now he attempted to render me and our relation-ship inert because he was starting to awaken to life and to loving contact and was naturally afraid of experiencing humiliation, frustra-tion, and loneliness. This defensive effort to remain in deadspace was revealed in a dream in which he caused his partner's death by suffocation in a desert sandstorm. At the same time, he rushed to sessions eagerly and even requested a double session so we would have more time. He, like John, began to speak of a feeling of "flow" between us. When I told him that it felt that a nourishing rain had finally come to replenish the dry desert where he had lived since childhood, for the first time in his analysis he became tearful. He told me he felt the deadening drought might end.

For Caleb, space had, indeed, felt like a rattlesnake-infested desert of paranoid anxiety and isolation. An image came to mind. I imagined him at the beginning of analysis as a thirsty infant clinging to a breast with an inverted nipple, a dry hole, rather than a breast that could feed him. He had approached any contact afraid that if milk began to flow, it would poison him, like the body fluids of AIDS contact, so he had refused either to suckle or to let go. Thus a dead-lock was created. Caleb could move out of the deadspace he had been inhabiting and release himself from this deadly object tie only over time and in a safe, nonintrusive analytic frame. For him, the analytic space came to represent the holding lap he had lacked with his anxious, intimidated, and paranoid mother. In this space he could detoxify his own paranoid projections of hatred toward his mother for betraying him by giving birth to a little brother when he was four, an event for which he had complete amnesia until after several years of analysis (see chapter 8). The rules and boundaries of the analytic frame represented the reliability and strength he wished he had felt with his father and grandfather.

SPATIAL RELATIONS

We believe narrative themes of space to be central to the separation-individuation process in normal and abnormal development. Normal healthy conditions during infancy lead to the internalization of a felicitous space between mother and child and within the child that fosters the emergence of imagination and symbolization.

Many seriously disturbed patients like John and Caleb, however, experienced space as if they were in the vortex of a black hole. Winnicott (1956), describing every infant's need for a holding environment, termed its lack

> impingement, reflecting a pattern of persistent empathic failure which interrupts the "going on being" of the infant. An excess . . . produces not frustration but a threat of annihilation. . . . a primitive anxiety, long antedating any anxiety that includes the word death in its description. (p. 303)

Patients who have experienced such inappropriate contact are unable internally to hold on to needed soothing and containing figures and lack a reliable sense of themselves as separate, sentient beings. Without the experience of safety or bodily integrity, they feel, instead, like bits and pieces of self dispersed in an annihilating void. Separateness is intolerable and must be denied to the point that others are kept flattened or at a great distance. Such people exist, instead, "high and dry," "lost in space." This makes psychological linking impossible because it signifies either dreaded persecutory attack, suffocating contact, or both.

When such patients finally internalize the safe space of analytic empathy, they begin to deal with separation issues. They become vulnerable to the pain of separation and aware of their desire for the presence of the missing loved one. This desire ushers in the capacity for mental imagery and the ability to co-author a new narrative of desire. Imagination and symbolization appear on the analytic horizon, as the accompaniments of desire for physical, sensual contact with the body of the longed-for mother. As the patient experiences consciousness of this bodily desire, however, he becomes frighteningly vulnerable. It is as if the specter of the "voluptuous" body of the analyst/mother may appear, bringing with it the attendant terror of being in the wilderness alone and being greeted by a frighteningly warm-blooded, lactating Brontosaurus. In chapter 8, we elaborate on the powerful specter of the early primitive mother and her ability to elicit erotic terror: in chapters 9 and 10 we discuss the crucial role of both the preoedipal and the oedipal father in the narration of desire.

IV
*Permutations
and Transformations
Related to Gender*

8

Erotic Terror in Men

Fear of the Early Maternal Erotic Transference

> Terror emanates from Medusa's head . . . the hairy maternal vulva
> seen by the son. The cut-off head itself stands for castration; the snaky
> hair both terrifying—as snakes, and reassuring—as so many penises;
> the petrifying effect: both death and erection. Athena, bearing this
> symbol . . . fends off all sexual lust. (Lederer, 1968, p. 3)

In Section III, we looked at "derangements of desire," psychically
crippling perverse internal arrangements that block many patient's
pathways to experiencing mutuality, intimacy, and healthy passion.
Such interferences as deadlocks, deadspace, paranoia, and perverse
distancing must be experienced, understood, and worked through by
both analyst and patient if they are to create the climate of safety and
playspace that we call narrative space, which is essential for transformation. We have also spoken of how therapeutically critical shared
story-making in this narrative space is to creating the conditions for
healthy desire, intimacy, and love.

Now we turn to a new defensive roadblock that arises to meet the
dangers of emerging intimacy. Here we address the primal panic in
the face of early erotic transferences, first mentioned in chapter 6 in
relation to Leonard and Suta, that we call erotic terror (Wrye, 1993b).
Surely not only patients but also some therapists struggle to avoid
encountering it. Nonetheless, intense and problematic transferences,
recognized, tolerated, and understood, can be properly interpreted
and worked through to provide access to the only true intimacy many
very seriously disturbed patients have ever experienced.

While preoedipal regression stirs degrees of anxiety in all men
(Tyson, 1982), the primal fear of intimacy experienced by many seriously disturbed patients, including schizoid men and women with

157

psychotic features, may provoke the terror of psychic annihilation. In this chapter, we illuminate the nature and implications of this erotic terror for male patients and their analysts as they encounter the primitive feeling states associated with early maternal erotic transferences and countertransferences.

As we indicated earlier, the possibility of experiencing the intense anxiety of erotic terror is in itself a developmental and treatment milestone for such patients who suffer from profound early ego faults. For those who have lived in the deadspace of an objectless, abject "horrible hollow," the entry of a passionate other into the landscape is indeed a move forward, but it often is accompanied by panic. In our first clinical example, we present a neurotic male's typically muted entry into shifting preoedipal and oedipal maternal erotic transferences. In the second example, to illustrate true erotic terror in a more disturbed male analysand, we return to the case of Caleb, introduced in chapter 7.

MASCULINITY AND EROTIC TRANSFERENCE AND COUNTERTRANSFERENCE

Returning to themes first elaborated in chapter 4 on gender and countertransference, we now develop them further and specifically in relation to male issues. Kumin (1985), whose phrase "erotic horror" we have found so useful, refers to the natural resistance to experiencing the inevitable shame and humiliation that is rekindled in an erotic transference. No patient wants to reexperience the horror of being the small, inadequate loser in the contest to dispossess the same sex-parent and enjoy exclusive sexual union with the opposite-sex parent. The term, referring to the horror of discovering one's separateness and exposing one's vulnerability to romantic humiliation, is a very useful, clinically sensitive one. Equating erotic with sexualized transference, Kumin focuses on both the intensely negative aspects of these transferences and the need of the analyst to refrain from erotic desire for the patient who desires him:

> The emotions experienced during a sexualized transference are, though genital, hardly pleasurable. The phrase *erotic horror* describes something of what most patients find the experience to be like. . . .
> (1) in direct proportion to the intensity of its need, the erotic transference is a form of negative transference deriving from past object relationships with exciting but frustrating objects;
> (2) genetically, erotic transferences can be related not only to the oedipal phase but also to preoedipal phases of development, can refer

to actual or fantasied seductions by either or both parents, and can involve both sexual and aggressive drives;

(3) the patient can also be an exciting but frustrating object to the analyst, evoking inevitable countertransference feelings in the analyst pertaining to both contemporary and past objects;

(4) the factor that most limits the elucidation of the patient's erotic transference is not the desire of the patient, but the desire of the analyst; and

(5) only the correct interpretation, whether spoken or silently understood, mitigates the frustrated desire and resistance of both patient and analyst. (p. 3)

Interested in working within the broadest spectrum of erotic phenomena, we posit that in the *pre*oedipal transference–countertransference situation, the countertransference problem is most likely one of inhibition, fear of "erotic horror" and fear of, as one supervisee expressed it, "messing around with cloacal mud babies." Involvement in preoedipal erotic experience is not about genital sexual intercourse: it is far more diffusely polymorphous and relates more to fantasies about feeding, bathing, diapering, and the like than to any focused genital activity. The most frequent danger to analyst and patient alike is that they may fail to recognize early erotism. Without recoiling in anxiety, the analyst must be able to permit herself to experience an array of primitive-sensual body states engendered by the patient. Analysts must be able to tolerate the anxiety that primitive erotic feelings will flood them, pull them away from a preferred analytic composure, and erode professional boundaries; male analysts must deal with fear of loss of masculinity. Surely, when the pathology is severe and self–other differentiation is not well established, the threat of regression into the mother's body stirs sheer terror and annihilation anxiety on both sides of the analytic couch.

A TYPICAL BOY'S DEVELOPMENTAL DILEMMA

Male Development and Psychosomatic Integration

A boy's entry into the oedipal conflict is fraught with danger (Ogden, 1989). He is alone with his

preoedipal mother as a primitive, omnipotent, partially differentiated object by whom he has been mesmerized and penetrated, whom he has ruthlessly used and omnipotently destroyed and recreated

(Winnicott, 1952, 1956, 1971). She also has the glow of warmth and safety that makes him "dissolve" in a way that is both blissful and terrifying at the same time, since this "dissolution" causes him to begin to lose touch with his accruing knowledge of where he stops and where she begins. (p. 148)

Liebert (1986) studying the history of male homosexuality from ancient Greece through the Renaissance, notes the

> struggle men wage their entire lives to resist the . . . yearnings for reunion with mothers and their female surrogates. To yield . . . is to invite dissolution of the sustaining integrated structures of thought, affect, and defensive organization that form the stable sense of self . . . to risk . . . primordial anxiety. (p. 205)

EARLY EMERGENCE OF SEXUAL-EROTIC FEELINGS

Freud (1933), writing of the origins of erotic feeling, stated, "the mother . . . by her activities over the child's body hygiene inevitably stimulated, and perhaps even roused for the first time pleasurable sensations in her genitals" (p. 20). Similarly, Lichtenstein (1961) wrote of "an innate body responsiveness . . . a specific kind of somatic excitation which . . . has no direction . . . [but] we may call sexual because it forms the matrix of later sexual development" (p. 280), and Kris (1951) speaking of the forerunners of genital sexuality, wrote of the "transfer from general affection to the genital zone itself . . . as a consequence of general body closeness" (p. 96).

The oceanic experience (Werman, 1986), which Federn (1952) described in ego-psychological terms, represents a breakdown of the outer ego boundary, giving rise to feelings of derealization, estrangement, and depersonalization. McDougall (1989) writing of the same phenomenon from the point of view of object relations theory, describes the earliest mother–baby body boundary diffusion, which has particular relevance for the genesis of "erotic terror" in adult male patients:

> I came to realize that, since the infant has intense somatic experiences in the earliest months of life, that is, long before it has any clear representation of its *body image*, it can only experience its own body and the mother's body as an indivisible unit. Although infants seek interchange with their mothers and early develop their own ways of relating . . . they do not make well-defined self–object distinctions . . .

When an adult unconsciously represents his/her body limits as ill-defined or unseparated from others . . . [it] may result in *psychosomatic explosion* as though in these circumstances there existed only one body for two people. (p. 10; second italics added)

McDougall describes the "psychosomatic explosion" that occurs when one body is perceived to be shared by two. This phrase offers a vivid clue to the origins of patients' avoidance of regressive erotic fusion for fear of psychic annihilation. Adult regression into the maternal erotic transference potentially gives rise to blissful reverie and creativity, but also to panic states. To offset this terror, a male patient must be able to find in his analyst of either gender both the phallic father who maintains strong boundaries and the "father-in-mother" who will protect him from dissolution.

Fogel, Lane, and Liebert (1986) suggest that adult men in analysis must contend with three complex, overlapping "problem areas": the first, which stems from the man's earliest relations with his mother, is his relation to the woman within, his own femininity, bisexuality, or androgyny; the second relates to his relationship with the archaic components of his psychosexuality and his need to be liberated from the dread of his preoedipality and narcissism; the third area unique to men relates to their need to find the archaic father of childhood, in order to "encounter the masculine" (pp. 11-12).

Schafer (1986) writes of common phenomena in male transferences of men with relatively firm ego integration, in which the same anxieties, albeit more contained and muted, appear:

Very often, men imagine sentimentality to be a shift of functioning in the direction of being a baby. As a baby, one is vulnerable to merging melting mindlessly into symbols such as the home or the flag. In this context, sentimentality means being passive, helpless, yielding, or surrendering. These men fear that they will lose touch with reality and expose themselves in naked emotionality to derision and abandonment . . . The orality of this regressive move is suggested by the common link between sentimentality and being a sucker and swallowing things whole, or in other words, lacking refined taste. p. (102)

Cooper (1986), arguing that uncovering castration anxiety in analysis reveals it to be a facade—an attempt to escape from active preoedipal fears—posits that the loss of the penis is still only a loss of a part, mild compared with total annihilation. He cites Bergler (1952), who enumerated a septet of baby fears—the fear of starvation, of being poisoned, of being choked, of being chopped to pieces, of being drained, of being trampled, and, finally, of castration. He sees these fears as arising out of the male patient's narcissistic need to attribute to the fantasied malevolence of the mother the injuries sustained as a result of the discrepancies between his infantile omnipotent fantasies and his passive reality, for example, his small size, and dependency on his overpowering mother.

We contend that the maternal erotic transference is frightening to male and female patients alike insofar as it threatens to suck them back into the intense body feelings toward the early mother and is thus a threat to separateness. Because girls' core gender identity, however, is not threatened by merger with the maternal body, they seldom exhibit the degree of erotic terror seen in males. Merger fantasies tend to evoke neurotic female patients' anxiety about loss of separateness and autonomy; whenever the mother–daughter bond is psychotically tinged, however, as in the cases of Suta and Rosie, for example, merger fantasies elicit annihilation anxiety.

For all males, the specter of regressive merger with an undifferentiated female other threatens core masculine gender identity in that it is equated with the loss of the penis in the female's engulfing body. Further, for those males whose core gender identity is already shaky, whose infantile experiences have led them to the "horrible hollow" of deadspace, the preoedipal maternal erotic transference threatens their schizoid isolation, their very identity and does evoke terror, as will be demonstrated in clinical material to follow.

CLINICAL ILLUSTRATIONS

Michael, Who Managed the MET

The following vignette, describing a comparatively well-functioning neurotic patient, illustrates a typically muted struggle around issues of early maternal erotic transference. Here, in contrast to the clinical material that follows from a more deeply disturbed patient, we see little evidence of the primal annihilation anxiety that characterizes males who exist in the "horrible hollow." In more seriously disturbed male patients, the maternal erotic transference can evoke terror because the ego is weak and core gender identity is often felt to be at stake.

The session described here was the fourth and final one of the week. As will be seen, Michael underwent analysis in his early 20s. His core gender identity was relatively secure, although he worried about being a "wimp." Sometimes, when he approached feelings associated with the early MET, he sought refuge in positive oedipal strivings or in the negative oedipal, passive, homosexual position. In the latter case he feared, yet sometimes seemed to invite me to be, the sadistically penetrating father who was going to "gun me down." I (HKW) experienced this impulse in the countertransference particularly on occasions when I felt he would become exaggeratedly obsessional and invite me to "cut through the bullshit" and set him straight with some pithy interpretation. He often moved from this position to positive oedipal stirrings toward the seductive mother.

Michael approached feelings about the separation from me in a way that illustrates three shifting transference paradigms: the maternal preoedipal, the paternal oedipal, and the maternal oedipal. Uncomfortable though he clearly was, this man's ego boundaries and reality testing remained intact. He was able to "play" with the possibility of experiencing me in all these roles, two of which are maternal erotic transferences.

During this session, Michael had been talking about his fear of being rejected for a job. From here, he associated to making himself vulnerable to powerful men and to a recent dream in which he was facing a "gunslinger's shoot-out." This association evoked memories of himself in high school, waiting to hear from the only college he had applied to. He acknowledged that he would approach opportunities for rivalry cautiously and typically retreat to a passive role. Recognizing that the prospect of "putting myself out there" (in rivalrous competition) was worse than withdrawal, he retreated to self-effacement, saying, "I didn't have enough going for me. Somehow, it may be I'm feeling it's Friday." After a moment's silence, he said, "It was going through my mind . . . maybe coming for a fifth session on Mondays . . . not wanting to have that feeling of being turned away for a long time, being asked to leave, being told good-bye."

Here I sensed that, intimidated by the prospect of oedipal rivalry with male competitors for a promotion, he was taking refuge first in self-denigration and then by regressing to a preoedipal maternal transference, which was signaled by his not wanting the session to end and wanting more time, in this case, a fifth session. I suspected that pattern stemmed from his often-described intimidated and humiliated retreats from rivalry with his father, and his returns to the fantasy of solace at the breast. Fantasied fulfillment at my breast, reflected by his wish for a fifth session, was frustrated following his thoughts of the pain of the impending weekend separation and associations to his sense of his mother's anxiety feeding him and her reports of pressing him to hurry with his bottle. The latter material had come up on several occasions following discussions with his mother about his early feeding history. With these formulations in mind, I interpreted, "Talking about the job application today leaves you feeling intimidated, shut out, vulnerable to the gunman. Perhaps I'll be the father shooting you down, getting rid of you. You would like to find solace in me as mother, but, as you anticipate the end of our session, perhaps you fear I will push you away. Then it may feel like I will be the mother who doesn't have time to feed you or hold you for however long you want me to."

Michael added "Yeah, right. I hate the session to end. I just want you to hold me, no words, you know, just humming, like we've talked about before. There's a third one. That's you as the attractive woman who I'm afraid even to look at. All three feelings are very powerful right now, and in the face of them, I don't feel very powerful at all! . . . "

Illustrated here are the typical oscillating paternal/maternal oedipal and preoedipal erotic transferences that characterize the relatively intact male patients in analysis with female analysts. In this case, even in the presence of neurotic anxiety, the patient approached the early maternal erotic transference without evidence of the pervasive annihilation anxiety and threats to core gender identity that characterize the case that follows.

Erotic Terror—"The Decapitated Kittens"

With this illustration we return to Caleb, this time in the sixth year of the completed lengthy analysis referred to in chapter 7. He was the male homosexual whose schizoid isolation and barren transference to me (HKW) had prompted us to develop the notions of dry space and wet space. I experienced his transferences to me as alternately "crackling" with rage and sadomasochism and perversely dissociated and distant. Typical of patients who exist in a kind of schizoid/compulsive deadspace, for years he could not tolerate experiencing me as a sensually alive woman and kept me as dismantled part object, another expensive artifact in his museum collection. Here we present material from considerably later in his analysis. This material reveals an emerging erotic transference marked by imagery of erotic terror.

The material occurred during one intense analytic week, after a lengthy period of addressing his need to portray both his mother and me as disabling bitches. This narrative was a defensive strategy to avoid the possibility of any sensual longings and to protect his total blocking of memories and feelings about his younger brother's birth when he was four. When he began treatment, his then aged mother had been institutionalized for what I inferred was a longstanding psychotic depression. The only memories of her he reported were of her harangues and complaints about him, and the few dream images about her seemed to portray his repulsion at her empty and smelly insides depicted by abandoned factories acrid with sulfurous smoke and the like. He had literally no conscious memories before age five, when he was able to recall a few incidents such as the rattlesnake joke with his grandfather and the hide-and-seek in the hassock with his father reported in chapter 7. His narrative was devoid of any intimation that a brother, his only sibling, had been born when he was four.

A selection from Dylan Thomas's (1957b) poem "Twenty-four Years" powerfully conveys Caleb's sensually deadened, perverse world through the feelings expressed by a young man. Thomas's poetic image of a crouching tailor sewing his own shroud powerfully evokes Caleb's erotic terror.

> (Bury the dead for fear that they walk to the grave in labour.)
> In the groin of the natural doorway, I crouched like a tailor
> Sewing a shroud for a journey
> By the light of the meat-eating sun.
> Dressed to die, the sensual strut begun,
> With my red veins full of money,
> In the final direction of the elementary town

Thomas's phrase "in the *groin* of the *natural doorway,* I *crouched*" suggests feelings of being trapped in a woman's pelvis or stuck in the birth canal—waiting to be born dead. The sun, like loving and devoted mothering, could bring warmth to this horrific vision, but this sun is "meat-eating," an image that evoked for me a son's paranoid fear of his mother's oral aggression. If the imagery of the poem gives you a kind of crawling feeling, then you have a sense of what it felt like, for years, for me to be with this patient.

In this unrelentingly deadened atmosphere, working with Caleb became the stimulus for thinking about erotic terror. Although he did not recall any memories of closeness to his mother or any feelings of warmth toward her body, I knew there had to have been some or he would have been psychotic, which he was not. In fact, though I saw him as having a severe schizoid character disorder with obsessional features, I believed that there *must* have been some very early closeness, perhaps even enmeshment, with his mother, that had ended traumatically for him and been repressed. I suspected that the birth of his brother when he was four might have been the traumatic disruption between him and his mother. Total amnesia of incidents prior to age five is unusual; something had felt like such a rejection that he had repressed all memory. I surmised that the loss of closeness with his mother, there being no one else available to him, must have felt so painful that he had ultimately internalized a view of himself as bad and of his mother as the bad, frustrating, and disappointing object of his hatred. This would perhaps explain his homosexual orientation and distrust of all women.

On this day, when I interpreted, as I had on many occasions, his denied yearning for the earliest time of sensual holding in his mother's arms when he had her all to himself, he stunned me with an entirely new reply: "Maybe it was she who gave me my creativity, but I never felt really held, like the object of her sustained attention. I did feel that with you. You've been holding me for a long time, even though I fight you."

As I had not mentioned his birth, I asked him if he could say more of what he had heard and felt: "Well, your talking about my longing for holding made me think of the erotic experience of one's whole body being enveloped in birth . . . and coming out and how that could have felt. . . sliding down that channel from the womb. . . and it being wet and warm and anticipatory, being so closely enveloped in living tissue."

I was struck by the powerful contrast between his typically dry, distant droning and this poetically evocative, sensually rich language and commented on that. It did not feel like the "literary" construction it may sound like as I report it—he was telling me something remarkably full of feeling. He said:

> Maybe that is what I did feel, and haven't wanted to know I felt . . . maybe after that I felt dropped when my brother was born, maybe I was so enraged, I wouldn't let anybody come near me, or let myself remember those feelings.
>
> I was thinking of that isolated landscape where I grew up . . . the prairie . . . the dust. Once we were driving in the car somewhere, and I was playing with my mother's scarf. I opened the window and it blew away into this barren desert. I don't know how I'd put myself into

something like that, but you know, I've told you how at different times I'd really be a rock, or part of the tire on the road. I guess I projected myself into that scarf, blowing alone in the desert, all unprotected and lost. . . . I have an impulse to give you a scarf as a gift . . . to hold me, to wear sometimes . . . my mother loved textiles and fabrics . . . maybe that's why I collect textiles.

As Caleb was speaking, I felt as if a dam had burst. He was languishing in the imagery of a slippery, sensual birth and in associations to his mother's scarf, then feeling lost, as he knew he had lost access to her containing womb. In this association he was reconnecting, through me, to the sensual side of her, which he had phobically denied for so long.

As the early maternal erotic transference unfolded in a series of shifting associations, he brought up material that was new after several years of analysis; and he revisited old memories linking his love for and identification with his mother's creativity, his rage at her unmindfulness of him, and his feeling of being the outcast due to his father's passivity and his grandfather's sadism.

We were banished by my grandfather. I remember moving from town to the ranch . . . sitting in the living room . . . you could hear the wind whistling into the windows . . . a bare bright light, gritty. It felt so despairingly bleak that it was almost romantic, but bald, unprotected. That's the house I used to sleepwalk in when I was 10 or 11. . . . It had ugly green linoleum . . . my mother dripped paint all over it— yellow, white, blue—to make it more alive. It was years later that I got to know Jackson Pollock's art, and I thought of my mother. It was all so conflicted.

I had a thing about claustrophobia tied to that house. But, I'd crawl under that house . . . a mother cat had had her kittens there. You had to crawl through the concrete footings, and then into this hole, this darker part; I crawled in with a flashlight and finally found the mother cat and kittens. There were these salamanders. It was icky . . . I found the kittens and their heads had been bitten off . . . I felt suffocatingly trapped . . . I couldn't get out of there fast enough—it felt like I was sinking into the earth, trapped. Later, I found out the tomcat did it . . . they do it if the kittens are left unprotected.

The Juxtaposition of Imagery of Birth: Sensual and Horrific

What was powerfully striking in that intense week of analytic work evoking the two juxtaposed images of birth is that, as the maternal erotic transference (the "wet, warm" vaginal birth) emerged after having been warded off for over six years of analysis, it was immediately coupled with a perverse fecal birth image (the decapitated kittens first mentioned in chapter 5), evoking erotic terror reminiscent of the cases of aborted desire and the male child's terror of predatory males. Caleb moved rapidly from a warded-off fantasy of the sensual pleasure and containment of birth out of a woman's vagina to an image of horror, of cloacal birth, of destroyed anal babies suggested by the decapitation of the kittens in the "icky" dark and dirty hole of the birth setting. The latter image was not new to the analysis. In fact, it had been a talisman for his counterphobic horror about contact with women's dark, smelly bodies; his rage at his mother for not protecting him; and his rage at his father for passively not protecting him against the sadism of his grandfather, the "rattlesnake man."

Significantly, father, like grandfather, was named Tomás. But Caleb's associations to Tomás the father were of an Uncle Tom to grandfather and of a Peeping Tom, as a model for his own isolated voyeurism as a museum curator of objects of other people's creativity. Grandfather was the executioner/castrator, the tomcat who terrorized everyone. And mother, fawning before her powerful father, never rose up to "protect her kittens." Although this screen memory certainly contained oedipal determinants in Caleb's fear of the tomcat's capacity for destructive attack on the "oedipal rival" babies, it also seemed to overlay his more primal rage at the father and grandfather for destroying the mother(cat)–baby(kitten) fusion. Similarly, Caleb felt that the family's "banishment" by grandfather from the Eden of the farm was, more poignantly, a destructive assault on Caleb's loving closeness to his maternal grandmother and the cornucopia of her garden:

> It felt like banishment. I hated that barren place—a square mile of a monotonous, barren trap . . . how could my father do that . . . driving up and down rows in the tractor. I'd hoe cotton up and down the rows, praying for rain so I could stop. It was used as a form of punishment. "Get out there and help your father, you lazy thing!" But really, my whole family felt banished by my grandfather's rage. He banished us all from his beautiful farm. It had willows to climb. All our meals my grandmother fixed from the garden—black-eyed peas, corn, okra, watermelon, squash, all from the garden. A cornucopia . . . with giant glasses of iced tea.

Caleb could approach the early maternal erotic transference only late in his analysis because erotic horror had been so much in the ascendancy; his fears of his symbiotic longings and of psychic annihilation threatened his very identity.

This material came up only when Caleb was able to find in his father some backbone that he had never recognized before. The material vividly illustrates the crucial role of father in offsetting this type of maternal erotic terror. Caleb finally realized that the "banishment" from his grandfather's "horn of plenty" (his hostilely guarded wealth) had occurred because his father had finally stood up to his father-in-law and said, "to Hell with you." It also represented the first self-respecting stand his father had ever taken. Through analytic reconstruction, Caleb was able to alter his long-held conviction that his father was a "wimp." Caleb was thus provided with a paternal phallus in his father and also came to a belated appreciation of my role as the father/analyst who had protected the analytic frame from his repeated assaults. He was enabled to tolerate emerging preoedipal erotic feelings for me and recognized that his mother's envied sister and her husband, remaining on the "farm of plenty," continued to grovel in impotent obeisance to grandfather.

Caleb's move from schizoid isolation in a horrible hollow to feelings of flow, erotic pleasure, and creative playfulness was marked by the emergence of more poetic imagery in his speech and a shift from barren dryness to imagery of fluids. He reported a dream of a waterfall springing forth in a desert and another dream of rusty pipes in an old house being repaired and returned to flow. He spoke of new creativity and risk-taking in his work.

His sexuality remained "on hold" as he felt committed to seeing his partner through his terminal phase, but he also realized that when he was sprung from that deadlock, he had a host of new issues to address regarding his choice of an asexual relationship with a dying partner and his homosexual choice.

AVERTING TREATMENT FAILURES THROUGH DIRECT ENCOUNTERS WITH EROTIC TERROR

Unconscious terror, based on fear of murderous rage, annihilation anxiety, and erotic timidity, impedes the recognition of erotic resonance in the treatment. Unanalyzed, it can result in treatment stalemates and reify internal object relations deadlocks and result in either prematurely terminated or interminable analyses.

Such severely pathological object relations states originate developmentally with early inappropriate contact or with the mother's excessive maternal absence, suffocating overinvolvement, unreliability, or cruelty. Typical of patients with severe early pathology is a history of maternal impingement or absence, a lack of appropriate, good-enough holding and mirroring. This pattern seriously impedes ego development and undermines the development of a secure gender identity. It interferes with the child's ability to identify with the positive aspects of the mother's leaving; instead the child identifies with the self-hating aspects of the mother and internalizes the mother's body as a bad object. The father's absence, emotional unavailability, and negativity forecloses the remaining avenue to positive gender identification. Paternal deficiency prevents the positive consolidation of daughters' femininity and robs sons of a positive model for male identification and self-esteem.

When patients' core gender identity has thus been so assaulted and the ego so faulted, they approach the early maternal erotic transference not with the anxiety most patients feel, but with terror. This erotic terror can take on psychotic proportions, because reexperiencing the feelings of body contact with the early mother in the transference threatens completely to overwhelm and dissolve the fragile self.

To protect themselves from psychotic fragmentation, these patients cannot really participate in the therapeutic relationship. Sometimes for long, deadening periods of time, they avoid any lively and meaningful contact with the analyst, who represents a threat to the survival of the internal bad object and to their shaky cohesion.

When such patients finally internalize the safespace of analytic empathy, longing for closeness, they become incredibly vulnerable to the pain of separation and aware of their desire for the presence of the loved one. Once, however, they experience any consciousness of body desire, they become frighteningly vulnerable. Who wouldn't retreat?!

Only the reliability and containment of the analytic space/frame and correct interpretation, both spoken and silently understood, ameliorate the frustrated desire and resistance of patient and analyst. Male patients are particularly threatened by the primal, inchoate feelings and regressive pulls accompanying the maternal erotic transference; symbiosis and early mother–baby boundary diffusion threaten core gender identity. The analyst must avoid the countertransference pull to distance from these feelings, or, so to speak, to "fill the room with, or rid it of, testosterone." (Attunement to the need for accompanying paternal transferences to defuse this panic is discussed in chapter 9.)

Transformations particularly accompany interpretations of the dreaded black hole and its origins and the fear of psychic annihilation due to loss of boundaries and internal impulse detonations and self-immolation (typically revealed by Caleb's recurring dreams of burning himself to death in a coffin).

Such transformations, sometimes marked by shifts from imagery of barren dryness and toxicity to imagery of moisture and flow were revealed in Caleb's "slippery vaginal birth" imagery. In this sense, then, feelings about primal body fluids and their role as sensual conductors between mother and infant color maternal erotic transferences and countertransferences. Analysts' and patients' fantasies—repressed to a greater or lesser extent—about the fetus enveloped in the body fluids of the mother and the vast preoccupation of mother and child with body fluids (urine, milk, feces, mucus, saliva) during the first year or two of a child's life—can be accessed. The flow of words and the evocation of feelings between male patient and the maternal aspect of his male or female analyst can create the associative transference and countertransference link to such early maternal care. The analyst's acceptance and tolerance of the patient's preoedipal fantasies is the matrix for consolidation of self and the advancement toward an oedipal transference.

9

Where's Poppa?

The Appearance of Paternal Transferences in the Face of Early Maternal Transferences

At times, in dreams occurring in the course of analysis, patients report the presence of a strange man or some unknown figure that stands for the primordial perception of the second object which must have been very disconcerting to the baby. (Gaddini, 1977, cited in Limentani, 1991, p. 583)

The presence of the preoedipal father provides a developmentally essential "otherness" and aids in the differentiation of the infant from its early mother, diffusing the intensity of the early erotic bond. Regardless of the analyst's gender, if and when early paternal trans-ferences appear in the company of unfolding maternal erotic trans-ferences and countertransferences, they are typically obscure and highly evanescent. It is difficult for both patient and analyst to foster the regression to and identify the preverbal bodily states associated with early maternal erotic transferences and even more difficult to locate and differentiate the early father in those transferences.

TYPICAL RESISTANCE TO EVANESCENT PATERNAL TRANSFERENCES EVOKED DURING MATERNAL EROTIC TREANSFERENCES TO FEMALE ANALYSTS

We all tend naturally to be rooted to our biological gender identity, and our patients see us according to our biological type as well. Thus, both parties in the analytic dyad may have difficulty recogniz-ing and appreciating transference to the parent who is the opposite sex of the analyst. Additionally, the "missing" father is also a painfully common theme in patients' entire narratives because far too many fathers are absent or weak or play only a minor role in parenting.

173

Add to this the sensory diffusion of early mother–baby boundary confusion, then locating the elusive presence of the third "other" in transferences between male and female patients and female analysts can indeed be slippery. The quest for the lost father is painfully common in many analysands' narratives (see Wrye, 1993c).

What happens to the mind of the analyst, the "thinking other," when there is immersion in these primitive maternally erotic bodily feelings? While father may be metaphorically "knocking on the door to the nursery," the analyst may be so "maternally preoccupied" (Winnicott, 1975) that she is deaf to the father's presence. She may miss his critical importance to the patient's consolidation of a sense of safety and self-esteem, separate wholeness, gender identity, and subjectivity. For a number of culturally engendered reasons, there seems a greater risk that "Poppa" will be shut out longer given these circumstances. To invite father into the nursery, the analyst must be receptive to her own internal early father. For analysts whose fathers were noticeably physically absent from the nursery, our only access to him was through the father our mothers revealed to us, the "father-in-mother" (Ogden, 1989). Crucial to analytic receptivity to our patient's early father is openness to the presence of our own paternal introjects and identifications. The female analyst needs to allow her patient to draw both from herself as father and from her own internal phallus. We also must distinguish early paternal trans-ferences when the father is sought as a "missing necessary ingredi-ent" or feared as a frighteningly inappropriate player on the analytic stage. We also need to recognize when the father is sought defen-sively as the prohibitor of forbidden oedipal wishes and when he serves as the protector against reengulfment with the preoedipal mother as well as the model for later romantic relations. Ross (1993) cautions us that much of what we intuit about the very early preoedi-pal father may be derived from encounters with the later father of more conscious memory. Typically, paternal transferences kaleido-scopicaly shift back and forth among these earlier and later functions, between their positive and negative valences, and in counterpoint to corresponding shifting maternal transferences.

A forcefully experienced father, possibly the most readily recogniz-able, may appear in the transference as the frightening, loud, or over-powering intruder into the mother–baby closeness (Solomon, 1978). He may appear, as in Suta's analysis (described in chapter 6), as the figure "we want to keep out of here." On the other hand, the early dyadic father (Blos, 1985) often appears in analyses as a gentler, reassuring other during the separation-individuation and differentiation subphases (Mahler, 1971; Mahler et al., 1975). His presence, if benign and palpable, is comforting. During rapprochement, he serves as a mirror of the child's subjective interior. His absence or his inadequacy is profoundly unsettling, particularly in the presence of an "impinging" mother figure.

In this chapter's title, the query "Where's Poppa?" comes from one of Caleb's dreams, in which he was seeking poppies in a field. Caleb was unable to tolerate the emergence of maternal erotic feelings and fantasies until his longed-for and previously missing father could be found within me. His heretofore successful analysis nearly died in the process but was resuscitated when I finally awoke to the dramatic meaning of his dream of searching for poppies in a field. We shall be speaking more of Caleb and this dream later in this chapter.

THE ROLE OF THE FATHER IN
THE DEVELOPMENTAL NARRATIVE

Ross (1982) traces the course of normal development in boys from early identification with the procreative and nurturing mother to a search for a generative father and final resolution in oedipal sexual identification with father: "Even a motherly mother and fatherly father cannot altogether spare their son from residual feminine or even homosexual wishes, or from his anxious, defensive, and often overcompensating protests against these threats to a newfound sense of masculinity" (p. 203). He suggests that the boy can, by way of the oedipal resolution, subordinate his early maternal identification to the newly formed identification with his father.

Benjamin (1988) stresses the boy's rapprochement love for his father as the prototype of ideal love, finding in the father his ideal image of the self:

> In rapprochement, the little boy's "love affair with the world" (of the earlier practicing stage) turns into a homoerotic love affair with the father, who *represents* the world. The boy's identificatory love for the father, his wish to be recognized as like him, is the erotic engine behind separation . . . through this homoerotic love, he creates his masculine identity and maintains his narcissism in the face of helplessness. (p. 106)

She emphasizes that this ideal homoerotic love is not equivalent to Freud's "negative Oedipus complex" in which the boy identifies with the mother and passively desires the father. She is not alone among critics of that concept (cf. Blos, 1985, pp. 6–10.) She also stresses the father's role in mirroring his daughter's subjectivity.

Drawing on their direct observations of little boys and girls, Galenson and Roiphe (1981) offer a developmental perspective on the origins of sexual identity. Their perspective on the critical role of the father in establishing a secure masculine identification and identity has signal relevance to the topic of erotic horror in males. Boys have great difficulty as they enter the oedipal phase, wherein their identifications with father are obstructed by intense rivalries, as their erotic feelings toward mother are intensified: "And above all, the boy's earlier sense of genital identification with his mother must be definitely disengaged at this critical juncture if he is to achieve a solid sense of masculine identity" (pp. 274–275)

Similarly, Tyson (1982) notes the significance of the preoedipal father in enabling a boy to develop a core masculine identity and male gender role that can withstand rivalry and aggression in relation to father during the positive oedipal phase. During the first year of life, core gender identity is established; for boys "disidentification from mother" (Greenson, 1968) requires a strong paternal presence. Greenson writes:

> The male child, in order to attain a healthy sense of maleness, must replace the primary object of his identification, the mother, and must identify instead with the father. I believe the difficulties inherent in this additional step of development, from which girls are exempt, are responsible for certain special problems in the man's gender identity, his sense of belonging to the male sex. (pp. 305–306)

Stoller (1968), studying the extreme disruption of gender identity in male transsexuals, emphasized that in each case studied there was an unbreakable symbiosis between mother and son, while the father remained passive and unavailable to the boy.

Diamond (1993), in a developmental perspective on the life cycle, enumerates 12 key tasks of a "good-enough" father with his son. It is the father's role when his son is (1) born, to provide a holding environment for mother and infant; (2) from six months to two years, to serve as an alternate attachment figure; (3) from one and a half to three years, to facilitate separation-individuation; (4) from two to four years, to modulate negative and aggressive affect during the anal stage; (5) at the same stage, to provide a male model of toilet training; (6) from two-and-a-half to teen years, to support gender and gender-role development; (7) from three-and-a-half to six years, to serve as the oedipal challenger; (8) in latency and middle childhood, to initiate and mentor instrumental and expressive masculinity as well as group relations; (9) an adolescent, to support the second individuation; (10) a young adult of 20 to 30 years, to provide mentoring; (11) a mature adult, to facilitate fatherhood, and (12) aging, to aid in reconciliation to that time of life.

Limentani (1991) focuses on those fathers who appear to have failed in these tasks with their sons and thus have contributed to the development of their sons' sexual deviation. His contention is that male and female analysts alike (including such well-established ones as Khan, Stoller, and Greenson) tend to "neglect" the father, often in complicity with patients' views and prevailing cultural norms that focus on the mother. He reports on a female analyst's account of an analysis of a fetishist in which she "suddenly realized that she could not remember the patient's surname. . . . the analyst had become the victim of the attempts to obliterate the man's role and potency. . . . [We] can only speculate . . . on the effect on the analysis" (p. 577). Limentani further decries the way in which in too many analyses of perversion

> fathers [are] relegated to the background. . . . It may take a long time before we become aware that something is missing and a state of stagnation ensues. But if the analysis continues, suddenly it comes to life again. A much denigrated father is discovered to be the source of much attraction and eroticism. An unconcerned and uninterested father is a source of fear, love and concern. (p. 582)

In a similar vein, McDougall (1978) describes how in male and female deviants the mother is often idealized and the denigrated father receives the split-off hostility. She suggests that behind the portrayal of the father as stupid, brutish, or castrated, available only for passive anal-submissive involvement, lies the image of a father who has failed his specific parental role.

Keeping in mind these perspectives on the role of the father in the crucible of preoedipal maternal relations, we turn now to a brief supervisory encounter and vignettes from three completed analyses, all illustrative of evanescent paternal transferences appearing in tandem with early maternal erotic transferences. Our focus is on the early sensate, bodily oriented tender impulses that are revealed alongside the sadistic, aggressive, and masochistic wishes that arise in relation to the body of the analyst in the transference. In this material, the early father is sought; later, oedipal, genitally focused sexual fantasies emerge more or less only in the shadow of the preoedipal paternal transference.

CLINICAL ILLUSTRATIONS

Nancy's Father Next Door:
A Supervisor Behind the Curtains

The first illustration reveals a common phenomenon: the supervisor as outsider/"father" intruding on the mother–baby closeness between analyst and analysand and the frequency with which early paternal transferences may be missed altogether. Dr. K contacted me (HKW) for analytic supervision, noting that she had been seeing her patient, Nancy, four times a week for nine months. She had called me because she felt that her patient's intense struggles were around issues of an early maternal erotic transference.

In the material of the first supervisory hour, I was struck immediately by the mutuality of the love affair in full bloom between Dr. K and her patient. Nancy wrote poetry to her analyst. She noticed each detail of her analyst's clothing, shoes, and office and seemed to live for and in her analytic sessions. Dr. K's report on her patient carried a similarly attentive, rich tone of her sensitive attunement and obvious love for her patient. I felt as if she were bringing me her baby. The lyrical quality of the material led me to muse on the meaning of the fact that this blissful, early erotic transference in an analytic case had continued unsupervised for about nine months. I wondered how both would feel about my intrusion into their snug dyad and why Dr. K had decided to call on me for supervision at this point in time. Dr. K smiled in recognition of her own ambivalence about inviting in an outsider and an "authority." I sensed that while she was resonating with aspects of her patient's early frustrations and longings toward her mother's body, she was also missing her patient's urgent search for her missing father.

The second supervisory hour was remarkable. It has been my experience that the entrance of a supervisor into an analytic pair often shows up in the material in a dream, similar to Gaddini's (1977) reports of the shadow of the father, the "unknown figure that stands for the primordial perception of the second object which must have been very disconcerting to the baby" (cited in Limentani, 1991, p. 583). Nancy, "sensing something different here," revealed her uncanny attunement to her analyst's anxiety about having the treatment intruded upon by my supervisory presence. In the very first session after her analyst had come to see me for consultation, Nancy reported a dream in which she mentioned my uncommon first name, Harriet. The patient actually reported a dream of "going to visit Aunt *Harriet's* very cramped house." Dr. K's description of many such unusual "slips of the mind" between herself and her patient illustrates the boundary diffusion characteristic of early maternal erotic transferences. In the early transference, Nancy's pre-occupation with the details and textures of Dr. K's body and clothing had reflected her longing for bodily closeness and reunion with her early mother.

Dr. K also mentioned parenthetically to me that she would soon be moving to the office next door, which happened to be the former office of a male psychiatrist who had seen Nancy for anxiety and antidepressant medication but who no longer treated her. While I concurred with Dr. K's initial description of a richly elaborated maternal erotic transference, I suggested my sense that a paternal transference was emerging in the "shadows" of the office next door. Dr. K then told me that her patient seldom mentioned her father, who had died suddenly when she was 13. She described her patient as the middle daughter whose anxious mother appeared unable to form an erotic resonance with her. Nancy's father had been an outdoorsman who had loved cooking and mountaineering, pursuits she enjoyed with her husband as they reminded her of the father whom she credited with the capacity to experience *with* her.

Nancy's early maternal erotic transference was tinged with repugnance for her mother, who arrived for an Easter visit bringing "disgusting sticky buns." She also expressed prudish disdain for her father's attention to her older sister's physical development. This disdain only thinly masked her craving for her father's interest and her jealousy of her father's oedipal choice of her sister. Behind this, what the patient appeared to be seeking, however, was not her sexual oedipal father but her earlier father, who had filled in the gaps in mother's anxious mothering with his own good cooking as well as the early father of separation from the mother, who could "take her off to explore the mountains."

Many female analysts, as noted earlier, may incline naturally toward the maternal erotic transference. While Dr. K had sought my assistance in relation to her patient's early maternal erotic transference, she actually did not need my help there at all. Although some are reluctant to immerse themselves in a primitive, undifferentiated transference, Dr. K had been gifted in enabling it to unfold and flourish in both its negative and positive valences. It was as if, within the nine-month, uninterrupted maternal erotic transference, Nancy had experienced previously missing intimacy.

As a pregnant mother may eventually need a midwife to assist her in birth, the analytic pair seemed now to need a father to provide the space for separation and differentiation. At this point, nine months into the analysis, Dr. K's unconscious awareness of her patient's need for a father, and perhaps her own need as well, may have led her to summon a third person, an "outside" supervisor. I picked this up in my own countertransference as supervisor, I was impressed with the work so far and felt concerned about intruding on the dyad. At that point, it occurred to me that that was what was wanted was the missing "other" to foster the triangulation required to develop intersubjectivity and the patient's moves toward autonomy. Such glimmerings of the *early* father within transferences and countertransferences suggest a kind of *éminence grise,* a literary term used to describe a cloudy presence that is not identifiable.

Dr. K's plan to move into the psychiatrist's empty office seemed to have evoked the shadow of Nancy's deceased father. He had died just at the onset of her adolescence, with its heightened oedipal excitement. She had experienced his death as an abandonment of her to "cramped quarters" with an anal, "sticky Easter bun" mother whom she felt frustrated by, but still longed for and yet despised. Her preoedipal longings for closeness with her early mother disgusted her and rekindled her desire for the father of rapprochement to mirror her subjectivity. Dr. K apparently had unconsciously sought supervisory help articulating, her patient's silent query, "Where's Poppa?" no doubt triggered by her awareness of her therapist's planned office move. The move had rekindled both Nancy's early need for a differentiating and attuned father to offset her mother's anxiously ambivalent care, and her grief-tinged memories of having been left by her father, alone in too close quarters with her mother.

In the parallel supervisory process, although patient, analyst, and supervisor were all female, what was being sought by patient and therapist alike was a third person, a shadow father figure, in this case a preoedipal father of differentiation and subjective attunement. Opening the door to let father in had a calming effect on Nancy and allowed further elaboration of the maternal erotic transference as well as preoedipal and oedipal paternal transferences, which gradually shifted from fantasies about the "supervisor behind the curtains" and the missing psychiatrist next door to the person of her female analyst.

Corrine: "Pungent Little Blossoms"

The appearance of the preoedipal father transference in the midst of an early maternal erotic transference in my (HKW) analytic work with Corrine was confusing to sort out. At the outset of treatment, Corrine, a successful professional woman in her 20s, entered into an alternately intensely idealizing and denigrating maternal erotic transference to me. This was marked by fantasies of becoming my "baby," moving into my neighborhood, replacing my husband and other family members, and more frankly erotic longings to perform cunnilingus on me. These fantasies alternated with angry accusations about my reserve, formality of dress, rigid schedule, and imagined preference for other patients. I linked her intense frustration and irritation to her experience of her mother's emotional overload, preference for her older brothers, and consequent unavailability to her as an infant.

Prior to analysis, Corrine had engaged in a series of affairs with married men. The triangular element suggested her efforts to repair both her sense of failure as a rival against her siblings for her mother's attention and her oedipal defeat. The men chosen contrasted with her father's abject failure as a provider for his family. On several occasions during the analysis, her father would rekindle her painful experience of him as pathetic and ineffectual by calling to borrow or beg rent money from her. For at least two years of the analysis, this denigrated picture obscured the more fundamental role of the preoedipal father in her internal drama.

Father appeared by way of an episode in which Corrine, seeking a "new look," went to a famous hairstylist. Her hair coloring did not turn out as she had hoped, and the stylist took great pains to assuage her disappointment; he even invited her to come back in the evening "after hours to try to fix it." Corrine arrived at her Monday session, flushed, her hair concealed under a hat to hide the obvious blunder. She felt no resentment toward the hairdresser; in fact she basked in his extracurricular attention to her. Corrine was deeply flattered by his care, especially as he was renowned and married to a well-known model. Initially, I focused on the more obvious oedipal aspects of this encounter. The next day, as if to help me "get it right," Corrine arrived with a large bouquet of richly scented blossoms carefully wrapped in paper for me. Aware of her narcissistic vulnerability, I accepted the gift while indicating that we would explore its meaning. I realized that she had offered me this floral bundle in such a way that I took it like a baby cradled on my arm. At the same time, my analytic inquiry as to its meaning immediately evoked her anger at my formality, distance, and lack of spontaneity. After a rather painful exploration, I suggested that she wanted to have, through the flowers, the kind of immediate and free contact with my body that she had felt so deprived of with her mother; she did not want to *talk* about it, she wanted to *experience* it.

It became clear that Corrine's excitement about her hairdresser's attention to her face and hair had rekindled far less an oedipal pleasure than a preoedipal enjoyment of her father's role as her physical caretaker in the nursery. This "paternal touch," which had apparently filled the void of the early bodily care she had missed from her mother, had evoked her present bodily longings for contact with me in the transference. She desperately wanted me to receive her like a floral bouquet, joyously and sensually, and to regard her as beautiful and sweet smelling like a freshly bathed and powdered baby. She agreed, saying she felt exhilarated by her hairdresser's physical attentiveness and desired that from me.

In subsequent sessions, a complex picture emerged of the confusion of roles of her early caretakers. Her mother, an anxious woman by nature with profound early deprivation of her own, had gone to work after Corrine's birth to support the family, her father being habitually unemployed. Thus, Corrine's father had been her primary caretaker from birth through adolescence. Memories flowed forth of his absorbed attention to her skin and bowel functions; she believed he had taken care of all her basic bodily needs.

It also emerged that her mother was an incest victim who seemed unconsciously to have colluded in this arrangement, which placed her daughter in harm's way in the primary care of a rather unreliable man who was often demonstrably inappropriate. As Corrine had approached puberty, it was her father who supplied the tampons and sanitary pads and developed a ritual of "cleaning" her face by close scrutiny to problem pores, which he would purge by squeezing.

This sexually provocative perverse behavior confused Corrine as to what she should expect from her analyst and from men.

Thus, unlike the differentiated early maternal and paternal transferences revealed in the previous supervisory case material with Nancy and Dr. K, Corrine's early paternal transference was not the transference of differentiation and distance from the symbiotic. In fact, Corrine's early father transference emerged as barely distinguishable from a maternal erotic transference, the perverse aspect of which sought to assault boundaries and space between the analyst's maternal body and the patient's infantile longings and fears. When she experienced her hairdresser in the context of the beauty salon, he evoked both the forgotten, early, nursery-stage, longed-for father of bodily caretaking and the "after hours/beyond the bounds" later father who could not succeed and who made her the unsuitable object of too much of his attention. The pungent blossoms were meant to clear the "rotten smell" in the nursery in which perverse, inappropriate fathering, with particular attentiveness to the pudenda, evoked both Corrine's guilty excitation and her profound sense of badness about her own body. The flowers Corrine offered me also were aimed at mollifying me as the jealous but collusive mother who in this case was outside the nursery closeness between daddy and baby. They were also meant to invite her mother/analyst back into the nursery of "sweet smells and little blossoms" to heal something that had gone seriously wrong in her early caretaking with her father.

Popeye and His Spinach: Who's Providing It —Mother Or Father?

In the next example from the completed analysis of an unmarried man in his 20s, we focus on one session in the early phase illustrating rapidly oscillating preoedipal and oedipal vicissitudes of the patient's quest for and fears of aspects of both his father and mother. Nils, "working as a drone in a huge accounting firm," had been working in his analysis on his passivity and denial of adverse, negative feelings toward me (HKW). At the end of his session the day before the hour we describe here, a female patient had arrived early and knocked insistently on the door. As he left, Nils told me the next day, he had became aware of his building rage at her intrusion. By the time he reached his van, he was muttering, "Get out of here, you bitch!" He associated to the probability of his early rage at his mother for prematurely rushing him off her lap and away from her breast to make room for his baby sister who was born just 14 months after him. This awareness was followed by blatantly aggressive fantasies of his returning to my consulting room, bursting in on "you bitches," and sexually accosting me—assertively taking off my clothes and "sticking my dick in you—having you."

At that moment, he realized that his "chronic flatness and lack of imagination" must have been a result of his defense against such fantasies, specifically about his sexual sadism and fears of inadequacy. He thought, "I must have to keep constant surveillance over my mind so the Nazi doesn't show." His next associations were to a fantasy of masturbating on the couch in front of me. This excited him, and he felt it was less physically threatening to me; but he anticipated feeling terribly humiliated, because, as the fantasy unfolded, he would stain his pants and I would show him to the bathroom. He then associated to a dream in which he had gone to a neighbor's house to help in the garden. The ostensible reason for the visit was that the neighbor had offered to teach him how to mow lawns and trim hedges so that he could earn some money of his own in the neighborhood. He confided that although he had no evidence, he had been afraid the man was a child abuser.

During this entire hour, he associated freely without any comments from me. As the session and the week were drawing to a close, I pointed out that throughout this hour he had given us a rich recital of his early psychological narrative—first, his feeling that his baby needs for his mother had gone unmet because he had been displaced by his sister's birth; then his defensive and precocious awareness of his young mother's sexual attractiveness as mirrored in his feelings for me as a sexual woman and fantasies of possessing me as a fully genitally adequate male. This sexuality was infused with sadistic and rageful fantasies toward women who made him dependent and then frustrated him. He had then shifted to his dawning awareness of his father's alternating absence and intimidating presence.

He could not recall memories of his father, also an accountant, as an enabling or reassuring presence; he had thought of him throughout his childhood as a "detail monger" and daunting critic. In Nils's mind, the best offense was a good defense, so he had joined his father in accounting, although he never enjoyed it. In the session, this paternal intimidation had forced his retreat into the humiliating masturbation fantasy where he stained or soiled himself like the "little boy bed wetter" we had been talking about in previous weeks. At this point in the transference I had become not the beautiful young mother whom he longed for yet raged against for displacing him, but alternately the oedipally prohibiting father and the humiliating preoedipal phallic mother who toilet trained him.

In confirmation, Nils associated further to the idea that the dream had revealed his early fears of his vulnerability in therapy, of being a child seeking help and being abused. He elaborated that in the dream he had taken his little sister with him to visit the neighbor (who was a member of his family's church congregation) to do the gardening chores. Nils felt he "needed the fortification of his sister" to protect against his fear of the man as a sadistic "meanie." He saw his sister in the dream as his castrated female self, associated with an emergency appendectomy he had endured as a child. In the dream, she represented his passive demeanor, his sense of his own weakened, hence effeminate, sexuality; the dream masked the rage at both his parents that we were beginning to expose in treatment. Taking her along also represented the baby sister that he wished to assault. He would accomplish this assault in the dream in the guise of the ostensibly helpful but mean neighbor he fantasied was a child abuser. By taking his sister into harm's way, the "meanie could do it for me." He also recognized his own defensive career identification with the aggressor, the split-off "Numbers Nazi" who said, "I've got the lawnmower and you're gonna get humiliated and cut up."

As this session drew to a close, I interpreted Nils's fears that I would be either the preoccupied mother, whose loving attention was focused on my other baby, or the unavailable and critical father. I also commented on his wish to bring his weakened self to me and to find in me instead the magic mommy with the healing breast and the instructive father who would infuse him with semen and testosterone. He agreed, acknowledging both his longing for me as the lullaby-singing mama who would soothe him and his fears of me as the "Computer Queen," a disguise for his intimidating father. Nils also recognized his desire for me as the early father who might have stepped in to assuage his feelings of rejection when his sister was born, as well as a later, empowering father as he entered the world. He recalled endless nights and weekends as a boy wondering when dad would come home from the office ("Where's Poppa?"). He also recalled spending considerable time in the neighborhood visiting with other "dads," helping them with chores, just to be close, as it were, to a possible wellspring of testosterone. He remembered a favorite fantasy he had had before entering analysis that centered on his wish for a magical cure from an analyst who would instill him with power, "like Popeye and his spinach," a conflation of the wish for a magical mammary and a testosterone-infusing phallus.

As the analysis unfolded, we followed these maternal and paternal transference threads of the preoedipal early mother and the enabling early father, sought as the bestower of blessings and for identification. We also explored his desire for me as a toilet-training oedipal father "who teaches me to be tough" and "to pee farther and faster" set against me as the seductive, sexual woman with the jealous husband who would either "initiate me into the club or club me to death."

Through the course of Nils's analysis, completed some years ago, we were able to reweave these threads together into a healthier and generative narrative of his masculinity. He called to report, post-analysis, that he had happily left the accounting firm to write a successful offbeat financial newsletter with a reputation for predicting trends in the market. No longer the droning "Number Nazi," Nils found he had a real flair for words and became a "narrator of financial desire." He also called on another occasion to report that he had fallen in love and married and was soon to become a father himself. His own narration of desire had been transformed from a story of debilitated emasculation and intimidation to one of masculine capability strengthened by lots of analytic spinach, alternately offered to him in engagements with his analyst as both pre- and postoedipal mother and father.

The Poppy Dreamer: A Male Homosexual's Quest for the Father

This chapter's title phrase, "Where's Poppa?" comes from Caleb's dream response to a countertransference block that nearly derailed his difficult analysis. My block, which had to do with my own father, really brought my attention to the powerful need of a male patient to find the elusive presence of the early and later father within his female analyst so that he can risk and creatively experience with her the transformational possibilities of a maternal erotic transference. This nearly paralyzing derailment occurred late in Caleb's analysis, as he approached feelings attendant to a maternal erotic transference.

Caleb (see chapters 7 and 8), in a kind of panic, had chronically denied any early sensual bodily feelings toward me until the session reported in the last chapter when he juxtaposed remembered images of decapitated kittens on the farm with fantasies of his own slippery, sensual ride down the birth canal. Indeed, his childhood narrative featured a mother who appeared to have been unpredictably punitive and seductive and a father who seemed quite passive. For him the absence of a father of boundaries and prohibition had been utterly threatening, leaving him unshielded from reengulfment with his early mother, humiliation by his phallic mother, or sexualized encounters with his oedipal mother.

Laborious work on his immobilization in a paranoid-schizoid "deadlock" occupied the first few years of the analysis. Work on triangular oedipal issues represented the first round of genuine analytic engagement following the deadlock. It also was less threatening to him than his long-denied and frightening earlier infantile longings for erotic contact and closeness with the body of his mother. For that crucial encounter, he needed to feel the presence of a reassuring father in the transference, but this father seemed perennially, disappointingly absent.

For most of the years of our analytic work, Caleb's paternal transferences figured more recognizably at oedipal levels in relation to either his woefully passive father or his powerfully sadistic grandfather. In a dream representing his wish and greatest fear within his remarkably undisguised oedipal triangle, his father permitted him intercourse with his mother and stayed in the room to watch. During the middle phase of his analysis, Caleb worked on the many triangles in his life, tracing the shifts in them. Initially, he had focused on his awareness of his triangular relations with his mother and older sister, who were always fighting. He also saw himself as a weak third in relation to his formidable mother and his nonentity father.

In another triangle, he saw each of his parents played off against his powerful and sadistic maternal ("rattlesnake") grandfather. Though working on these triangles signaled work on the oedipal conflicts of his lengthy analysis, actually these triangles seemed more like a debilitated tripod, incapable of shouldering analytic resolution. They also represented safer, opener ground for him than the "squishy, trapped" feelings of the earlier dyadic relations on which they stood.

He became aware of the early period of idyllic bliss when he and his mother were "wrapped in a beautiful silk scarf." His bliss was disrupted by his feeling of banishment when his baby brother was born. He conveyed this depressive loss in a screen memory of riding in a car when he was about four years old, playing with his mother's silk scarf until it was sucked out of the window by the

wind and disappeared over the horizon in the vast desert near
their home. While he had difficulty accessing early memories of his
mother, he vividly remembered the color, texture, and feeling of
her scarf and his aching at its loss. On his travels, he searched for
such a scarf to give to me until finally he designed one and had it
specially silk screened and handmade.

As we approached the preoedipal material, he became more
openly depressed, questioning the point of continuing his analysis
and preferring to retreat into interminable deadness. I interpreted
his fear of being alone with me as fear of a close encounter with
a loving mother who would leave him or a critical mother who
would emasculate him, drain all his resources, and humiliate and
trap him.

Patient and Analyst Stifled in a Danse Macabre

In a manner similar to his adolescent depressive withdrawals, and
disconsolate at the lack of "testosterone" in his father, in the analysis
Caleb resorted to his old mode of cruising the gay scene, and, worse,
he reported images of self-immolation, like the burning coffin dream
reported in chapter 7. I interpreted his fantasy of turning to men
with "big dicks" as lovers as an attempt to find the strong father
he lacked and to ward me off and even destroy me as both intimidating older sister and, more deeply, as his longed-for yet feared and
intrusive mother.

At this point, Caleb reported a dream about his friend who was
dying of AIDS:

> He was completely different from real life—sexually responsive,
> allowing, reciprocating. It seemed we were younger, almost brothers.
> We were having to keep quiet because someone's father was in the
> next room. We couldn't make any noise to draw his attention. We
> were sort of in a little nook, like walls around a bed but with an open
> ceiling.

He associated to my small consulting room and couch and to feeling caged but exposed. Throughout the analysis he had associated
images of confined spaces—cages, alcoves, room around the bed,
the trunk of a car, a hassock, a coffin—primarily with the stifling and
sadistic presence of his grandfather, the strongest male figure in his
childhood, who had dominated the presence of both his father and

his mother. Caleb recognized that the dream strikingly portrayed his wish to find his dying friend not only healthy but also sexually responsive to him. It also revealed both his wish for loving repair with his brother and his wish that, instead of inhibited desire dampened by the presence of a father "who was never present, but always in the next room," he could receive a vital seminal infusion from a healthy man.

His sense of "having to keep quiet because someone's father was in the next room" stirred me to recognize my own depressed preoccupation with the imminent loss of my own father, who was very ill. The specter of his presence, figuratively "the sleeping father in the next room," left me feeling very identified with Caleb's conscious sense of loss of his dying friend and his father's weakness. Thoughts of death and the loss of my father, a brilliant, looming presence in my internal world, rendered me temporarily unable to provide Caleb access to the needed generative father within me. In a kind of *Danse Macabre* we had unconsciously traded projective identifications with a deadened Tiresias-like old man unable to bring new life to the wasteland of toxic AIDS, malignancy, and heart failure.

In this state, I resorted to a kind of false maternal posture, hoping to pour a transfusion of hope into my patient, like a mother who stuffs food into her distraught offspring in an effort to mask her real distress. In fact, because of the nature of his object ties to a passive and disappeared father, Caleb needed the presences of both an authentic, nonintrusive mother and a strong yet benign father to enable him to assimilate his best facets as a man. He seemed to require in me both a mother to introduce him to the father and a father to make mother safe.

He lamented, "I feel my manhood will never be enough for a woman. I tried to get it from my father but it's been futile. I've been trying to confirm my manhood but no one has confirmed it. The most I can hope for is a gentle man. Manhood, stripped from me years before I ever had a chance to claim it. Cheated." He associated to his efforts to capture an affirming but gentler masculinity through homosexual encounters with black men, which stemmed from his identification with the "Good Samaritan" black man who had fainted at his grandfather's sadistic motorized rattlesnake joke. Then he thought of his fear of sexually transmitted diseases from "swallowing the semen of infected men." He dreamed that he and a friend with AIDS "were being put in a hospice with six months to live." As his depression deepened, he ruminated on his parents' failing health, the economic recession, his fear of bankruptcy, and the possible loss of his analysis.

Gender Confusion—Searching for "Balls of Steel"
While Making Anal Doghouse Babies

Caleb remembered an episode when he was four, just after the birth of his brother. He and his best friend, hiding in his doghouse, placed stones in each other's anus and then removed them to sniff the results. This transparent childish fascination, at the time of his mother's having given birth, with what is "inside"—creating magical cloacal babies in play—was disrupted when a neighbor woman, finding them, bellowed, "Don't you *ever* play with little girls, or little boys . . . or yourself!" Concluding that his father's masculinity was too weak, that attempts to swallow it from another man would be disastrous, and that he was not allowed to identify with mother's procreative role, he had no path but asexual impotence.

Still preoccupied, I remained "dead" to his plight. Persisting in trying to wake me up, like Dr. K's patient who had finally resorted to screaming, Caleb said, "I have this sculpture I *have* to do—it's of a hand in a glove, holding a steel ball." I *finally* understood this as his plea for the missing father in me, the empowering father of the baseball mitt, the father with with "balls of steel." In contrast to his experimentations with maternity via stones pulled from the anus like babies, or his fantasies of "Cruising for the Big Dick" in which he had hoped that physical insemination by the large penis of a random male would magically masculinize him, he was poignantly beginning to seek an internalized, beloved, functional father to metabolize. He wished he could figuratively reach into me, "like a glove" and find a steel ball, the strength of his father there. I saw this as a graphic description of any child's search for the needed same-sex parent inside the body/psyche of the opposite-sex parent, touching Ogden's (1989) conceptualization of the "father-in-mother. "

When I understood this quest and interpreted my sense of the meaning of the image of the gloved hand holding the ball of steel, Caleb's depression lifted dramatically. Experiencing a breakthrough in his creative work, he artistically executed a sculpture of the ball in the gloved hand with sunflowers ("son flowers"). With a burst of new ideas, he was excited by the possibility of finding his flowering as a son. For the first time, he began to recall and identify with long-forgotten aspects of his father's quiet refusal to acquiesce to the overpowering grandfather.

Just as this positive shift was occurring, I unfortunately had to depart for a week, leaving Caleb feeling untethered and deflated, "as if my little ideas are not enough to keep you with me. If you don't care for me, I won't care for you." On my return, he spent 15 minutes in session almost sleeping: "I'm back in the same place, stuck. I'm feeling drugged. Want to go to sleep." While I felt that this lethargy indicated the narcissistic injury inflicted by my absence, it turned out that his sleepiness reflected his relief at my return; he could relax at this point into a holding and calming maternal presence. "It's odd. It's like receiving a gift. I would love to surrender to the joy and excitement, but there is something else in the wings that says I can't have it."

This blissful reunion was followed by oscillating maternal and paternal transferences, where I interpreted his wish to have me as the mother who would pick him up when he felt dropped and untethered and also as an available father who would protect and support him. He agreed. My voice at this time lent cadence to a new narrative thread he was developing. My role could be conceptualized as offering support for a "loving and beloved superego" (Schafer, 1960), providing a new model of strength, tolerance, and reliability in contrast to the demeaning sadistic paternal imago of his grandfather, whom he chronically heard berating him for being a "weak wimp."

At this point, Caleb mused about enrolling in a workshop on "Father Hunger and Male Bonding": "I'm struggling with how much I need you. I'm afraid of falling into a lifelong depression. When I brought you my sculpture, I was afraid I would let you down, not be good enough . . . and yet you appreciated it." A tearful silence followed, as we encountered another level of his underlying chronic depression.

I reframed the emerging narrative: "When you were little you sometimes had wonderful contact with mother, good but unreliable, like the beautiful scarf that blew away. When you were four, and quite in love with her, you were heartbroken when she gave birth to Jake, the cat boy." (Here I was referring to his memory of the decapitated kittens he found in the dirt under his farm house, their heads bitten off by the tomcat—as he would have wished to destroy Jake.) "You felt betrayed, dejected, and inadequate, knowing you could never make a baby with her. You could not breathe life into stones. I sense that was the beginning of your feelings of abject failure."

He responded, sobbing, "That's when I began to run away and have all those accidents. I felt so puny." I reminded him that all this had happened when he was about four, the same age he remembered playing in the dog house with the neighbor boy, inserting stones in each other's anus and smelling them. I suggested that the play may well have stemmed from his curiosity about where babies came from and his wish that he could produce a baby that would win his mother's heart, as baby Jake seemed to have done. I said, "If only you could have been as big as Daddy. I think this may have been the beginning of your urgent interest in big dicks."

Caleb was moved by this interpretation, which finally put together many separate images and themes in the context of the birth of his brother, about whom he could retrieve practically no conscious childhood memories at all. (His only image was of a nameless baby in a crib. The baby made horrible noises, and he wanted to kill it, he hated it so much.) He had only recently realized, after retrieving the memory of the dead kittens, that the nameless baby was his baby brother. He also saw the marauding tomcat as his grandfather attacking unprotected kittens that, like him, needed a protective father. The following week he brought two dreams. In the first:

> I was in Armani's, not intending to buy anything, when a woman said, "There's an incredible deal on a trench coat." There was a man helping me try it on. It was a little big in the shoulders. I thought I didn't really need it but I tried it.
>
> The woman was you helping me to be a man—like trying on my father's clothes, instead of dressing up in my mother's like I used to do. The big shoulders suggest I'm not sure I can manage it but you think I can. Armani's is the best! I can get out of the trench I've dug into; the clothes are part of my new personality.

In the second:

> I was in New York with President Reagan. There was an entourage but we were walking together under a bridge toward a hotel. He was trying to figure out whether to repair it with steel or concrete. It had needed to be repaired for a long time. He asked me if it needed steel or concrete and I didn't know. Then he cried because he cared so much. I said it would be great if he could do it with dispatch like in his cowboy movies. When we got to the lobby, Nancy Reagan was there in cowboy hat. I told her that if she wrote "White House" on hats like that, she could sell them.

He realized that walking with Reagan and worrying about re-
pairing bridges related directly to his sense of strengthening the
bond to his father. Just as he would not imagine the president cry-
ing, he had been unable to imagine his father's strength. Maybe
a man who could cry or appear weak could also care deeply and
have considerable power as well. Further, as Caleb was politically
opposed to Reagan's presidency, his obvious appreciation for Reagan's
fatherly qualities in the dream represented his emerging ability to
tolerate ambivalence and to form a whole object relationship. The
presence of Mrs. Reagan revealed an emerging oedipal couple; his
"talking business" with her reflected both his practicing the role
of mentoring father he was experiencing from me and his acceptance of the fact that his previous sexism, which consigned women
solely to the kitchen and men solely to the office, was undergoing
change. At the close of the session, he mentioned that he was going
to a co-ed beach party and worried about how he would look in a
bathing suit, revealing emerging oedipal rivalry and concerns about
measuring up.

A Genuine Oedipal Phase Emerges:
Locked Outside the Parent's Bedroom

A few weeks later he became inexplicably cross and stalemated; I
was puzzled by this rupture following the earlier analytic excitement
and rapid growth. After days of inquiry, he reluctantly revealed that
while waiting for me to enter the consulting room one morning, he
had overheard a man's voice, presumably that of my husband, saying
affectionately, " 'Bye, Doctor, have a good day." Caleb said sheep-
ishly, "When you came in that day, I saw a shy, girlish side of you. I'm
outside of that. I don't belong. I can fantasize all I want to, but it's
not real. The door closes and I'm outside . . . the whispering behind
closed doors." For the first time, he revealed erotic fantasies about
me in which he had imagined me reciprocating, until his dreams
were dashed by the presence of the oedipal rival. He felt humiliated
and shamed.

I was chagrined at my carelessness in leaving the consulting room
door open but realized that the extent of this oedipal depression was
significant. Was the carelessness the unconscious enactment of my
desire to bring my relationship with my husband to his attention? I
pointed out that he had not transgressed—the fault had been mine
as he had been unable to avoid overhearing my husband's voice. If

he felt that he had been caught at the keyhole to his parents' bed-room, so to speak, his curiosity was natural. He had anticipated the dismissive or critical response of his strict, religious mother, who typically accused him of having his mind in the gutter, or of his hapless father who typically acted befuddled, ashamed, or as if nothing were going on.

I posited his need for an empathic father who would acknowledge his desire, jealousy, and curiosity and who would "take him on his knee" and tell him something about sex, who would encourage him to look forward to the day when it would be his turn for sexual love. This newly forming notion of a father who could be both rival and pal greatly comforted Caleb. He looked forward to the possibility of talking to his aging father in a different way when he went home to visit his family.

The following week, however, before Caleb's planned departure to visit his ailing mother and father, I unexpectedly again had to cancel his sessions owing to my father's critical state. On his trip home, Caleb faced the fact that his mother's mental deterioration had left her completely dysfunctional, and she required full-time care. He found his father overwhelmed and listlessly depressed. Deeply disturbed at seeing both parents' physical and mental deterioration, on his return he spoke about his mother and his sadness about her, describing himself at home as a "court eunuch serving the queen. I identify with my father serving a brain-dead woman. I see myself as damaged goods—no balls—they fell off 'way back when'."

His return to analysis was marked by a period of late arrivals, missed sessions, and laments that the analysis had drained him of all his resources. The recession, he said, had robbed him of prospects for either creative or remunerative work; he lacked energy for the lengthy drive to his analytic hours, which simply made him feel angry and depleted. I commented on his frustration that his desire had left him so vulnerable that he hated it and wanted to get rid of it by experiencing me as the one who wanted so much of him. He succeeded in constructing me as the demanding, draining, utterly undesirable bitch who humiliated him. This defensive system worked to maintain his denial of grieving for his mother's mental deterioration and killed his recent tentatively emerging awareness of desire. At this point, I was partly correct that his love and longing had been defensively turned into hate, but my own depressive countertransference clouded my capacity to experience him freely and neutrally and unwittingly corresponded closely to Caleb's depression.

Morphine and Poppies

Although I had never said so, the last-minute cancellations were due to my own father's terminal illness and death. Grieving myself, I was unable to summon a vital internal father for Caleb. He spoke of giving up analysis entirely, as he was broke and drained by the long drive to sessions. Listlessly, I thought he might do better in a men's group than in analysis and that it would suit his economic state. He reported a dream in which he was going up a hill:

> I was with someone. It was wonderful. We stopped at this lighted ranch house. Then we were in a walled garden. There were gorgeous huge poppies. The plants were at least four feet high. I thought they must be Matilaja poppies. One was way over by the side and different, in the last stages of bloom and rust covered. The owner came forward and said "Help yourself. If you want some, take them." I worried if you cut them, they wouldn't last.

The poppies reminded him of Soldiers' Field and the red paper poppies the Veterans of Foreign Wars sell on Armistice Day to remember the dead soldiers. Thus, he associated to his mourning over the warrior father he wished for but never had. He also felt that going backwards (Chasseguet-Smirgel, 1985) had to do with his backward search for that father's strength in homosexual encounters, particularly rooted in his fourth year, when his brother was born and he felt cut adrift. But as he drove "up the hill with someone" he was reminded of the drive to my office and its garden. When the owner (my paternal aspect) offered him the poppies (fathering), he was deeply moved and appreciative. He worried about leaving to visit his parents and feeling cut off from me. He feared that the paternal strength I was offering him would not last, especially as he associated to his father's aging and decline (the rust-covered poppy).

Finally, it dawned on me that the poppies he was drawn to represented the father in me that he so desperately needed, the father, whom he called Poppa, whose reassuring and enabling presence he had needed when he was four and his baby brother was born. His intuition was that my poppies were dying, "rusty, in the last stages of bloom . . . and wouldn't last." The connection between poppies and morphine reflected his uncanny attunement to me. It was really quite chilling when I recognized what I hadn't wanted to see, namely, that my dying father was in the hospital on morphine, and I myself wished to remain drugged against the pain of his death. Caleb had experienced this opium-poppy deadness in me and needed desperately to regain in me the vibrant, colorful, and huge Matilija poppies of springtime. I finally woke up to Caleb's need for the strong father in me to guide and protect him as he approached early erotic longings for the mother of his infancy.

I was able then to interpret the dream to him. Pointing out his uncanny sensitivity to me after seven or eight years of our working together, I told him that his trip home had coincided with events he seemed to have sensed in my life. I posited that in my canceled sessions, which had been last minute due to a critical illness of a family member, he had intuited a death—and had fallen into despair.

Confirming his unconscious perception, I tied in his accusation that I had been particularly wounding to him in a session a couple of weeks earlier, when thinking I was making some trenchant and insightful comment, I had subliminally registered that I was also taking a sadistic pleasure in "nailing" him. I let him know that this was uncharacteristic of me and wounding to him. (In fact, in self-analysis, I realized that the acerbically penetrating aspect related to an identification with that aggressive aspect of my father; my behavior had evoked for Caleb memories of his demeaning grandfather.) This session proved to be a breakthrough. Caleb felt reaffirmed by my willingness to be "present" and to acknowledge my contribution to his painful feelings. He felt verified and "a lot less crazy"; he felt like a "snake about to shed old skin."

The Preoedipal Erotic "Slip-Slide" Between Genders

Following this session, Caleb excitedly reported a dream of me as a man:

> You'll love these dreams! The first dream was very sexual. I have a feeling I was in a three-some. This one person I was making love with didn't have a face—it was really like I was swimming—like a fluid! This person was pulling me toward him (or her) and we were kissing—giving and receiving.
>
> Then you were both yourself and your husband and both of you welcomed me into your home. Then it was like you were also your husband who knew and loved you as a woman!! You were wearing a Wizard of Oz outfit—you were an older man—50s or 60s—your hair was gray. I was dumbstruck to discover you were a man.

"These dreams are significant," he said."You told me I was need-ing a man—that perhaps I could find that man in you. I recently got a Bergdorf Goodman catalog and it had this very handsome tuxedo dress. It would look great on you. Maybe my anxiety in thinking of going away to a men's group—if you were a man, I wouldn't have to leave to find that."

I commented on the sense of fluidity and the pleasure he experi-enced in both dreams. In the first, he "tried on" making love to me as a male/female; in the other, he shifted from my husband and me welcoming him to my becoming my husband loving me. I saw this material as bridging the early erotic ties to both the father and the mother. It was characterized by the limitless possibilities of preoedi-pal omnipotence, with its capacity to slip and slide between both genders, followed by the triangular love bonds between the child and differentiated sexual parents of the oedipal phase.

He said, "In the fluid dream, I associated to that time when I almost felt like I was actually being born—a kind of warm, fluid, exciting, wet feeling"—that warm, erotically sensual feeling of being contained in mother's vagina traversing a bridge to feelings of sen-sual eroticism. I noted that in the dream, "love is in a threesome—perhaps you and mother and father, or you and me and my husband. But at this point, you seem to want it all and don't want to relinquish any possibility—love with a man *and* love with a woman. The world *is* your oyster! And you can *be* both sexes, an oyster!"

He laughingly acknowledged this and noted that he could finally imagine himself as a desirable and desiring man, a man desired by women, though "of course I'm not interested in that." This dramatic transformation in the narration of his desire occurred only after I had been sprung from my own countertransference deadness by the recognition of my identification with my dying father. Only then was I free to become once again available to my patient for an erotic resonance within the shifting roles of maternally erotic mother and powerfully enabling father.

In the week after this breakthrough, Caleb made a remarkably creative sculpture that was a sort of "love poem to analysis; it depicts an image of a head in deeply resonant multihued light—a brain with areas of feeling and thought inscribed on it." He stated that this image reflected the richness and complexity of his analysis. He began to take on more and more self-assurance, calling the shots, managing problems surrounding his mother's deteriorating medical condition and his father's depression. He felt a new sense of himself as a "take-charge guy." His father "crowned" him, telling him that he felt ready to turn over the family's financial affairs to his son. Finally, gaining the investiture he had long sought, he started to do financial research on investments and planning regarding the family estate and began to move with the assurance of a man who had some control over his destiny.

Castration by Father's Ineptitude

This triumph was short lived. His father soon recanted and decided not to relinquish control to his son as yet. Caleb felt "beheaded, stabbed in the back, castrated, and turned into shit." He felt he had been robbed of a son's birthright, his "father's blessing" (Blos, 1985). His sister, adding insult to injury, chose the occasion to attack him. She recited all his shortcomings and, as he put it, "worked me over" until he felt completely debilitated. He was furious when he came into his session the following Monday. He announced, "I'm sick of all you women!" and said he would end his analysis because "it hasn't helped at all. I feel just like I always did—impotent, paralyzed, and with nowhere to go. There's nowhere to turn and you're just draining me of my few remaining resources." The self-immolating monk was back.

We explored his pattern of self-destructive withdrawal into an impotent rage, where he was unable to differentiate between one woman and all women. Caleb rather quickly regrouped, acknowledging that he did not want to cut himself off from my support. In the sessions that followed his father's recanting the request that Caleb take over the family finances, he sat up, "refusing to take this lying down." Caleb began to sort out his valid anger and frustration at his father, who once again had "wimped out" and undermined him just when he had given Caleb something. Caleb recognized his pattern of enfeebled withdrawal when confronted by his sister's negativity. He began to consider the possibility that his anger was legitimate. Knowing that his anger would not produce good results if "blasted" at the family, he could nevertheless "own it" and perhaps distill it into something that might effectively clarify and right the situation.

In the session after recognizing his anger at his father, Caleb reported an erotic dream in which he was invited to a banquet in the "south of France or Italy." While his host prepared a meal,

I found an open shower near the garage. It was beautifully tiled. I didn't think my host would mind if I used his shower and soap, so I took my clothes off and was enjoying a shower. I looked up to see a woman photographing me. At first I felt embarrassed. Then I realized that with the southern light, the beautiful tile, the country in the background, and the sun on my body, it would be a very aesthetic shot, so I didn't mind. After I toweled off, she wanted to continue shooting, and though I felt self-conscious I decided there would be a great shot of me swinging in this big swing. I was swinging back and forth. For some reason I had to duck my head each time, but it was great. Then I noticed that she had lost interest.

Caleb immediately linked the woman photographer to me and his new-found pleasure in having me see that he could be attractive. He linked the "south of France or Italy" to my Mediterranean-style home/office. That in the dream I had photographed him without his permission evoked two ideas. One was my having asked his permission to use some of our work for a scientific paper; did he feel excited by the attention? fearful that I would grow bored? The other was his feeling that sometimes I would catch him off guard when he preferred to be left alone, as when I had actively interpreted his intention to quit his analysis.

My "shooting" him revealed his castration anxiety, as well as his guilt that his host (my husband) would shoot him if he knew what pleasures he was enjoying with me on my couch. He linked his nudity to his recently sitting up on the couch to face me and allowing me to look at him. At the same time, deciding to continue the photo session to "play," he entered into more exuberant swinging, but feared I would lose interest. This reminded him of his mother's being interested in him only until he began to describe his separate interests. We both agreed that his sitting up represented frightening and exciting feelings of a "real encounter" without the dispassionate "scientific or artistic" removal of me as the camerawoman/writer behind him or him as the distantly asexual sculptor/museum curator. It also reflected his redoubled efforts to respond with playful vitality to rework his castration anxieties and imagined oedipal defeat.

This dream speaks of the combined excitation and anxiety elicited by a patient's discovery of his analyst's gaze and narrative interest. Pleasure in "composing the scene" is safe, as long as both are engaged in "aesthetic appreciation"; but analytic distance raises questions as to whether the analyst would "really be interested in real life." The additional masturbatory aspect of "swinging sexuality" and the bisexual "back and forth" elicited fear that I would see him as "just going over and over the same old stuff." I suggested that perhaps he felt tired engaging only in masturbatory sex and shunning heterosexual stirrings to avoid sexual rivalry.

Caleb told me that he was reading *Mambo Kings Sing Songs of Love* and felt embarrassed by the "dirty parts." When I inquired, he revealed his fear that I, as his mother had, would chastise him for his prurient sexual curiosity and interest in pornography. The book had, in fact, received a Pulitzer prize, and a friend had recommended it because it told of a man's love of women's bodies and described women's vaginas in earthy, loving detail. Caleb was excitedly enjoying the book because he felt so "ignorant and behind the times."

This led to associations about his rivals for my attention. A psychiatrist whom he met socially gave him one of my published papers about a heterosexual patient. It described the patient's getting to a point where he could say he loved his analyst and found her attractive; Caleb had read the paper enviously. I pointed out that his envy of the other male patient might touch feelings we had spoken of earlier—his feeling that he had been displaced in his mother's embrace both by his father and by the birth of his rival baby brother. Caleb agreed that perhaps his feelings of inadequacy and ugliness, and his fear of boring me, had emerged as he began to feel the "in love sort of feelings" he had felt for his mother when he was her only and special boy. He associated to his anxiety that my husband would be the rival who would humiliate and shame him; he further associated to feeling "cut off at the knees" by his father over and over when he sought his blessing.

The Trumpeter Swan's Song

Caleb expressed relief that he had not quit the analysis and had made contact with these feelings. He talked about his awareness of his need to be assured of his absolute specialness, recalling an incident in the school band. Totally absorbed with the trumpet since the age of 12, Caleb was thrilled when he entered his high school's large orchestra. The band teacher, "Chief," had given him lessons every Saturday. "But I felt I was way out of my league with all these seniors and big guys," Caleb said. However, he distinguished himself and made the "first chair" locally, then in the state, and finally in the regionals. When Chief, however, told Caleb he had not expected him to win the regionals, Caleb was utterly crushed and humiliated. "This confirmed all my worst fears, that people were thinking negatively of me and didn't tell me." I commented on how crushing this kind of experience would be for an adolescent boy seeking from his valued mentor the affirmation he had been unable to find from his father or grandfather.

We also talked, as we had before, about the thinly veiled metaphor of his horn as his adolescent manhood, his penis, which he was thrusting forth into the world to be admired. What Chief had said was like a psychological castration, like his father undoing the blessing he had offered when he first offered Caleb financial responsibility for the family estate and then took it away. I indicated that, although this sense of defeat and fear of ever "putting it out there" had dominated his lifelong narrative, it was not necessarily destined to be so now that he was no longer a little boy. The analysis moved into fully elaborated working through of Caleb's oedipal issues, as well as his mourning for his father's too briefly experienced support.

In this case we have seen a dramatic process of reworking the preoedipal, oedipal, and adolescent male patient's quest for his father. The father was sought in shifting and often evanescent paternal transferences to a female analyst to perform several developmentally vital functions: to assist in the differentiation from a mentally disturbed and sometimes psychotic mother; to affirm his masculine sexual strivings; to provide the paternal blessing for his autonomous functioning in the business world; to mirror his effectiveness; to foster his vitality; and to engage playfully in a nonlethal sexual oedipal rivalry for the mother. These represent typical pre- and postoedipal paternal transferences that oscillate and interweave among preoedipal and oedipal maternal erotic transferences.

In the clinical situation, it is often necessary to uncover paternal transferences embedded within maternal transferences; the early father is particularly elusive, especially when the analyst is female. Sometimes, in contrast to the actual father and occasionally merged with him, either a denigrated or an idealized father figure appears in the transference as an object of both intense longing and frequent despair. Encounter, contact, and sometimes confrontation with this paternal figure is necessary to resolve preoedipal issues as well as oedipal ones. This task is particularly difficult in the search for the early father of the nursery years, whose presence is often shadowy at best and who is often perceived through the later layering of the patient's oedipal drama and more consciously remembered adolescent history.

In this chapter, we have noted the gauzy layers that may obscure early paternal transferences in supervision; with patients where early caretaking arrangements vary; and with male patients in analysis with female analysts. We have also illustrated how, at the same time, the early father may insistently call out to be heard. In the supervisory example, a deceased father appeared both in the shadow of the supervisor's presence on the treatment and in the "ghost" of a former psychiatrist in the office next door; with Corrine, he appeared in the bodily attentions of a hairstylist and in a bundle of blossoms; with the latter two male analysands, the father appeared in the person of the analyst's husband, in dreams, and finally in the search for "the father in mother" within the person of the female analyst.

We have also discussed many of the powerful resistances female analysts may have to struggle through to make this contact come alive. Male and female analysts alike may easily connect to oedipal paternal material but may be slower to recognize the preoedipal paternal presence in the transference nursery. As fathers have only recently taken active roles in the nursery, analysts of both genders not accustomed to finding him there in their own childhood may miss his presence in ways that lead to treatment impasses, stalemates, and enactments.

10

Oedipus and the Spruce Goose

A Narration of an Oedipal Transition

It is the true desire of every artist to impose his or her vision on the world. . . . I build imaginary countries and try to impose them on the ones that exist. I, too, face the problem of history: what to retain, what to dump, how to hold on to what memory insists on relinquishing, how to deal with change. . . . My story's palimpsest country has, I repeat, no name of its own. (Rushdie, 1992, p. 87)

PALIMPSEST: A METAPHOR

Palimpsest is a kind of parchment, or vellum, used by ancient scribes, which could be repeatedly inscribed and erased; often imperfectly eradicated text was still visible in the final version. This seems a particularly congenial metaphor for the textural qualities of narratives of desire.

Over the course of an analysis, the bits and pieces of the patient's current experience, personal history, emotions, attitudes, beliefs, and fears slowly evolve into a series of analytically informed narratives. To the extent that she provides the loom to the patient's narrative warp and woof, the analyst's personal history, beliefs, and so on are also inevitably woven into the background of the patient's narrative.

Composed of an ordered array of interrelated concepts, psychoanalytic narratives form and abridge, authorize and prohibit, privilege and exclude what can be said, heard, and understood by the small community of meaning that is the analytic dyad. Each successive narrative the dyad produces contains traces of earlier attempts at understanding, partially apparent and partially erased.

In this book, we have looked primarily at those narratives related to desire, as they can be focused and understood in erotic transference and countertransference. The major narrative threads that constitute what we call maternal erotic transference include 1) the birth of desire and body-based aspects of the self; 2) anal eroticism and permutations of desire; 3) the sensual matrix in the formation of object relations; and 4) erotic desire as transitional opportunity fostering the solidification of gender identity. Comprehensive understanding of the range of the concept entails the palimpsest-like superimposition and differentiation of these narrative threads not only against each other, but against the broader context of the clinical situation.

How do we know what we know? In our view, transitions within the patient and within the dyad provide the most serviceable, although imperfect, points of comparison available to the analyst. A narrative represents the personal meaning imposed on a series of events. It takes the form of a story that tells who, what, where, how, and why. A noticeable shift in any of these elements, or in the stylistic and syntactic aspects of the narrative, may be correlated with other changes in the interior world. Specifically, we think that transitions can be described by recognizable shifts in narrative accounts, particularly represented in dreams, fantasies, the transference, and the countertransference.

In this chapter we present a case in which a male patient, Ray, and his female analyst (JKW) rework a preoedipal and oedipal narrative that had precluded success. Important changes in Ray's key narrative accounts accompany the progress of the analysis and offer examples of structural changes in the ego and progress in object relations.

EROTIC DESIRE AS TRANSFORMATIONAL OPPORTUNITY

This chapter is mainly concerned with the fourth narrative theme of the MET; that is, erotic desire as a transformational opportunity to foster the solidification of gender identity. Secure gender identity is based on adequate identifications with parents of both genders. Such dual identifications provide flexibility and the dialectic tension that prevents defensive stereotypic adjustments. Developmentally, a secure gender identity is formed in part through the oscillating eroticism involved in making the transition from a primarily two-person maternal engagement to a three-person oedipal triangle, and back again. We identify such transitions within the clinical material.

For male patients with female analysts, the narrative oscillates from chivalrous and aggressive courting of the mother/therapist as love object, to fear of oedipal defeat or success, and back to baby/mommy closeness. The last position is fraught with the dangers of imagined loss of the masculine self through merger with the preoedipal mother. To stave off this anxiety, the oedipal courting returns. This love dance/war dance, and its attendant dangers for patients who are particularly threatened by, yet drawn to, closeness to the mother's body was elaborated in chapter 8 on erotic terror. When the boy-in-the-adult male analysand fantasizes that an intolerably high price will be extracted for the security and bliss of maternal reunion, he fears loss of his masculinity, sacrificed in the at-one-ment with a female body. If his terror does not result in flight, or the defensive reinstatement of rekindled sexual romantic overtures toward the female therapist, the opportunity appears for the male patient to reengage gender development through a series of paternal transferences, described here and in chapter 9.

CLINICAL ILLUSTRATION

Ray: An "Epic Hero"

By age six, most children realize that to tell a story requires that events be related to each other. There must be a point to the story; it must have a proper beginning and end. Western culture is particularly interested in success or failure stories, lives that spiral up or down. One particularly attractive format is the narrative of the epic hero: "Some individuals adopt the 'epic hero' narrative, in which one strives toward success, only to be turned back, and then to battle again to the top, and so on in a series of heroic recoveries" (Gergen, 1991, p. 162).

In this chapter we present a case in which a male patient and female analyst (JKW) engage in reworking such an "epic hero" narrative. This particular patient, who asked to be called Ray, did not suffer from erotic terror so much as he felt himself to be erotically horrifying. Like the patients in chapter 5, who sought rebirthing, he believed he needed to be transformed; Kafka's "Metamorphosis" was, he believed, the story of his life. In particular, he so loathed the masculine gender that he attributed all desirability and goodness to females. At the same time, he tried to convey a notably masculine impression, halfway between "hippie" and "biker." For Ray, the only way to redeem himself from the dreadfulness of being male was to become heroic.

The negotiation of reality, and the making of meaning, were the ever-present subject, purpose and dilemma of the treatment process. Although Ray was not psychotic, he heavily defended himself against recognizing that the world was other than his own omnipotent creation. Relying heavily on manic defenses, he believed in his creations more robustly than in the people around him. Consequently, suffering a profound loneliness, Ray described his heart as encased in a monolith, with only the barest aspect engaged in the world.

A creative writer, bartender, and college lecturer on literature, Ray was a consummate storyteller. In the years of our working together, I seldom heard him use a word carelessly. Sentences, whole paragraphs, seemed crafted either in advance of the meeting or on the spur of the moment. Ray was driven by a ferocious need to make himself understood.

Specializing in phenomenology, Ray envisioned himself as among the preeminent writers of our time. A latter day hippie, he was *au courant* with theater, cinema, and writing, and had achieved some success in each of these fields, including writing a successful screenplay about a fairly obscure cult hero. His dreams were peopled by the mythic and the dead: James Joyce, John Lennon, Howard Hughes and the New York Knicks. No living man genuinely captured his imagination. For Ray, humanity consisted of monkeys and sacred cows, rather than men and women.

According to the original narrative Ray elaborated in treatment, his apparently ordinary, middle-class childhood had been ghastly and chaotic. A saintly, bountiful, and magnificent mother (also a sorceress) failed repeatedly to subdue a barbarous, blundering, proletarian father. Like Oedipus, Ray had for a father a callow, murderous rival. This Laius arrogantly absconded with the mother when Ray was only two weeks old, leaving Ray with his maternal grandmother. Thus, like Oedipus', Ray's abandonment was almost immediate. Mother, although a sorceress, had no choice but to go with her husband. Throughout his childhood, Ray's father was the undisputed villain of the piece, portrayed as extremely dangerous and despicable yet, at the same time, stupid and inconsequential.

Ray was the youngest son; the eldest had ostensibly been driven to a psychotic break by hatred of the father. Only Ray recognized the magnitude of this event and had the brother committed. This was one of the early pieces of heroic rescue that formed Ray's favorite, and in some ways most nourishing, self-image.

Ray's conscious wish was to be as different as possible from his "bean counter" father. Since his father had been financially successful, Ray made it his business to bring down the entire world of finance like a house of cards. In a book that unraveled the intricacies of the credit system, he delineated a method for demolishing the credit industry. Chronically in debt, he lived on this scheme, justifying these shenanigans as necessary to sustain himself while developing his profound literary talent.

The Magical Hero Born of Sorceress and Beast

Because the theme of Ray's narrative, which can be distilled to a magical boy born of a sorceress, required an entirely inadequate father, any positive memories of his father had to remain secret. This narrow focus extremely limited Ray's ability to identify with his father and, as a consequence, interfered with his capacity to feel himself a real man. Later in the treatment, other, more benign aspects of his father were to be retrieved, including his staunch paternal protectiveness and unflagging financial support of his extended family. Eventually, Ray was able to see his father as a "stand-up" guy, and this phallic construction corresponded to his own increasingly appropriate aggression. In the early stage of his analysis, however, every negative aspect of Ray's mother was denied or repressed. As he brought her forth, she was a goddess of tremendous stature who gave birth to him and was at once unique and doomed. Ray considered himself the product of a mismatched couple, a beast, grotesque, yet blessed with the talent to make his acts sublime. An immediately idealizing maternal transference and corresponding countertransference were the initial enactments of the original narrative and were to undergo very erotic development.

A charming and attractive man, he cultivated darkness with tattoos, opaque glasses, antediluvian jeans. Costumed as a "Hell's Angel" and living by the code of Sherwood Forest, he saw as his mission the protection of whatever helpless creature wandered into his path. Ray unhesitatingly gave away all he had to whoever needed it. He delighted in presenting himself as an outlaw, daring the world to see through him. He became the "dirty darling" of more successful, liberal friends who could be relied on to prevent total fiscal disaster.

By his mid 30s, Ray had managed to defeat most of his opportunities. A prime example was that although he fulfilled all the requirements for an advanced degree from a major university, he declined
to pay his fees and never collected the degree. Determined to live
his life in a swashbuckling way, he moved to Paris. For a number of
years he traveled on a credit scheme, using one line of credit to
finance the next and amassing debts he never intended to pay. In a
quasi-revolutionary scenario, he considered it his moral duty to bam-
boozle Credit America, the Real Oppressors of the People. In some
ways, this frenzied white-collar crime amounted to no more than a
hobby, because Ray's soul was dedicated to literature. Ray was convinced that in his writing he was contributing to a better world
in which there would be decency and honor; for him, to make literature was the ultimate act of love. Notwithstanding his credit
schemes, he was generally impecunious. On some days, he spent the
little money he had on feeding a large collection of pets, while he
literally went hungry.

Cycling through manic and depressive periods, he nevertheless
maintained a cadre of childhood friends who grew to prominence in
their respective artistic endeavors while continuing to revere and
finance him, the perpetually unsung genius of his generation. In his
20s and early 30s, his considerable talent as a writer had often been
recognized, but his work—raw, angry, experimental—was only rarely
published. People would become tremendously excited by it, and
then, somehow, it all came to nothing. Additionally, Ray kept up a
correspondence with some truly astonishing figures in the arts,
entirely on the basis of his ability to write remarkable letters. Although collaborations were mentioned, Ray could not follow up on
these offers. In some ways, the letter of intent was enough, more
than enough.

Ray's presenting complaint included his inability to sustain a sexual relationship with the woman he loved. His erotic encounters
tended to be episodic, mostly with prostitutes because with them he
could be sure of not being rejected and not giving offense. Over
time he revealed some mildly perverse masturbatory practices,
including the use of pornography and telephone sex.

A major focus of the analysis was the extent to which Ray was
isolated and imprisoned in a world he had created. He could not
relate to the "idiots out there." Men could not understand his
pain, his humanity, his talent, or his love. Women were sacred
cows who could not be touched, even if he starved. It was a long

time before he acknowledged my presence in the room as other than a rapt audience.

Oedipus and the Spruce Goose

The following dream and associations illustrate some of these issues:

> I was the Howard Hughes persona. It was my Spruce Goose, flying over the water. I was explaining the importance of it being built. It does not matter if it flies. It's the forerunner. People thought it was a failure, but it was a symbol of limitless imagination.
>
> I was in bed with Paulette. Feeling content, and then a menacing character with a gun came in. He was pointing it at me. I didn't take it seriously. The character Alice Cooper takes the gun and shoots himself in the stomach.

He associated to the dream:

"I was just visiting Paulette. My reaction is it has to do with my mother and father and how I was trapped in their dynamic. Alice Cooper, the rock singer, the smeared sexual identity. And he didn't really want to kill me but himself. Alice Cooper's a bourgeois guy who plays golf. He's all hype, a marketing scheme that worked. Reminds me of Mitchell, my oldest friend since kindergarten. He's a VIP in business but a bean counter. I pick on him. Howard Hughes, that was my brother's hero growing up, a maverick entrepreneur. I admire these people to some extent, Ted Turner, William Buckley. Cool guys, even if they might be assholes. [*pause*] I have a good time with Paulette and I'm on the edge. Nervous and depressed. The further I go into the full and rounded way I'm writing, I never proved it before. I never lived up to my own billing."

I said, "You've been more comfortable with big, beautiful failures."

"Yes. And I'm changing it. I'm bucking the system. I was programmed to fail."

"Ray as The Spruce Goose."

"I see that my mother used me. It's weird to see this."

At this point, I challenged his picture of his mother as saintly and asexual. I reframed his unfocused feeling of being used within the specifically sexual context of the manifest dream, with a comment halfway between a statement and a question: "She was seductive with you."

He immediately supplied new pieces of history that supported my tentative construction: "She let me see her in her underwear. She asked me to do up her bra. She used me in between her and my father. One time she almost left him and it was because of me. My mother was voluptuous and feminine, really a woman. I'm getting a little hard on, to think of it. She was a real woman."

He began to weep as, for the first time, he began to deconstruct the defensively cherished narrative of a saintly mother. He moved immediately into the present tense and the now unavoidable and, for the moment, defensively erotic maternal transference: "What is happening here? I'm challenging the dynamics. The big beautiful failure. This is life and death, man [*weeps, hard*]. I like your stockings [*little boy voice*], how they look."

"You like my being a woman, having a woman's body."

"Yes. I love women. I love the way they look."

"Yet when you become sexual with a woman, someone gets killed. So you make wonderful planes that can't really fly, so no one has to be killed. You settle for the fantasy of limitless omnipotence, because real potency is fatal."

"Yes, I need to get in touch with the bean counter. I need to allow myself to identify with my father, his presence and his being a stand-up guy. I've been thinking a lot about that lately."

The Developing Erotic Transference and Countertransference

In this session, when he first indicated awareness of my physical presence, an erotic transference became apparent. I had been picking up the resonance for a long time in the countertransference. I felt him to be a very young and tender manchild and was most concerned about acknowledging his masculine presence without fanning the flames, rather like a high-school teacher with an ardent freshman.

Ray's false picture of his mother was tethered to his manic self-construction as limitless and brilliant, bisexual, but self-destructive. This is the sort of selfobject situation that limits elaboration of the depressive position with its opportunities for repair. Ray had begun to use my presence and his erotic response to me to create the kind of analyst who could oversee his transformation. The analyst he required at that time was a sexual woman who could, but would not, seduce and abandon; who could, but would not, despise the father. In retrospect, it occurred to me that perhaps it would have been useful to explore the erotic avenues further before imposing a genetic reframing of the material, since feet and tickling later emerged as important aspects of his sexual fantasies. I may, however, have unconsciously retreated from the perverse aspects of the erotic moment centering on his interest in my legs and feet.

The avenue I chose, which consisted of a partial oedipal interpretation, did bring us to a positive image of his father, now seen as a stand-up guy for the first time. I think this comment may have permitted Ray's tentative identification with a real and living man. His shift to the father in this maternally erotic moment also underlies our thesis in chapter 9 that the presence of the preoedipal father of boundaries and protection interrupts an erotic regressive merger with the primitive early mother. Segal (1991) put it this way:

> I think one of the important functions of the father is that of an object seen as stopping a stream of mutual projective identifications between child and mother. When the depressive processes are initiated it enables the child to recognize the father as a separate object and that object in turn becomes a necessary factor in the further elaboration of the depressive position. (pp. 46–47)

Ray's intensive weeping was an indication that his manic defense had been punctured and he could begin a more efficacious self-construction than that of Howard Hughes or Alice Cooper.

Alice Cooper: A Symbol of Confusion

Ray described the Alice Cooper character in his dream as a false self and a counterfeit. Most salient in his description was what he named as "the smeared sexual identity." The Cooper image represented Ray's preoedipal, omnipotent, limitless, bisexual self. The image presents an interesting counterpoint to Margot's Aunt Alice dream. In chapter 3 we described that dream image as follows.

> "Aunt Alice" may refer to fused symbols for "falling down the rabbit hole," "phallus," "all ass," and analysis. If so, it typifies a primary developmental characteristic of the preoedipal period, the combined attempt to make confusing and disparate part objects and body parts into a whole. It also may represent the effort to deny triangulation by fusing mother and father into one available parental object. . . . This waystation, or "bridge" . . . represents an erotic container in which father's phallus is fused with mother's body.

A sturdy and serviceable gender identity is based on a continuing dialectic tension and partial resolution between masculine and feminine aspects of the personality. If the child feels that choosing a gender is tantamount to destroying one parent, she or he may seek to resolve this unbearable dilemma by creating a hermaphroditic, or sexually ambivalent, self representation. Alice Cooper, a singer and performance artist, is not altogether such a figure. Alice Cooper is blatantly self-invented, a man in heavy harlequin makeup using a woman's name—a travesty and essentially an illusion.

Ogden (1989) has summarized the child's gender predicament this way:

> Disorders of gender identity can be understood as disturbances of the intrapsychic dialectical relationship of masculinity and femininity. An attempt to make the painful (matricidal or patricidal, and always suicidal) choice leads to the construction of . . brittle pseudo identities [which] lack the subtle resonance of the masculinity and femininity that characterize mature gender identity. The triangulation that is the outcome of a satisfactory Oedipal transitional relationship represents a restructuring of the individual's fundamental bisexuality in such a way that femininity need not be a flight from, or denial of, masculinity (and vice versa). (p. 139)

When Alice Cooper entered the primal scene, he turned the gun on himself; for Ray, suicide was preferable to patricide, or matricide. In subsequent weeks and months, as we worked within this evolving masculine narrative, Ray elaborated more aggressive and phallic themes, as Sam (chapter 4) had done. This masculinization reverberated in the countertransference as well. Ray's work began to sell, and just before my vacation he brought in a large chunk of cash he owed on the bill. He tossed the money casually on the table in front of the analytic couch and told me to "spend it on your vacation, gambling." I was surprisingly offended by his action and noted the manic and hostile aspects of this act and its resemblance to an act carried out with a prostitute. On the surface, Ray's gesture seemed to resemble Leonard's denigration of his analyst described in chapter 6.

Later, upon reflection, I realized that I had neglected another aspect of the gesture. Ray was using this money as a kind of transitional object. He wanted me to carry with me something he had held. Indeed, when I asked him about this later, he remarked that he had carried it around all the previous week, not spending a penny of it, although it was virtually all the cash he had. His wish for fusion was obscured for me by the make-believe oedipal resonance in the countertransference; I momentarily forgot who the Spruce Goose was. It is interesting that Ray did not correct, or refine, my prostitution interpretation, as he so often did when I was off base. He later told me he liked the idea of prostitution because it seemed more adult and acceptable, more what a man would do. Why I fell in with the masquerade is another story, which traced back to my own history with an idealized parent.

Aspects of Paternal Erotic Transference

As Ray struggled to feel and express aggression towards me, he often constructed me as masculine and spoke to me within the male idiom of his adolescence. For example, he often threatened to "kick my ass." I never had a moment's anxiety about this; on the contrary, I found myself sizing him up, wondering if I could kick his ass. Despite his considerable advantage in height, weight and age, I was quite confident that I could. In this way, I was resonating internally with his desperate need for a father to curb his impulses. On the female side of the transference, he loudly and repeatedly proclaimed my specifically female vanity. He maintained that I was trying to seduce him solely in order to be adored by one of the greatest artists of all times. Inadvertently revealing a little about his own erotic transference, he imagined that I went home and masturbated over this triumph.

As his false construction of his mother was repeatedly exposed and identified in the transference, he became terrified of having hurt me in some vital but unspecified way. He was mortified that he had hurt my feelings, deflated me. At other times he was afraid he might kill me or that I might kill him. He was afraid that if he used the couch, I might lie down with him and be sexual. He wanted to carry me in his arms all day and became more and more troubled by the separations. He believed I was deliberately misunderstanding him: when he said he wanted me, he meant it all literally, not figuratively, and felt diminished and insulted by interpretations. Over and over, he asked me to explain how it would help, what good it could do. If we were not to engage in sex, why were we discussing it? Resonating with erotic horror (Chasseguet-Smirgel, 1985; Kumin, 1985), Ray saw only one reason: to humiliate and torture him.

The Monkey Woman and the Gosling

The growing intensity of the erotic transference led to the next important change in the analytic narration. Early in the week, Ray came in and announced that he was "crazed with frenetic energy, wild." His appearance matched his description. He was unable to sit; he paced, peered out the window. Looking at me, then away, he began to tell the following dream:

> It was a busy urban street where you come to change currency. I was with my father, and asked," Should I try to do this? He doesn't really say. I go in anyhow, and while I'm in line I get harassed by this monkey woman. The scene shifts to a big restaurant. She's still harassing me. I go to hit her and I realize she's pregnant. I don't hit her but she falls to the ground. I'm in tears as I cock my fist. She starts rolling around on the ground and turns into a midget black stump and bares her horrible teeth. The owner of the restaurant, a woman, chases her and catches her. As the owner is about to catch her, she realizes she is pregnant. The monkey woman kills the owner and then turns into a repulsive log creature.
>
> Then we're home and I'm eating with some combination of my father and mother, but we're in this little bedroom. Someone says, 'what's wrong?' and I suddenly feel in a profound way that moment of being abandoned as an infant. I suddenly begin to howl. I start screeching the John Lennon song, "Mother. Mother don't go!"

Immediately following the dream, he associated,

> In order to get my mother's ministrations I had to allow my father's abuse. She protected me from his hatred. So here I am today, you minister to me, you soothe me, to go to the center of this hatred. I wouldn't have gotten Mother's love if he hadn't hated me so much. To assure I could stay that close I made him hate me more. I associated my mother's love as a direct product of being hated, so any real affection on my father's part was a threat to that love from mother, which was narcotic, sustaining. The male abuse and humiliation kept me unearthly and attached to my mother. If I go to my father and ask him to help me, my fear is I'll lose mother. You [*Pointing at me, intensely underlining my presence*], you can't stop supplying love now!

This was the first indication that he felt that anything like "love" was between us. This dream signaled a profound internal change in Ray. The log creature, we came to understand, represented the terrifying and denied aspects of his mother, starkly visible beneath the shredded counterfeit image. This unmasking, produced by interpretive work in the transference–countertransference matrix, created the nearly unmanageable anxiety he experienced and also the new narration he was beginning to articulate.

I understood the action of the dream to represent his shifting away from the sorceress mother, whom he had made grotesque in his hatred and the agony of abandonment at two weeks old. He had been unable to tolerate a construction of her as a monkey woman, a primate, a mate for the monkey father, because he would have been the monkey baby, howling endlessly, not even human, unable to speak. So he had transformed his agony into the godling/gosling self, using his art to cleanse and glorify the grotesque act of being human. I was able to convey some of these ideas to him in the following weeks. This episode marked a significant narrative shift, because it was followed by a major alteration in his dreams, which were suddenly athletic, competitive, and very blatantly male. Here are two short examples.

The first dream:

I got into a fight with Humphrey Bogart in our jockey shorts. I just defeated him; not that I killed him or hurt him.

The second:

I was playing basketball with the New York Knicks. I'm unconscious. I can't miss. The lights are so glaring I can't even see the basket but I make it every time. People are screaming. I'm my normal size and these guys are the NBA. My teammate, when there's a time out called, puts his cheek next to me with congratulations.

In these dreams, for the first time, there was the beginning presence of a male figure with whom to struggle, by whom he is encouraged, and to whom he is drawn, "cheek to cheek." This narrative shift sees the emergence of a paternal figure in whom he places blind faith, and suddenly he can't lose, can't miss. It is significant that he manages to stay his real size among the giants of the NBA and is still able to hold his own. These new dream figures illustrate our belief that adequate analysis of the early maternal erotic transference leads to early paternal erotic transferences. When the patient achieves identification with the father within the female analyst, this serves to clarify, support, and solidify gender.

It is also of note that in these dreams Ray portrayed a way of dealing with fathers, aggressively and assertively, but stopping short of destruction. Because the rules of the game are followed, no one gets hurt. Many weeks later, associating anew to this dream, he remembered the one time his father had ever come to see him play basketball. On that night, he played the best game of his life. He could not see his father in the crowd, but in a sudden silent moment, he heard his father say, "Atta boy, Ray!" He wept as he recalled this incident affirming his father's support of his aggressive and competitive strivings. Ray had consciously longed for, and now could only barely glimpse, the father who "initiates and mentors instrumental and expressive masculinity" (Diamond, 1993). We followed this narrative trail to his bitter resentment of his father's lack of availability, due to his preoccupation with work and his wife.

Ray soon brought this conflict directly into the transference. Later the same week, Ray brought in and read to me some of his most successful work. Afterward, he had two thoughts: "Don't show this to your husband." Silence, then, "If you need money I can kill my father and get my inheritance." Somewhat surprised, I asked him if it wouldn't be easier to just ask his father for the money. He laughed and said, "No, it would be far easier to kill him than to ask for money." This construction pleased him enormously; he felt that it was the key to his relationship with his father, and with me. He felt that I must understand this to understand him. He then began to speak more directly about his feelings about the essential perversion of all sexual acts.

In the following weeks, he solidified his new understanding of the way he had constructed the relationship between himself and his mother to lead him to a feeling of limitless greatness, but at the cost of his ability to identify with his father and to learn how to live in the real world with anything like success and satisfaction.

Revising a Counterfeit Narrative

In chapter 6, on perverse narratives of desire, we presented the concept of the deadlock, in which a healthy and enlivening sense of self was not fostered within the early mother–infant relationship. Consequently, an enlivening internal object position could not be achieved. We proposed that under such circumstances a coordinated series of fantasies are unconsciously converted into attempts at a normalizing narration of one's life in order to make it endurable. A male patient who realized how much of his "normal" life he had fabricated used the phrase "This must be love" to stimulate and describe his constant, feverish reworking of parental indifference into demonstrations of "freedom and trusting me." These normalizing fantasies over time result in counterfeit objects, false in that they do not provide transitional opportunities. These counterfeit objects are complementary to a false self; the defense of the false self is related to the maintenance of the counterfeit object and vice versa.

The cumulative defensive posture resulting from excessive fictionalizing one's ongoing life has a marked effect on the ability to learn from experience, making it difficult for new experiences to occur. If in early development the object is not authentic—that is, partially encountered outside the omnipotent control of the self—genuine intimacy is not possible, for the other person is not quite real. Indeed, the idea that the object might be outside the omnipotent control of the self remains a constant threat that must be constantly answered in the negative: "No. You are mine. I control you." Such false objects do not add anything new to the relationship. The developmental crisis becomes a lifelong event, and the object is essentially a counterfeit object, held together by more massive and primitive defensive efforts. In the analytic situation, the potential playground becomes a graveyard, as discussed in chapter 6.

A patient in this state desperately tries to manage a morass of undifferentiated primitive wishes but lacks the proper object environment and narrative space in which to achieve this. That proper environment is what is meant by "good-enough" mothering. A "good-enough" mother/analyst is both found and invented, experienced by the patient as allowing herself to be controlled, destroyed, or ignored as the patient requires for normal development.

The therapeutic environment is woefully incomplete if it excludes the sensual body of the analyst as part of the transference playground. The analyst must allow, limit, and survive this process, which occurs, of course, entirely in the *minds* of the patient and the analyst. If she does, she permits the patient to split her into good and bad aspects, to fathom the essential elements of her loved and hated maternal and paternal bodies, and then gradually to reconcile them. In this way, the analyst enables the patient finally to make, as we have suggested in chapter 3, a whole beloved object out of a series of contradictory fragments and primitive shards.

Ray, whose narrative closes this, our final, chapter, represents such a failed attempt at transformation. For him, maternal reparations and oedipal transition had been attempted and had failed, leaving gender less than solid, his self-esteem friable, and his mood labile. The clinical crisis occurred as Ray had to face his horrified belief that his aggression and hatred for his once idealized and subsequently disappointing mother had, in the transference, irredeemably destroyed his analyst. All of this was played out in the erotic transference and countertransference duet of his narration of desire.

Transformations do considerable damage to sorcery (as in Saint-Saëns's *Sorcerers's Apprentice*, in which the sorcerer is gradually dissolved after a seemingly fiendish and macabre erotic dance frenzy). Mutative encounters with the mind/womb of a creative analyst cultivate the patient's transformation, and newer and more healthy narratives are born. They are fostered within the rich dominions of early erotic transferences and countertransferences. Transit within analytic therapy through this developmental crisis lends to both the internal objects and the self a solidity and vitality.

Ray came into treatment with a counterfeit mother whose life he was preoccupied with saving, and a denigrated father, with whom he could not identify. He was not able to move into and through oedipal issues and left with important implications for issues of gender, generativity, and reality. He was managing ongoing unconscious rage toward his counterfeit mother by idealization and other manic devices.

He came into the treatment prepared to offer me the same deal. If I would acknowledge his greatness, he would be my slave. He would forego phallic considerations and content himself with oral, and anal, and narcissistic gratifications. The dream image of the Spruce Goose, the pathetic wooden creature that flew only once, and the echoes of the manic psychosis of Howard Hughes, provided me with a chunk of constructs to understand his dilemma. In his "smeared sexual identity," he was shooting himself in the belly, and I needed to help him find a way out of the deadlock.

Learning from the Patient: Goosing Mother Goose

The image of the Spruce Goose—the anality of the goose image and its relation to Mother Goose, the maker of fairy tales—added something essential, but hard to verbalize, to my comprehension of preoedipal male development. At the time, the image seemed transparent; it seemed to speak directly to me, clarifying my thinking on the meaning of manic reparation and the outcome of fear of success. I wonder if the heightened intellectual excitement represented a sublimation of erotic interest on my part.

In the following months, Ray was able to put words to, and elaborate in my presence, explicitly sexual wishes about me. They did not, at this point include intercourse but, instead, were variations on the themes of naked embrace, tickling, nursing, and holding. As space was made for these fantasies in our narration, they changed. Next, he imagined being entirely contained somehow within me. Again, he found these fantasies humiliating and horrifying. He felt as if I were torturing him, masturbating with his very soul, triumphant in having secured his devotion and his great talent.

He despaired of telling me any fantasy because, in his manic state, they came in such overwhelming numbers and were so incredibly real that he momentarily lost track of primary and secondary process. Having struggled throughout the session to do so, he painfully revealed an intense, savage wish to put me across his knee and insert a finger into my anus. As he spoke, he trembled in fear, shame, and confusion.

Clearly, to him, this was not a fantasy or a wish, but an act. He was so regressed I felt as if only my presence were holding him to earth and to sanity. At the same time, I saw this as a chance for him to feel himself to be fully human. In my mind was an image of a man climbing the sheer face of a mountain, losing his footing, and needing to be steadied by his companion. I felt extremely strong and more masculine than feminine in that moment. I felt that if I had to pick him up and carry him, I could do so. If this was an erotic countertransference, it was decidedly paternal. As we sat together and quietly discussed his experience and the intensity of his wish and shame, we both understood a final dimension of the Spruce Goose.

That this was another important narrative transition was indicated by Ray's diminished perverse masturbatory activity. As these acts decreased in frequency they were replaced by more appropriate sexual behavior. Also at this time his mother began to appear as a ghost in his dreams; she had something to tell him, but he could not or would not hear it. I took this as a sign of the return of repressed material (Fairbairn, 1943), specifically, the theme of mortality. As his manic defenses continued to fray, Ray elaborated the theme of limitations in a short series of dreams. In the first dream, he needed to move his mother to higher ground to prevent her from being flooded. Accomplishing this, he then took himself though a series of complicated, fantastical acrobatics to a steeple, where he just barely hung on. In the next dream, waiting for his mother to come back, he was terribly thirsty. Although he drank gallons of apple juice from his own refrigerator, he could not slake his thirst. He realized he must have milk. In the third dream he was in a doctor's office, confronted by the possibility of mortality: he could tolerate the certainty of death if his mother would promise to see that his book was published.

We understand the dream narratives in the following way: Ray had to take his mother to higher ground, that is, he had to remove her to protect her from his sexual hunger and his rage. Having done so, he developed the manic vision of himself as immortal, but terribly high in the air. In our years of working together, Ray came to realize that what he had in himself, sweet apple juice squeezed from the tree of knowledge, and poured endlessly into his writing, was indeed delicious, but not a substitute for the breast. His recognition of a need for the other—me, mortal woman—with the womb, breast, and mind of a woman, brought with it the acceptance of mortality.

Here was, finally, a mother who was able to take care not only of herself but of him too. The dream spoke of both a much more adequate maternal object, and a self who was capable of finishing a project. In this context, instead of the presumptive, preemptive act of parthenogenetic male birth his work had manically represented, the book depicted a legitimate bid for recognition and provided him considerable solace. This dream series was followed in a few months by Ray's being able to find and relate to a woman in an appropriate sexual relationship.

Although Ray continued to struggle with his inability to turn his talents into real-world profits, he no longer believed that talent was all that was required of him, and that everything else must flow from that.

The Analyst's Empty Nest

The countertransference was complicated by Ray's unusual literary talent. From the beginning, I found him fascinating to listen to, enchanting. Perhaps this was the resonance of the much-needed maternal preoccupation he seemed to have missed the first time around, when, as he felt it, he was deserted at two weeks of age.

Ray engaged me as an actor in his narration and altered me with his shifting demands. For him I took on a more masculine identity, as the need for fathering and his projections had their effect. He needed me to infuse the bean-counter father with the magic previously reserved for his mother/sorceress. As I called on male identifications, I became Alice Cooper, Howard Hughes, the New York Knicks, and, eventually, a good-enough father.

Perhaps every analytic termination leaves the analyst with unresolved internal issues. Sometime in the last several months before he was scheduled to terminate, I dreamed that Ray had packed his suitcase and was leaving me for another woman. I was furious but accepted the inevitable. Weeks later, I dreamed that I had produced a marvelous piece of sculpture, a head, that was so magnificent that it suddenly burst into life. But this bursting into life also marked the beginning of its destruction, and it, unlike the portrait of Dorian Gray, soon began to age. Before the aging process began, the original image of the head, a little neonatal, had not entirely formed. In particular, one of the eyes was closed. The figure looked sad and confused, because he understood that this was the beginning of our eventual separation. I woke up thinking that this was a dream about Ray.

Ray's leaving me for another woman, as he did in the first dream, was of course, the best outcome of the mother–son situation and implied a resolution Ray had not previously achieved. In the second dream, the artistic action of casting his head so realistically that it brought him finally to life bore clear remnants of a manic/grandiose alternative to birth; it almost seems to be the original transference–countertransference matrix condensed into a single symbol. The provision of aging adds the human dimension and reflects the existential dilemma of life and death inevitably intertwined, the very issue of mortality we had hoped to bypass. The neonatal quality of the head, and in particular the one sleepy eye, reminded me of a hospital photo of my tiny newborn daughter, moments old in the photo. At the time the dream took place, she was entering high school, and moving toward autonomy, yet still deserving and requiring parenting but with much altered demands.

As I continue to reflect on the requirements of the maternal role, in life and analysis, I am mindful of the magnitude of effort, the magnitude of the reward, and the hope and trepidation with which one watches the generations in their inevitable advance away from home. In these dreams, I cast myself as accepting the situation Ray was only beginning to deal with; in life, it is not always so. Without delving too far into my personal dynamics, the manic and grandiose countertransference meanings of the dream seemed painfully self-evident when I awoke. They are the familiar anodyne for loss. I had been enrolled in the analysis as a kind of birth goddess, uncomfortably reminiscent of Ray's image of me, but we had both struggled to the recognition that the work of becoming is, finally, an individual matter and cannot be accomplished in any other way. Alice Coopers can't make babies; wooden birds can't fly; analysts can't erase a patient's history and start from scratch. And for me, most poignantly, live birds, once named, nourished, and nested, must, in contrast to the Spruce Goose, fly into their own destiny.

THE PALIMPSEST OF NARRATIVE TRUTH

In psychoanalysis, the most important sources of understanding are reverberative rather than predictive. This is inherent in the ideas of repetition, reconstruction, and transference. What the patient once was, he will be again; what the patient desired, believed, fantasized, and has forgotten will again be apparent as derivatives, plucked from dreams, associations, slips, symptoms, and, most especially, the ongoing interwoven threads of the transference and countertransference. These reverberations result over time in narratives, which, in turn, influence and shape the analysis. Narratives may either support mutative change or obscure and impede it.

A patient enters treatment with a story, including some ideas about the way life works and the way his own life in particular works or fails to work. Individual responsibility for outcomes and the ownership of action are key aspects of the story, as are cohesiveness and self-consistency. The quality and character of the objects and object relations the patient describes are equally vital. In the analytic process, the patient discovers, selects, and elaborates symbols, objects, and memories. As these are grouped together in a more or less complete narrative account, the resulting palimpsest may serve as a kind of working truth of the analysis. Such a narrative would contain within it a summary of the state of the self, the state of the object, and the state of the analysis.

Spruiell (1993) has pointed out the overwhelming masses of information that analysts are regularly expected to deal with. When confronted with overwhelming data, we, clinging to the slender reeds of the settled to avoid being washed away in chaos, take refuge in organization. We strive to listen without prejudice but must necessarily listen within the context of our own system of meaning, including the very real filter of the countertransference. No special claims can be honored for the pure reality of the analyst's observations, which Spence (1992) has called the "doctrine of immaculate perception."

Yet we cannot simultaneously question every aspect of our belief system without incurring the paralysis of the obsessive-compulsive and essentially ignoring the patient. Having acknowledged the partiality of our theories, and keeping in mind the fallibility of our ideas and of our ability to live up to our own ideals, we still need a working truth to be getting on with. Freud maintained his conviction that memories, embedded in the unconscious, could be coaxed or compelled to speak for themselves through the synchronous processes of the patient's free association and the analyst's evenly hovering attention. Contemporary analysts, questioning Freud's basically archaeological perspective on the nature of memory, have rejected the notion that splintered shards of memory lie, pristine and undiluted, under the obscuring mud of repression.

At the outset of this book, we defined stories as containing a character undertaking action, mental or physical, real or imagined, within the interrelated series of events that constitute the narrative or story itself. We defined narration more broadly as the developmental capacity for verbally describing internal and interpersonal experience, some of which is preverbal, body based, and inchoate. Narration is a form of internal organizer through which a person attempts to balance and orchestrate narcissistic, aggressive, and sexual intentions. Narration also names and defines important internal objects and potentially reveals a great deal about internal psychic structure.

It is no easy matter, though, to "read backwards" from a narrative, to arrive at statements about drives, objects, self-states, and belief systems. First of all, there are, in the very telling, the distortion and limitation inherent in transducing thoughts into words. This is particularly relevant when dealing with images and affects, which may not be available to the person in anything like a speakable language. Second, once a story is established, changing it causes anxiety and disruption. Third, there is the issue of unconscious compliance, the ways in which patients tend, over time, to dream and produce material in ways that confirm the theories of their own analysts.[1] Finally,

---

[1] I must leave aside for now the issues of how much of this is attributable to compliance and how much to genuine identification. There is also the corollary consideration of resistance, where seeming agreement prevents uncomfortable change.

and most specifically on the analyst's side of the couch, there is the double helix of analytic theory and countertransference, which serves as the frame of comprehension through which constructions are created. All these factors are endemic aspects of resistance and make it difficult to deconstruct the existing narrative in the service of analytic change.

So where must we look for our working truth? It is our conviction that analysts, working within a narrative analytic space, find the most powerful and therapeutically transformational elements of truth within the rich, powerful, bodily based phases of primitive maternal erotic transferences and countertransferences. Within the slowly and cautiously created safety of the analytic space, primitive and then oedipal erotic transferences are elaborated in the kind of mutual story-making process we have come to call the narration of desire.

Thus, it is our way to do our analytic work mindful of the body–mind relationship, tracing patients' songs and stories of their bodies from before birth onward and into the analytic relationship. Attunement to bodily experiences evoked through words brings forth the themes and leitmotifs of their particular narration of desire. Once this process is completed, each patient moves on with the capacity for new ever-developing sagas of his or her generative love stories. To return to the "romance of the rose," both patient and analyst move within the earthy origins of desire—with the worms, snails, dirt, and the moisture of impulsivity, bonding, and sensual hunger—into longing for the other, tolerance for ambivalence, then desire, and finally the "rose," the capacity for love. To have that capacity is to recognize the separateness and integrity of the other, and to be able to incorporate tenderness and aggression. Ultimately the rose can come into full bloom—into mutuality, love, and genuine intimacy.

References

Anzieu, D. (1989). *The Skin Ego*. New Haven, CT: Yale University Press.

Balint, M. (1968). *The Basic Fault*. London: Tavistock.

Bateson, G. (1972). *Steps to an Ecology of Mind*. New York: Ballantine Books.

——— (1979). *Mind and Nature*. New York: Dutton.

Benjamin, J. (1988). *The Bonds of Love*. New York: Pantheon Books.

Bergler, E. (1952). *The Superego*. New York: Grune & Stratton.

Bernstein, D. (1991). Gender specific dangers of the female dyad in treatment. *Psych. Rev.*, 78:37–48.

Bion, W. R. (1957). Differentiation of the psychotic from the non-psychotic personality. *Internat. J. Psycho-Anal.*, 38:266–275.

——— (1959). Attacks on linking. *Internat. J. Psycho-Anal.*, 40:308–315.

——— (1962). The psycho-analytical study of thinking. *Internat. J. Psycho-Anal.*, 43:306–310.

Blos, P. (1985). *Son and Father*. New York: Free Press.

Blum, H. P. (1973). The concept of erotized transference. *J. Amer. Psychoanal. Assn.*, 21:61–76.

——— (1980). The value of reconstruction in adult psychoanalysis. *Internat. J. Psycho-Anal.*, 61:39–52.

Bollas, C. (1987). *The Shadow of the Object*. New York: Columbia University Press.

——— (1992). Colloquium on a paper in progress on erotic transference. Santa Barbara, CA, July 25.

Boothby, R. (1991). *Death and Desire*. New York: Routledge.

Brenman Pick, I. (1985). Working through in the countertransference. *Internat. J. Psycho-Anal.*, 66:156–166.

Breuer, J. & Freud, S. (1893-95). *Studies on Hysteria, Standard Edition*, 2:21–47. London: Hogarth Press, 1955.

Call, J., Galenson, E., & Tyson, R. L. (1983). *Frontiers of Infant Psychiatry,* Vol. 1. New York: Basic Books.

Cardinal, M. (1983), *The Words to Say It*. Cambridge: Van Vactor & Goodheart.

Carpy, D. V. (1989). Tolerating the countertransference: A mutative process. *Internat. J. Psycho-Anal.*, 70:287–294.

225

Chasseguet-Smirgel, J. (1978). Reflections on the connections between perversion and sadism. *Internat. J. Psycho-Anal.*, 59:27–35.

———— (1984). The femininity of the analyst in professional practice. *Internat. J. Psycho-Anal.*, 65:169–178.

———— (1985). *Creativity and Perversion*. New York: Norton.

———— (1986). *Sexuality and Mind*. New York: New York University Press.

Chehrazi, S. (1986). Female psychology: A review. *J. Amer. Psychoanal. Assn.*, 34:141–162.

Coen, S. (1986), The sense of defect. *J. Amer. Psychoanal. Assn.*, 34: 47–67.

The New Columbia Encyclopedia (1975). New York: Columbia University Press.

Cooper, A. M. (1986). What men fear: The facade of castration anxiety. In: *The Psychology of Men*, ed. F. M. Lane, G. I. Fogel & R. S. Liebert. New York: Basic Books, pp. 113–131.

Diamond, M. J. (1993). Fathers and sons: Psychoanalytic perspectives on "good enough" fathering throughout the life cycle. Presented at spring meeting of Division 39 of the American Psychological Association, New York.

Eco, U. (1992). Overinterpreting texts. In: *Interpretation and Overinterpretation*, ed. S. Collini. Cambridge: Cambridge University Press, pp. 45–66.

Eliot, T. S. (1952). The hollow men. In: *A Little Treasury of American Poetry*. New York: Chas. Scribner's Sons.

Emde, R.N., Gaensbauer, T. & Harmon, R., ed. (1976). *Emotional Expression in Infancy. Psychological Issues,* Monogr. 37. New York: IUP.

Erikson, J. M. (1988). *Wisdom and the Senses*. New York: Norton.

Fairbairn, W. R. D. (1943). Repression and the return of bad objects (with special reference to the "war neuroses") *Brit. J. Med. Psychol.*, 19:327–341.

Federn, P. (1952). *Ego Psychology and the Psychoses*. New York: Basic Books.

Fliegel, Z. O. (1982). Half a century later: Current status of Freud's controversial views on women. *Psychoanal. Rev.*, 69:7–28.

Fogel, G. I., Lane, F. M. & Liebert, R. S., ed. (1986). *The Psychology of Men*. New York: Basic Books.

Freud, S. (1913). On beginning the treatment. *Standard Edition*, 13:121–144. London: Hogarth Press, 1958.

———— (1917). Mourning and melancholia. *Standard Edition*, 14:243–258. London: Hogarth Press, 1957.

———— (1919). "A child is being beaten." *Standard Edition*, 17:175–205. London: Hogarth Press, 1955.

———— (1933). Femininity. *Standard Edition*, 22:112–135. London: Hogarth Press, 1964.

Gaddini, E. (1977). Formazione del padre e scene primaria. *Riv. Pscianal*, 23:167–184.

Galenson, E. (1985). Preoedipal influences reflected in the transference, with special reference to women in the transference in psychotherapy. In: *The Transference in Psychotherapy*, ed. E. A. Schwaber. New York: IUP.

———— & Roiphe, H. (1981). *Infantile Origins of Sexual Identity*. New York: IUP.

Gay, P. (1988). *Freud, A Life for Our Time.* New York: Norton.

Gergen, K. (1991). *The Saturated Self.* New York: Basic Books.

Goldberg, P. (1989). Actively seeking the holding environment. *Contemp. Psychoanal.,* 25:449–479.

Goldberger, M. & Evans, D. (1985). On transference manifestations in male patients with female analysts. *Internat. J. Psycho-Anal.,* 66:295–309.

Gornick, L. R. (1986). Developing a new narrative: The woman therapist and male patient. *Psychoanal. Psych.,* 3:299–326.

Greenson, R. (1967). *The Technique and Practice of Psychoanalysis.* New York: IUP.

———— (1968). Disidentifying from mother: Its special importance for the boy. *Internat. J. Psycho-Anal.,* 49:370–374.

Grotstein, J. S. (1978). Inner space: Its dimensions and its coordinates. *Internat. J. Psycho-Anal.,* 59:55–61.

———— (1980). A proposed revision of the psychoanalytic concept of primitive mental states: I. an introduction to a newer psychoanalytic psychology. *Contemp. Psychoanal.,* 16:479–546.

———— (1990a). The "black hole" as the basic psychotic experience: Some newer psychoanalytic and neurosciences perspectives on psychosis. *J. Amer. Acad. Psychoanal.,* 18:29–46.

———— (1990b). Nothingness, meaninglessness, chaos and the "black hole": Parts I & II. *Contemp. Psychoanal.,* 26:257–290, 337–467.

Guntrip, H. (1969). *Schizoid Phenomena, Object Relations and the Self.* New York: IUP.

Hirsch, M. (1989). *The Mother/Daughter Plot.* Bloomington: Indiana University Press.

Horney, K. (1926). Flight from womanhood. In: *Feminine Psychology,* ed. H. Kelman. New York: Norton.

Jacobsen, E. (1965). *The Self and the Object World.* London: Hogarth Press.

Joseph, B. (1982). Addiction to near-death. *Internat. J. Psycho-Anal.,* 63:449–456.

Keller, E. F. (1985). *Reflections on Gender and Science.* New Haven, CT: Yale University Press.

Kernberg, O. (1975). *Borderline Conditions and Pathological Narcissism.* New York: Aronson.

Khan, M. (1979). *Alienation in Perversion.* New York: IUP.

Klein, M. (1975). *Love, Guilt and Reparation and Other Works, 1921–1945.* New York: Delacorte.

Kris, E. (1951). Some comments and observations on early autoerotic activities. In: *Selected Papers of Ernst Kris.* New Haven, CT: Yale University Press.

Kristeva, J. (1982). *Powers of Horror.* New York: Columbia University Press.

Kuhn, T. (1962). *The Structure of Scientific Revolutions.* Chicago: University of Chicago Press.

Kulish, N. M. (1986). Gender and transference: The screen of the phallic mother. *Internat. J. Psycho-Anal.,* 13:393–404.

———— (1986). The shadow of the object: notes on self-and object-representations.

Psychoanal Contemp. Thought, 9:653–675.

Kumin, I. (1985). Erotic horror: Desire and resistance in the psychoanalytic situation. *Internat. J. Psychoanal. Psychother.,* 11:3–20.

Lacan, J. (1977), *Ecrits,* trans. A. Sherican, London: Tavistock.

Lane, F. M. (1986). Transference and countertransference: definition of terms. In: *Between Analyst and Patient,* ed. H. Meyers. Hillsdale, NJ: The Analytic Press, pp. 227–256.

Lederer, W. (1968). *The Fear of Women.* New York: Grune & Stratton.

Lester, E. P. (1985). The female analyst and the erotized transference. *Internat. J. Psycho-Anal,* 66:283–293.

Lichtenberg, J. (1981). Implications for psychoanalytic theory of research on the neonate. *Internat. Rev. Psycho-Anal.,* 8:35–52.

——— (1983). *Psychoanalysis and Infant Research.* Hillsdale, NJ: The Analytic Press.

——— (1991). What is a selfobject? *Psychoanal. Dial.,* 1:455–480.

Lichtenstein, J. (1961). *The Dilemma of Human Identity.* New York: Aronson.

Liebert, R. S. (1986). The history of male homosexuality from ancient Greece through the renaissance. In: *The Psychology of Men,* ed. G. Fogel, F. Lane & R. Liebert. New York: Basic Books, pp. 193–215.

Limentani, A. (1991). Neglected fathers in the aetiology and treatment of sexual deviations. *Internat. J. Psych-Anal.,* 72:573–584.

Mahler, M. (1971). *A Study of the Separation-Individuation Process and Its Possible Application to the Borderline Phenomena in the Psychoanalytic Situation.* New York: Quandrangle.

——— Pine, F. & Bergman, A. (1975). *The Psychological Birth of the Human Infant.* New York: Basic Books.

McDougall, J. (1964). Homosexuality in women. In: *Female Sexuality,* ed. J. Chasseguet-Smirgel. London: Karnac Books, pp. 171–123.

——— (1972). Primal scene and sexual perversion. *Internat. J. Psycho-Anal.,* 53:371–384.

——— (1978). *A Plea for a Measure of Abnormality.* New York: IUP.

——— (1986a). Eve's reflection: On the homosexual components of female sexuality. In: *Between Analyst and Patient,* ed. H. Meyers. Hillsdale, NJ: The Analytic Press, pp. 213–228.

——— (1986b). Identifications, neoneeds and neosexualities. *Internat. J. Psycho-Anal.,* 67:19–31.

——— (1989). *Theaters of the Body.* New York: Norton.

Moss, D. (1989). From the treatment of a nearly psychotic man: A Lacanian perspective. *Internat. J. Psycho-Anal.,* 70:275–286.

Natterson, J. (1991). *Beyond Countertransference.* Northvale, NJ: Aronson.

Ogden, T. (1985). On potential space. *Internat. J. Psycho-Anal.,* 66:129–141.

——— (1986). *The Matrix of the Mind.* Northvale, NJ: Aronson.

——— (1989). *The Primitive Edge of Experience.* Northvale, NJ: Aronson.

Person, E. S. (1985). The erotic transference in women and in men: Differences and consequences. *J. Amer. Acad. Psychoanal.,* 13:159–180.

Piontelli, A. (1989). A study on twins before and after birth. *Internat. Rev. Psycho-Anal.*, 16:413-426.

Plaut, E. A. & Hutchinson, F. L. (1986). The role of puberty in female psychosexual development. *Internat. Rev. Psycho-Anal.*, 13:417–432.

Racker, H. (1968). *Transference and Countertransference*. New York: IUP.

Rosenfeld, G. C. & Ochberg, R. L., ed. (1992). *Storied Lives*. New Haven, CT: Yale University Press.

Ross, J. M. (1982). In search of fathering: A review. In: *Father and Child*, ed. S. Cath, A. Gerwitt & J. M. Ross. Boston: Little, Brown.

———— (1993). Panel Discussion on "The father of the nursery years and beyond." Spring meeting of Division 39 of the American Psychological Association, New York.

Rushdie, S. (1985). *Shame*. London: Jonathan Cape.

Sanville, J. (1987). Creativity and the constructing of the self. *Psychoanal. Rev.*, 74:263–280.

———— (1991a). *The Playground of Psychoanalytic Therapy*. Hillsdale, NJ: The Analytic Press.

———— (1991b). Review of *Wisdom and the Senses* by J. Erikson. *Child & Adol. Soc. Wrk.*, 8:431–434.

Schafer, R. (1960). On the loving and beloved superego in Freud's structural theory. *The Psychoanalytic Study of the Child*, 15:163–188. New York: IUP.

———— (1976). *A New Language for Psychoanalysis*. New Haven, CT: Yale University Press.

———— (1978). *Language and Insight*. New Haven, CT: Yale University Press.

———— (1980). Action language and the psychology of the self. *The Annual of Psychoanalysis*, 8:83–92. New York: IUP.

———— (1983). *The Analytic Attitude*. New York: Basic Books.

———— (1986). Men who struggle against sentimentality. In: *The Psychology of Men*, ed. G. Fogel, F. Lane & R. Liebert. New York: Basic Books.

———— (1992). *Retelling a Life*. New York: Basic Books.

Segal, H. (1964). *Introduction to the Work of Melanie Klein*. New York: Basic Books.

———— (1991). *Dream, Phantasy and Art*. London, Tavistock/Routledge.

Shengold, L. (1967). The effects of overstimulation: Rat people. *Internat. J. Psycho-Anal.*, 48:403–425.

———— (1971). More about rats and rat people. *Internat. J. Psycho-Anal.*, 52:277–288.

———— (1985). Defensive anality and anal narcissism. *Internat. J. Psycho-Anal.*, 6:47–64.

———— (1988). *Halo in the Sky*. New York: Guilford Press.

Siegelman, E. Y. (1990). *Metaphor and Meaning in Psychotherapy*. New York: Guilford Press.

Solomon, J. (1978). Transitional phenomena and obsessive-impulsive states. In: *Between Reality and Fantasy*, ed. S. Grolnick & L.B. Boyer. Northvale, NJ: Aronson, pp. 247–255.

Spence, D. (1982). *Narrative Truth and Historical Truth*. New York: Norton.

———— (1992). The hermeneutic turn: Soft science or loyal opposition? Presented at spring meeting of Division 39 of American Psychological Association, Philadelphia.

Spruiell, V. (1993). Deterministic chaos and the sciences of complexity: Psycho-analysis in the midst of a general scientific revolution. *J. Amer. Psychoanal. Assn.*, 41:3–44.

Stern, D. (1985). *The Interpersonal World of the Infant*. New York: Basic Books.

———— (1992). Development of the narrative self. Presented at UCLA Conference on "Narratives: Creating Meaning from Birth through Adulthood." Depts. of Humanities, Sciences & Social Sciences, Los Angeles.

Stoller, R. J. (1968). *Sex and Gender,* London: Maresfield Reprints, 1984.

Thomas, D. (1957a), Poem on his birthday. In: *Dylan Thomas: Collected Poems*. New York: New Directions.

———— (1957b). Twenty-four years. In: *Dylan Thomas: Collected Poems*. New York: New Directions.

Tolpin, M. (1971). On the beginnings of a cohesive self: An application of the con-cept of transmuting internalization to the study of transitional object and signal anxiety. *The Psychoanalytic Study of The Child*, 26:316–354. New York: Quadrangle.

Tyson, P. (1982). The role of the father in gender identity, urethral erotism, and phallic narcissism. In: *Father and Child,* ed. S. Cath, A. Gerwitt & J.M. Ross. Boston: Little, Brown, pp. 175–189.

Van Buren, J. (1991), The psychoanalytic semiosis of absence. *Internat. J. Psycho-Anal.*, 18:249-263.

Welles, J. K. (1989). Deadlocks: The construction and maintenance of counterfeit objects. Presented at spring meeting of Division 39 of American Psychological Association, Boston.

———— (1993). Counterfeit Analyses: Maintaining the illusion of knowing. Presented at spring meeting of Division 39 of American Psychological Asso-ciation, New York.

———— & Wrye, H. K. (1991). Maternal erotic countertransference. *Internat. J. Psycho-Anal.*, 72:93–106.

Werman, D. S. (1986). On the nature of oceanic experience. *J. Amer. Psychoanal. Assn.*, 34:123–140.

Winnicott, D. W. (1952). Transitional objects and transitional phenomena. In: *Playing and Reality*. New York: Basic Books, 1971, pp. 38–57.

———— (1956). Primary maternal preoccupation. In: *Collected Papers: Through Pediatrics to Psychoanalysis*. New York: Basic Books, 1958, pp. 300–305.

———— (1967). The location of cultural experience. In: *Playing and Reality*. New York: Basic Books, 1971, pp. 95–103.

———— (1971). *Playing and Reality*. New York: Basic Books.

Wolf, D. (1992). Narrative attunement. Presented at UCLA Conference on "Narratives: Creating Meaning from Birth through Adulthood." Depts. of Humanities, Sciences, & Social Sciences, Los Angeles.

Wrye, H. K. (1991). Space as a narrative theme. Presented at spring meeting of Division 39 of American Psychological Association, Chicago.

——— (1993a). Hello the hollow: Deadspace or playspace? *Psych. Rev.,* 80:101–122.

——— (1993b). Erotic terror: Male patients' horror of the early maternal erotic transference. *Psychoanal. Inq.,* 13:240–257.

——— (1993c). Where's poppa? The appearance of paternal transferences in early maternal erotic transference. Presented at 38th Congress of the International Psychoanalytic Association, Amsterdam.

——— (in pressa). Narrative scripts: Composing a life with ambition and desire. *Amer. J. Psychoanal.*

——— (in pressb), Perverse narratives: A female patient's panic at the maternal erotic transference. *Psych. Psychol.*

——— & Welles, J. (1989). The maternal erotic transference. *Internat. J. Psycho-Anal.,* 16:673–685.

Index